This is Your Century/Geoffrey Trease

Heinemann : London

William Heinemann Ltd
London · Melbourne · Toronto
Cape Town · Auckland

First published 1965
Copyright © Geoffrey Trease, 1965

0434967599

Illustrated overleaf:
Symbol of a divided world: The Berlin Wall

Printed and Bound in Great Britain by
Bookprint Limited, Kingswood and Crawley

This is Your Century

Books by Geoffrey Trease

Biography

The Seven Queens of England

Seven Kings of England

Seven Stages

History

The Italian Story (Macmillan)

Contents

Maps

Maps drawn by Joan Emerson

1 Hope and Glory

As twilight deepened into darkness on January 22nd, 1901, a tired old woman slipped out of a world in which, ever since most people could remember, she had been the dominant individual.

Queen of England, Empress of India, Victoria had ruled nearly a quarter of the globe. At the end over a quarter of the human race were actually her subjects, and indirectly, through a network of family relationships with other royalty, she affected the government of many millions more. The Emperor Nicholas, Tsar of All the Russias, had married her grand-daughter. The German Emperor, Kaiser Wilhelm II, most devoted of her grandsons, was at her bedside as she died. Even his arrogant personality yielded to hers. 'It was strange,' recalled one of his suite after an earlier visit to England, 'to see the Kaiser ill at ease and almost tongue-tied in the presence of the little Queen.' To the German Emperor she had been 'dearly beloved Grand-mamma', and in a sense she had become with the years a grandmother figure to the whole world.

Even in the United States, where people had little reverence for monarchs, the strong-minded old widow had won admiration. It was almost incredible that she was only the grand-daughter of that remote monarch whose memory they detested, that George III who had provoked the Declaration of Independence in 1776. But now it was 1901, and they did not hold the ancient quarrel against her.

She had been Queen for sixty-three years. Few Englishmen alive had ever sung 'God Save the *King*'. It had seemed unthinkable that one day she must die. But now she was dead, and nothing, at home or abroad, would ever be quite the same again.

That is why, if we must choose one day when the nineteenth century really ended and our own began, it is hard to think of one more significant than that January day in 1901.

The imperial crown passed to her eldest son, 'Bertie', the Prince of Wales.

1

He was already in his sixtieth year but only lately had his mother reluctantly begun to treat him as a man, and to give him a chance to prepare for the work ahead.

Few modern parents and sons can have been more at odds than these. The Prince was gay, sociable, extravagant, a lover of sport and the theatre, preferring people (especially pretty women) to books. He had charm: his interest in human beings might sometimes involve him in scandals but it was a powerful asset in dealing with foreign statesmen or making himself popular with a whole nation. When, as a young man, he visited the United States he won all hearts, not only by such symbolic gestures as planting a tree beside Washington's grave but by such normal actions as paying his own hotel bill. When he left, a voice from the crowd summed up the verdict of America: 'Come back in four years and run for President!'

Unluckily the father of this Prince Charming had been the worthy, well-meaning, deadly serious German, Albert, the Prince Consort, who had planned his upbringing on the strictest lines. The unintellectual youth was sent not to one university but to three, Edinburgh, Oxford and Cambridge, in crushing succession, till he must have been punch-drunk with lectures and tutorials.

When he was twenty his father died, but he found himself with less independence than ever. For Albert was no fool and if he had lived might have modified his methods. But Victoria had always done blindly as **2** Albert said; his wishes had been law. Now, shattered by grief, she began a widowhood of nearly forty years during which his memory was kept alive by every possible method. She even maintained a morbid old German custom whereby his room was treated exactly as though he were still alive. Every day, from December 1861 to January 1901, the dead man's clothes and shaving-tackle were laid out, a can of hot water brought. Everything must go on exactly as before, including her husband's programme for forming the character of their problem son. She wrote to the Belgian King, 'I am anxious to repeat *one* thing, and *that one* is *my firm* resolve, my *irrevocable decision*, viz. that *his* wishes—*his* plans—about everything, *his* views about *every* thing are to be *my law*! And *no human power* will make me swerve from *what he* decided and wished.' So the Prince Consort's views had to be deduced from what they were supposed to have been in 1861 and there was no way of bringing them up to date. Victorian children could not argue with their parents, Victoria's own children least of all. Bertie could only shrug his shoulders and go his own way behind Mamma's back.

Some day, she admitted gloomily, he would be King. He must call himself Albert Edward, unEnglish though it might sound. The glorious name of the father must certainly be included; but as there could never really be another Albert he had better tack on Edward as well.

'Bertie' did not contradict Mamma. But when, three days after her death, the heralds and trumpeters filed out on to the balcony of St James's Palace, the crowd were delighted to hear Garter King of Arms proclaim that 'the High and Mighty Prince Albert Edward is now, by the death of our late Sovereign of happy memory, become our only lawful and rightful Liege Lord, Edward the Seventh.'

Victoria had died at Osborne in the Isle of Wight, and her body was to be transported in the yacht *Alberta*, her son sailing behind in the *Victoria and Albert* with the unwanted company of his nephew, the Kaiser. Going aboard, King Edward asked why the royal standard was flying at half-mast not only above the crimson-draped coffin on the deck of the *Alberta* but also over his own vessel. 'The Queen is dead, sir,' the captain explained. 'But the King is alive,' came the retort in that guttural German voice which Edward had inherited. So, with his own standard flying at the masthead, the new sovereign followed the old, sailing proudly between double ranks of cruisers and battleships for eight miles under a blue wintry sky, guns firing and all the bands playing Chopin's Funeral March, thin and sad and sweet across the water.

Europe then contained only two republics, France and Switzerland. Every other state had its monarch, from the Emperor of Austria to the Grand Duke of Luxembourg. It was tactfully agreed, to avoid the ticklish problem of sorting them out in order of importance, that these sovereigns should not attend the funeral in person but send their sons. As usual the **3**

Kaiser upset things, and, as the coffin was drawn slowly through the London streets, he himself rode directly behind it, level with the King, and after them unwound a cavalcade of lesser royalties from Europe, China and Japan.

An ordinary person, watching bare-headed and respectful from the pavement, might reasonably have thought that he was seeing most of the men who would shape world history during the first half of the new century. He would have been wildly, unbelievably mistaken. A few, a very few, of these royal mourners were to have even moderate influence upon events. Most would be swept into oblivion.

The real shapers of the future were elsewhere and otherwise employed.

A young Russian lawyer, newly released from exile in Siberia, was directing revolutionary propaganda from Switzerland. Born Vladimir Ilyitch Ulyanov, he was to adopt the undercover name of Lenin.

Working in the same movement, but inside the Tsar's dominions, was a twenty-one-year-old Georgian, recently expelled from a theological college. He too, Joseph Vissarionovitch Dzhugashvili, was to take a shorter name: Stalin.

Also in Russia, and in the Hunan province of the Chinese Empire, two little country boys, both seven years of age, could not foresee how often they would be bracketed in the newspaper headlines, Nikita Khrushchev and Mao Tse-Tung.

In the United States everyone knew the name of Roosevelt. But they thought of Theodore ('Teddy') Roosevelt, the picturesque, swashbuckling Vice-President who had just taken over the White House after the assassination of President McKinley. Franklin Delano Roosevelt, his distant relative and destined to be a far greater statesman, was just entering Harvard University.

In Italy there was a young school-teacher named Mussolini. In Austria there was Adolf Hitler, eleven-year-old son of a minor Customs officer.

In India Jawaharlal Nehru, son of an eminent lawyer, would soon be leaving home for an English education at Harrow and Cambridge. But the teacher from whom he would learn most was another Indian lawyer, M. K. Gandhi, at that moment working with a Red Cross unit in South Africa, where the war between the British and the Boers, the original Dutch settlers, was drawing to an end.

In London, waiting to take his newly-won seat in Parliament, after a series of adventures as soldier and war-correspondent in Africa, India and Cuba, was an ambitious young man named Winston Churchill.

Of all these ten only the last name, it is safe to say, would have meant anything whatever to the watcher on the pavement at Queen Victoria's funeral. But it was these ten, and others equally unknown, not the riders

4 in the plumed helmets, who were to make the twentieth century.

Queen Victoria's funeral procession in Windsor. Straw-hatted sailors draw the gun-carriage. Immediately behind it walk King Edward and the Kaiser

Horse-drawn traffic jam: the scene here is the Royal Exchange, London

What was it like to live in 1901? What would strike us most if we were able to travel back in time?

First, perhaps, the horses. Though the railways had achieved high standards of speed and comfort, often higher than those we know today, other transport was horse-drawn. When a baby was coming into the world the doctor's carriage signalled the news to the neighbours, and the last journey of all was made in an ornate hearse behind black horses. From birth to death the horses were always in the picture. Splendid sleek creatures drew the carriages of the rich, with coachmen and grooms in glossy boots and cockaded top hats. Massive beasts with feathery legs and hoofs like sledge-hammers pulled coal-carts, brewers' drays and all kinds of heavy waggons, not to mention the plough. The milkman came spanking up the street in his float, a little two-wheel vehicle open at the rear, in which he stood like a Roman charioteer, dismounting, pail in hand, to ladle milk into the customer's jug. The horse-drawn fire-engine, going full pelt through the city, had a dramatic urgency unknown to us. There were traffic jams, but only in a few congested centres, and people *were* run over, though there was nothing to match the road casualties of today. A commoner excitement was when a horse ran away and was stopped by some

6

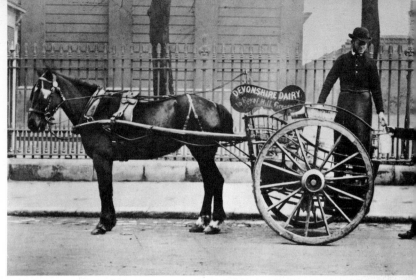

The milkman served his customers direct from the tall can on his 'float'

heroic policeman or passer-by, or fell down and lay struggling, when a sympathetic crowd would gather, all suggesting that someone else should sit on its head.

The automobile, or 'motor', was just coming in. Henry Ford had founded the Detroit Automobile Company in 1899, nine years after Daimler started his company in Germany, but the mass production age lay in the future. King Edward was an enthusiast for the newfangled 'horseless carriages' and did much to make them fashionable in England. Royal motorists were not spared the frequent breakdowns suffered by lesser men, but at least His Majesty did not himself 'have to get out and get under', in the words of a comic song then popular. As a great journalist (later Lord Northcliffe) wrote in 1902:

A prime difficulty of the establishment of a motor-car is the chauffeur or engineer. The perfect motor servant should be a combination of gentleman and engineer. He is a new type of man, and will require the

The automobile or 'motor' was just coming in

SLOW AND SURE

John: 'I've noticed, Miss, as when you 'as a motor, you catches *a* train, not *the* train!'

7

wages of other engineers. I do not think that a competent cool-headed, skilful, well-mannered engineer will ever be obtainable for thirty shillings a week.

The King was lucky. He could afford an engineer to sit beside the chauffeur and cope with emergencies.

The automobile brought other problems. Horses bolted at sight of them and nervous ladies fell off their bicycles, though some unchivalrous males thought this was their own fault for riding in long skirts because they were too modest to show their legs. The bicycle had established itself a few years earlier. This was its age of glory, unforgettably depicted in some of H. G. Wells's novels, when the countryside was still unspoilt and the roads quiet, though very dusty and covered with puncturing grit. Cycling was recommended for physical exercise, but so was motoring, for, as one medical expert enthusiastically declared, the continual jolting shook up the liver as effectively as horse riding. Only the legs, he admitted, got no exercise. This disadvantage, he had found, could be 'overcome by alighting at the end of a drive of twenty miles, and running smartly for about two hundred or three hundred yards.' No one foresaw the real problems created by the new invention, problems of parking and traffic movement which, when cars multiplied into millions, would destroy the old beauty of town and country alike and, having first revolutionized daily life, threaten to bring it to a halt.

The Wright brothers' aeroplane making its first flight

It was not till 1903 that the American brothers, Wilbur and Orville Wright, flew the first aeroplane (for just twelve seconds) and it was another five years before Wilbur achieved a really significant flight of fifty-six miles in ninety minutes. A year later, on a Sunday morning in July, 1909, the Frenchman Blériot flew the English Channel from Calais to Dover. People grasped the significance of the aeroplane more quickly than that of the automobile. Baden-Powell, just then founding the Boy Scout movement, declared that Wilbur Wright was 'in possession of a power which controls the fate of nations.' And in 1908, the year of Wilbur's first considerable flight, H. G. Wells wrote *The War in the Air*. 'I'm bored with the future', Queen Victoria had once exclaimed, 'I don't want to hear any more about it.' There were many who disagreed.

8

The future was crowding in, whether one liked it or not. Telephones were spreading. For ten years it had been possible to speak between Paris and London, though it was not till 1911 that they were taken over in Britain by the Post Office. One thing we should certainly notice if we went back to those days is the speed of the ordinary postal services in Britain. Postmen tramped round from early morning until late at night. There were half a dozen deliveries daily. It was common to receive after supper a letter posted at the end of the office day or one despatched that morning from some quite distant town. Not everything has grown quicker during the twentieth century.

In 1901 the Italian, Marconi, sent the first radio signals across the Atlantic, but it was only in 1920, in the United States, that radio broadcasting began as a means of mass entertainment, the B.B.C. following in Britain two years afterwards. In the first years of the century people were more dependent on home-made amusements like the piano, the banjo and amateur theatricals, if they could not reach the playhouses and concert halls. The phonograph or gramophone was coming in, but it sounded scratchy and tinny, a miracle, but unsatisfactory by musical standards, until electrical recording and reproduction arrived in the 1920s and long-playing records (about 1950) made it possible to play major compositions without cutting them up like a string of sausages. No one had heard of jazz, although it had originated just before 1900 in New Orleans, a blend of negro rhythms and other musical elements creating the 'blues' and the now nearly forgotten 'ragtime'. It did not conquer the world till the 1920s.

The first cinemas, on the other hand, were opened at Pittsburgh, Pennsylvania in 1905 and another in Britain in the same year. The new 'picture palaces' sprang up like mushrooms. The legendary Mary Pickford made her first film in 1909, Charlie Chaplin in 1911. It was almost another twenty years before sound films arrived. The earlier pictures had to convey dialogue by captions. They were accompanied by the tinkling and thumping of a tireless and (usually) quick-witted pianist, or occasionally by a small orchestra.

Another mass entertainment owed nothing to scientific discovery. Professional sport was developing in the Anglo-Saxon world, soon to spread beyond. In Britain it was chiefly football: in 1901 a crowd of 110,000 watched Tottenham Hotspur and Sheffield United battle in the Cup Final at Crystal Palace, and sport was becoming such good business that one club would buy a player from another for as much as a thousand pounds. In America it was baseball: the World Series contests began there in 1903.

A hundred other changes were taking place in industry, science, and every department of life. Some were homely and obvious to all, like the spread of bathrooms and similar modern conveniences in ordinary houses. **9**

Dress marked the difference between rich and poor. Contrast the elegantly-dressed ladies with the barefoot children on the opposite page

G. L. SCARPA.

SPEEDING THE STAYING GUEST

Hostess: 'Won't *you* sing something, Mr Borely?'
Mr B: 'Yes, if you like. I'll sing one just before I go.'
Hostess: 'Well, *do* sing *now*, and perhaps Miss Slowboy will accompany you.'

Other developments were stealthier, their importance, or even their very existence, unknown to the common man. X-rays were just coming into use. A British doctor, Ronald Ross, was about to receive a Nobel prize for proving that malaria was caused not by 'bad air' but by mosquitoes, a discovery destined to save millions of lives throughout the world and yet later, unwittingly, to increase the population problem. In Europe and America a growing minority of educated people now knew how to control the size of their families, but the great mass of humanity, in every land, struggled endlessly to feed and clothe more children than they could afford. Some knowledge spread slowly. On the other hand, when King Edward was stricken on the eve of his coronation and underwent an emergency operation for appendicitis, which few of his subjects had heard of before, the new complaint became familiar, and even fashionable, almost overnight.

Perhaps the outstanding thing which would strike a young person today, if he could magically step back into the world of 1901, is the *inequality* between man and man, and between man and woman, of an extent now unbelievable.

It showed in their dress: in the long elegant dresses of the ladies, the flamboyant hats, the furs or parasols or jewels or ostrich feathers, according to the occasion, the appropriate, impractical costume of women who

10

had nothing more strenuous to do than to ring the bell for a servant; and in the silk hats and frock coats, the curly bowlers and fur-collared overcoats, of the 'men-about-town', who might do no more work than the women. In those days the rich really *were* rich and income-tax was so low that they were left with nearly all their money to spend as they wished. Much of it went on clothes, houses, horses and carriages, creating the legend of 'Edwardian elegance'.

Some of the more thoughtful might feel embarrassed, even guilty, at enjoying so much luxury, but most of them, though often kind to their own servants, were not worried about the population as a whole. They might see ragged, barefoot, undernourished children as they sailed across the pavement to their waiting carriages, they might give generously, when asked, to charity, but they clung to the Bible text, 'The poor always ye have with you,' and assumed that nothing could be done to abolish such conditions. They saw no reason to be ashamed of being rich, or of displaying their wealth as conspicuously as they liked, or of leading a life of utter idleness. Many men, of course, did choose to sit in Parliament, follow a profession, or even enter business, but others felt no need to. Why work, they argued, and rob some poorer man of employment?

Dress not only marked the difference between rich man and beggar but it graded people in an infinite variety of stages between. The shop assistant, the humble bank clerk, the respectable working man, each was **11**

A street scene in Putney: an eager crowd gathers round a man with a barrel-organ

expected to dress 'according to his station'. To rise too high above this standard, or fall too far below it, spelt trouble, even dismissal. One must not 'ape one's betters'. The prettiest maid must not dress up on her free afternoon so that she could be mistaken in the street for her employer's daughter. She must remember that she was only a 'young person' and could never be a 'young lady'. Such miracles happened only in Bernard Shaw's play, *Pygmalion*, which many know better in its modern musical version, *My Fair Lady*.

If the rich were really rich, so were the poor really poor. The American writer Jack London, who had known the hardships of the Klondyke gold rush, was horrified by the conditions of the English working class, which he exposed with savage indignation in *The People of the Abyss*. His description was supported by the sober facts collected by the Quaker sociologist, **12** Seebohm Rowntree, in the outwardly beautiful cathedral city of York.

When we day-dream of living in earlier historical periods, we tend to
assume that we should have been born into the comfortable and interesting stratum of the upper class. The odds are against it. For a change let us
suppose ourselves born into the lowest stratum, one quarter of the entire
population, which Rowntree reckoned to be living in actual poverty.

Home would probably have been a dank, cold, verminous tenement.
Two rooms for the whole sprawling family. No conveniences of any kind.
In the yard outside, one closet and one cold water tap for a dozen or more
households. All dirty water and slops to be carried to a grating in the
street. But we might never grow old enough to notice these conditions:
in the poorest parishes one child in three died before it was a year old, and
in many other districts the proportion was one in four.

What would the food have been like? We have typical diet sheets for
children up to eight years old as provided in the workhouse. Breakfast **13**

was dull but filling: half a pint of milk and five ounces of dry bread. Dinner was more interesting: roast beef (but it is worth stopping and trying to visualize the slice which, with its fat and gristle, would weigh an ounce and a half), with another four ounces of potatoes or other vegetables, and a formidable six ounces of pudding. Supper comprised a half-pint mug of cocoa (half water) and a quarter-pound hunk of seed-cake. If, instead, we picture ourselves the children of a steady working man, bringing home his regular twenty shillings (then just under five dollars) a week, it is even worse. According to the experts who studied prices and conditions, the average wage earner with several children could not spend as much per head on their food as was allowed for by the workhouse regulations. Thirty shillings was reckoned quite a good weekly wage. A skilled uphol-sterer might make as much as forty-two, but a woman in the same trade, matching him in output and quality of work, could not hope for half as much pay.

Our parents would have worked long hours for these low wages and been haunted continually by the fear of unemployment. Trade unions were weak, the law gave little protection, and there was no system of unemployment insurance. A man could be dismissed at short notice or turned out into the street by his landlord.

Supposing after all that we *had* been born prosperous, one thing that would have struck us would have been the excellence of the service. In shops and hotels, outdoors and at home, we should never have lacked for people to take our orders, eagerly and respectfully, whatever secret resent-ment gnawed their hearts. Some of them, it is true, would have been reasonably secure in their jobs, and even some who were not had too much self-respect to put up with treatment that went beyond reason. But resis-tance required courage. The customer was always right and so was the employer. Working men and women had to accept indignities which their great-grandchildren find incredible.

Inequality between the classes was not so bad in the United States or throughout the 'White' Dominions, where there was less of an old-established upper class and much more chance for a poor man to change jobs or set up on his own. But actual inequality was still worse in the colonies where coloured races were governed by a small European group. In Africa and south-east Asia almost every scrap of territory belonged to one of the European powers. Britain, France, Belgium, Holland, Spain, Portugal, Germany, Italy, all had their colonies. The treatment of the subject peoples varied a good deal (the Belgian Congo and the German East African territories had particularly unsavoury reputations) but even when the white man was most benevolent he never doubted for one moment that he belonged to a superior branch of humanity, sent by

14 Heaven to teach hygiene, efficiency, and Christianity to the lesser breeds.

Racial segregation, which today survives only in a few countries, though as a problem of acute world concern, was accepted at the beginning of this century as the natural thing.

Finally, there was the inequality of the sexes. For a generation or two women had been fighting to get education as good as their brothers', to gain entrance to professions and skilled occupations, and to be recognized as intelligent individuals. They had won many victories, but the really independent woman was still a rarity, and the vast majority were still subordinate to fathers or husbands or even brothers. It was, they complained, a man's world, run by men for men. In Australia and New Zealand they had recently won the right to vote, and in four of the American states they could take part in state elections, but elsewhere they had no say in the government of their countries. Here again, though, some lively changes were at hand.

A good way to catch a living echo of Edwardian days is to listen to Elgar's 'Coronation Ode' and 'Pomp and Circumstance' marches. At its best Elgar's music is stirring, solemn, and noble. It expresses the simple faith in royalty and tradition that most people accepted without question. But when, at the King's suggestion and to Elgar's later regret, one of the tunes was fitted to A. C. Benson's lines to make the song, 'Land of Hope and Glory', the result was brash and sentimental.

'Wider still and wider,
   Shall thy bounds be set.
God who made thee mighty
   Make thee mightier yet!'

When those words were first sung the British Empire was reaching its limit. The Boers had at last been beaten and soon the new Union of South Africa would be added to the other Dominions. Apart from minor adjustments the bounds were already set as wide as they would ever be. The next sixty years would see the old Empire, as King Edward knew it, shrink in upon itself almost to nothing, though that would not stop mass audiences from bellowing forth the vainglorious lines which have long been meaningless.

'Land of hope and glory' was a phrase which would have been much better applied to the United States, then coming to the fore as a tremendous economic force but not yet a great military power outside the American continent. 'Hope' brought millions of emigrants from the poverty and oppression of Europe, filling the empty lands and building up the new cities. And there was 'glory' in the realization that a young nation was coming to its full strength and outstripping the kingdoms of the Old World.

Between the Declaration of Independence, in 1776, and 1901 about 21 **15**

million immigrants entered the United States. In the next few years, until the 1914 War stopped the ships from sailing, another 12 million poured in. The flow was becoming a flood. And the newcomers were of a different type. In the nineteenth century the immigrants had been British and Irish, with a fair number of Germans and Scandinavians. In the twentieth century they were Jews, Poles, Ukrainians, and other refugees from the oppressive government of the Russian Tsar, or Italians and Greeks driven by sheer poverty from their Mediterranean homes. They spoke neither English nor one of the kindred Teutonic languages. They had different customs, different religions, different living standards from the earlier Americans.

A great effort was made to absorb the newcomers. The United States were thought of as a 'melting-pot' in which all these elements were to be blended into a new nation, and considerable success was achieved. But outsiders (and particularly the British) did not sufficiently realize that it *was* a new nation, that it was no longer exclusively 'Anglo-Saxon', that its language would no longer be 'King's English' but an English hammered into new forms by millions who had learnt it as a foreign tongue and never mastered its grammar. British people would go on speaking of 'our American cousins' and assuming that all of them regarded Britain as their ancestral home, forgetting that, while this was true of some, it was untrue of others. This was to cause much disappointment and ill-feeling in the years to come, when United States support for Britain was too easily taken for granted.

A young man named Winston Churchill

Few foresaw this at the beginning of the century. The new King liked Americans. More and more appeared at his court and in London society. The link between the upper classes of the two countries became stronger. **17**

Hope brought millions of emigrants from the poverty and oppression of Europe to fill the empty lands of America

For some time there had been increasing intermarriage (two future British Prime Ministers, Winston Churchill and Harold Macmillan, had American mothers) and under King Edward this process developed. He swept away the Victorian stuffiness, the rigid German-style exclusiveness which had cut off his predecessors from so much of real life. Aristocrats were freer to marry as they chose. Many chose wealthy American girls, and thus, while the mass populations of the two countries were loosening the ties of kinship, the upper strata, dukes and earls, senators and millionaires, were making new ones.

And America was the place for millionaires. J. D. Rockefeller, the richest man in the world, had built up the Standard Oil Company and spread his power over mines, banks, and railways. He was the classic type of multi-millionaire, making his money by pitiless competition and later giving much of it away to education, science, and charity. In his long life (1839–1937) he gave away more than 500 million dollars. Andrew Carnegie, whose name is commemorated on countless public library buildings in Britain and the United States, was a penniless Scottish boy who built up what became, in 1901, the United States Steel Corporation, in which year he retired to a castle in Scotland and devoted his time and money to good works. There were many other such men, 'tycoons' as they are now sometimes called, but they did not all put their immense riches to such good purposes. Nor was America the only place for millionaires, but it was the country which produced the most and the wealthiest. It was truly the land of opportunity.

The United States had no empire as the great European nations had, but she wielded a powerful influence over the republics of Latin America, the former colonies of Spain and Portugal. Long ago, in 1823, when those colonies were newly free, President Monroe had declared what is still called 'the Monroe Doctrine', making it clear that the United States would not allow any non-American nation to interfere in the affairs of the continent. (Similarly, the American countries were not to get involved in the wars and troubles of the Old World.) Thus, if we leave aside Canada and some smaller territories, mainly West Indian islands, which still belonged to Britain, France, or Holland, the American continent was a kind of 'closed shop', in which the wealth and power of the United States outweighed those of all the less developed republics put together. Merely by lending money or refusing to lend it, the United States could put pressure on their governments. 'Dollar diplomacy' was the term used by critics to describe this process, and they argued that there was an American imperialism, without an emperor, but as ruthless as the European imperialism which had devoured Africa.

The President at this time was that flamboyant character, 'Teddy' Roosevelt, who had come unexpectedly to office after the murder of **19**

That flamboyant character 'Teddy' Roosevelt, President of the United States

President McKinley. He was a vigorous, versatile, aggressive man, who, if he had been British, would have been termed an 'Empire builder'. In the recent war with Spain in Cuba he had raised his own volunteer regiment, the Rough Riders. He wrote books about the history of the Wild West and his favourite hobby was big game shooting. When he came to London someone put a notice on the sculptured lions in Trafalgar Square, 'Not to be Shot', and it is said that Teddy bears got their name from him.

It was this first President Roosevelt who began building up the United States Navy. He decided that, no matter what the difficulties, a canal must be cut through the Isthmus of Panama so that the Navy could concentrate either in the Pacific or the Atlantic without half the ships having to steam round Cape Horn. A previous French attempt to build the canal had failed for various reasons, including the fever which killed off the workers like flies. Americans knew that they could overcome the engineering, financial and health problems, but there was still a political stumbling-block. Panama did not then exist as a separate republic, but only as a province of Colombia, and Colombia would not agree to the United States plan. The province of Panama thereupon revolted, declared its independence, was quickly recognized by Washington and entered into a treaty with the United States, giving her the right to build the canal and to maintain a 'Canal Zone' on both sides. The Panama canal was opened in August, 1914, when the historic importance of the occasion was overshadowed by even more fateful events in the same month.

By then Theodore Roosevelt was no longer in power. In Britain a Prime Minister can govern as long as the majority of the House of Commons will support him. He is part of that House: there has never been a Prime Minister in the House of Lords since Lord Salisbury, who resigned just before King Edward's coronation. He stands for election with all the other candidates for Parliament and those elections are held when the situation requires, but at least every five years. In the United States, by contrast, President and Vice-President are elected regularly every four years, and there are elections every two years for the two bodies forming Congress, the Senate and the House of Representatives. So, once elected, a President is safe for four years (if he lives) and another four if he is re-elected; but the Americans have always had a prejudice against Presidential 'third terms' (they finally prohibited them by amending the Constitution in 1951). The other Roosevelt, Franklin Delano, was to be the only other President elected a third time, in the special conditions of the Second World War, but Theodore, though he fought rumbustiously as ever to return to power, was unable to do so. In the end he split his own (the Republican) party and stood as a Progressive candidate, which merely had the effect of letting in the Democrat, Woodrow Wilson.

20   Most of his life Wilson had been a university professor. He was an idealist and a reformer, but it was his misfortune to seem cold and aloof compared with Theodore Roosevelt, so that he had difficulty in carrying the people with him. Also, big business usually supported the Republican Party and disliked this dangerous Democrat. They remembered what he had said in 1911, when Governor of New Jersey: 'The great monopoly in this country is the money monopoly. So long as that exists, our old variety and freedom and individual energy of development are out of the question . . . The growth of the nation and all our activities are in the hands of a few men.'

When Wilson was elected in 1912 he was very little interested in foreign affairs. Yet within two years he was to be thrown into them at the deep end. Reluctant though he was to be drawn into the quarrels of the Old World, he was destined to be far more involved than any American President before him.

*The horse-drawn fire engine going
full pelt*

2 Drifting to Disaster: 1914

What had been happening meanwhile in Britain?

In 1910 Edward VII was succeeded by his son, George V, grandfather of Queen Elizabeth II. He was very different from his pleasure-seeking father. Duty came first with him and, though kindly enough, he had a brusque manner, sometimes treating his own boys like defaulters in the Royal Navy. He was always a naval officer at heart and would have made his career at sea, but for the death of an elder brother which made him heir to the throne he occupied until 1936.

Though Edward VII's reign lasted only nine years, it saw such a gay reaction from Victorian gloom that it left a vivid legend behind. The mere word Edwardian conjures up a picture of elegance: the sun always shining on garden-parties, race-meetings and regattas, and at night the lamps gleaming on necklaces, tiaras and starched shirts. This picture was of course only one tiny fragment of the truth, distorted by memory, but many who were young at that period went on boring their children and grandchildren for decades afterwards with rose-tinted and inaccurate recollections. They remembered how cheap everything had been: they forgot the miserably low wages. They vowed that the summers had been finer and hotter: in fact, Britain had several good summers including 1914 (which they naturally remembered with special poignancy, since it was the summer when their pleasures were cut short by the war) but records show that there were about as many wet cold summers as their descendants were to endure.

'Everyone was so contented in those days . . . ' This was true of many good simple folk who expected little of life in this world and who in some cases were (not to speak too harshly) rather lacking in spirit and imagination. Of others it is truer to say that they wore a mask of contentment because they dared not speak their minds. Not only could a man lose his job for voting the wrong way or for joining a trade union but even the

22 shopkeeper dare not offend Conservative customers by revealing Liberal

sympathies, and vice versa. As for being a Socialist, and voting for the newly-founded Labour Party, that was as unpopular and as dangerous as being a Communist sixty years later.

How 'contented' people in Britain were may be judged from the election landslide of 1906 which swept away the Conservative Government after twelve years. The Liberals took office with 397 members against 157 Conservatives, and even Labour had 51 seats. There were also 83 Irish Nationalists, because the whole of Ireland was still governed from London, though the struggle for independence had been raging for years. The Liberal Cabinet was a gifted team and included a fiery Welsh lawyer, David Lloyd George, destined to become Prime Minister. Among its supporters, first as an under-secretary but soon to be promoted step by step, was Winston Churchill, who had recently 'crossed the floor' of the House of Commons and for this period of his life become a Liberal.

As Churchill was destined to play an important role throughout our period (the sole character 'on stage' from start to finish) it is worth pausing to glance at him. He was a man of immense vitality and versatility. One life was not enough for his passionate interests. If he had not made politics his career he might have been a general. A best-selling author he became, in any case, and a historian, though he never went to university and did not appear one of the brighter scholars at Harrow, where his main distinction was to win the public schools fencing championship. He was a fearless adventurer and a tireless traveller, he could paint very passably and build a brick wall. He had a warm tempestuous nature that responded to a fight or a friendship, yet a mind that could withdraw from petty details and ponder world issues in long perspective. A duke's grandson, he had no aristocracy of feature: according to mood, he resembled a dour bulldog, a cross baby or a mischievous cherub. Instead, he cultivated distinctive tricks, wearing unusual hats and a bow tie when the other kind was usual, **23** and clamping a cigar between his lips whenever the occasion permitted. He was genuinely a 'character' but he also knew the value in politics of emphasizing the fact.

The 1906 Government brought in various laws to help the poorer people. Old Age Pensions, insurance stamps, Labour Exchanges, all began at this time. When the Conservative majority in the House of Lords tried to block such measures, the Liberals passed the Parliament Act to reduce the power of the Lords. Meanwhile the Trade Disputes Act helped the unions to organize the workers. In the three years before 1914 the men showed their 'contentment' by a month-long miners' strike, two dock strikes, and the first general railway strike against the numerous private companies then owning the system.

The same kind of thing was happening in other countries, especially Germany and the rest of Western Europe. Social security was developing along with trade union organization, labour unrest, and the rise of Socialist parties. The United States saw much less of these changes, because Americans had a tradition of 'rugged individualism' and expected a man to stand on his own feet without help from the State or anyone else, although the American Federation of Labor did make conspicuous progress in these years, organizing unions in the skilled trades and pressing for reform. In the less developed countries, Russia especially, such changes were slowed down by the poverty and ignorance of the masses and by the overwhelming strength of rulers determined to clamp down on any kind of protest.

In Britain there were other struggles mounting at this time. Women were now better educated. For a generation they had been going to the newly-founded girls' schools and even taking university examinations. Many were earning their livings: the female typist (originally called a 'typewriter') had transformed the old-fashioned office depicted by Dickens. More and more women demanded the suffrage or right to vote, and, though many men were amused or indignant, others supported their campaign. One sympathizer was H. G. Wells, then coming to the fore as a novelist and a pioneer of science fiction. A rumbustious, untidy little man, always in shapeless tweeds, always laughing and talking fast in a rather squeaky, indignant, yet at the same time good-humoured voice, Wells had a heart and brain which belied his unimpressive exterior. He loved life and he loved argument. He flung himself into both with equal enthusiasm. He walked, cycled, played tennis, badminton, croquet, and even elaborate war games with toy soldiers on the floor. He made friends, quarrelled, married and was divorced with similar intensity. But most of all, as a rebellious young man sprung from the lower classes, who never wanted to become a 'gentleman', he enjoyed attacking the established

24 order, and, as a first-class science graduate of London University, attack-

Suffragettes, arrested after a demonstration at Buckingham Palace, are marched away by the police.

ing especially the unscientific bias of the governing class. 'If the world does not please you, you can change it,' he declared. 'Determine to alter it at any price, and you can change it altogether.' In his novel *Ann Veronica* he made one of the 'New Women' his heroine. The book caused an outcry at the time. It lives on, both for its story and for the picture it gives of the period.

The Liberal Government would not promise votes for women. Some Suffragettes, finding that orderly meetings got them nowhere, decided on militant action. They were led by a remarkable Manchester woman, Emmeline Pankhurst, the widow of a liberal-minded lawyer. She had had experience in the kind of work already open to women, administering the Poor Law and serving on educational committees. It seemed to her extraordinary that she was debarred from any say in the government of the country, whereas no male was judged too stupid or ignorant to vote. She was now about fifty, and her two grown-up daughters, Christabel and Sylvia, supported her loyally as she resolved to carry the struggle further.

Mrs Pankhurst and her 'militants' stopped at nothing to draw attention to their cause. They smashed shop windows with hammers concealed in **25**

their handbags, slashed a famous Velasquez painting in the National Gallery, raided the House of Commons, attacked cabinet ministers with horsewhips, and chained themselves to the railings outside 10 Downing Street, swallowing the padlock keys. One woman broke from the crowd at the Derby, threw herself under the hoofs of the King's racehorse, and was killed.

Whatever is thought of their methods, their courage was undeniable. So was their ingenuity in using every kind of trick and disguise to deceive the police and reach the places chosen for their dramatic demonstrations. When caught, they were often handled with a roughness that was remarkable for those days. Their opponents were frightened and indignant, it was felt that Suffragettes had forfeited the right to be treated as women, let alone 'ladies', and all the weight of the law was thrown against them. When sent to prison, some went on hunger-strike and endured the revolting brutality of forcible feeding. Yet on release they renewed their campaign and were at once rearrested under what became known as the 'Cat and Mouse' Act.

By 1913 Mrs Pankhurst herself had served several prison sentences. In that year there was an attempt to burn down the house of Lloyd George, then Chancellor of the Exchequer. She was charged with inciting her followers to do this. She conducted her own defence at the Old Bailey, and, though the crime was never proved to have been the work of Suffragettes, she was given three years' penal servitude.

It is hard to say just how much these acts of sacrifice did to win votes for women, because the war cut short the agitation—and then gave women such opportunities to prove their abilities that afterwards there was no question of denying them the vote. Similarly in the United States 1920 saw victory for the women's cause, after a long campaign as dogged, if not always as sensational, as that of their British sisters.

Another, equally bitter, struggle was taking place to win Home Rule for Ireland. Over the centuries the Irish had suffered conquest, massacre, enslavement, famine and exile disguised as 'emigration'. They were a Celtic, Roman Catholic peasantry ruled by an Anglo-Saxon, Protestant upper class. Since the Act of Union in 1800, abolishing their short-lived separate Parliament in Dublin, their affairs had been controlled from London, where the Irish M.P.s kept up a constant fight for independence.

It was no simple question. North-east Ireland (Ulster, or the Six Counties) had long ago been colonized by English and Scottish Protestants. Their energy and enterprise had made this the most prosperous part of the country. They were fervently loyal to the British Crown and determined not to be swamped by the southerners in an independent Ireland. They were in a cruel dilemma which has been repeated in many **26** other countries since. When, in that eventful year 1914, Home Rule was

This steamer has been detained in Ayr docks by the authorities for taking guns illegally into Ulster

at last about to be granted, Ulster was willing to fight a civil war to prevent it. Many British officers sent in their resignations lest they be ordered to put down a rebellion with which they sympathized. Here again the struggle was broken off, the crisis postponed. That summer the troops marched out against a very different enemy.

Many British people believed that their country could never again be involved in war with another civilized nation. Apart from a stupid and unnecessary conflict in the Crimea half a century before, they had never fought in Europe since Waterloo. Their navy had dominated the oceans of the world since Nelson's day: it was kept equal to the next two largest foreign navies put together. A small professional army was enough for local wars in distant corners of the Empire, usually against ill-armed enemies, so Britain had never needed conscription. The man in the street took peace and security for granted.

Other countries were less fortunate. In 1904 there was war in the Far East between Russia and Japan. The Japanese had been a backward oriental nation, living in almost medieval conditions. Then, in a single generation, they modernized their country, copying everything the West had invented. A quarrel developed with the Russians. Without declaring war, the Japanese torpedo-boats attacked the Russian Pacific Fleet in harbour. The land struggle which followed in Korea and Manchuria was **27**

'Bloody Sunday': the demonstrators faced suddenly by troops

fought with courage on both sides, the Japanese showing a suicidal disregard for their own lives. Their commanders knew just what they were after. The Russian generals were muddle-headed and over-confident, nor were their admirals any better. When their Baltic fleet set off to sail round the world to the scene of the conflict, it mistook British trawlers in the North Sea for Japanese torpedo-boats and fired on them. On reaching the Pacific it was caught in the Tsushima Straits between Korea and Japan and annihilated. Four Russian battleships, seven cruisers, and five destroyers were sunk, and most of the other vessels were captured. The Japanese had lost only a few destroyers and had won the war.

Disaster in war often brings revolution. The Russian revolution of 1905 was touched off by the events of 'Bloody Sunday'. About 200,000 people marched through the snow one January afternoon to the great square in

28 front of the Tsar's Winter Palace in St Petersburg. It was a peaceful,

Clearing the streets in St Petersburg

respectful demonstration, led by a priest, carrying sacred icons, and singing 'God Save the Tsar'. The troops however opened fire and shot down some hundreds of men, women and children. Strikes and armed risings followed throughout the country. In the Black Sea the sailors of the new battleship *Potemkin* hoisted the Red Flag, the traditional symbol of revolt, and sailed to a neutral port in Rumania. This 1905 revolution (in which the word *soviet* came into common use to describe a workers' committee) was damped down at last, partly by brute force, partly by promises of reform. But it had been a rehearsal for a greater drama soon to come.

There were other wars. The Turks still ruled a crumbling empire mainly in Asia (what is now Arabia, Iraq, Jordan, Israel, Syria and Lebanon) but also extending up the Balkan peninsula. Their African possession (now Libya) was lost to Italy in 1911, and much of their Balkan **29**

Europe in 1914

territory was wrested from them by a league composed of Greece, Bulgaria, Serbia and Montenegro: these last two countries are united today in Yugoslavia. Then in 1913 the victors fell out, Greece and Serbia attacking Bulgaria, with Rumania joining them. Not for nothing was this eastern peninsula called 'the powder barrel of Europe'. Its ever-shifting boundaries and age-old racial feuds were a constant threat to peace, and there was always the risk that bigger countries would be drawn into the quarrel.

So it happened in 1914.

The Serbs belonged, like the Russians, Poles and Czechs, to the Slav race. Much as they hated the Turks to the south-east, they detested even more the Austrians in the north-west. At this time the Austrian Empire embraced Hungary, bits of Italy, modern Czechoslovakia, and much of **30** what is now Poland and Yugoslavia. The Austrians were a Teutonic race, like the Germans, but they had many unwilling Slav subjects, including millions of Serbs. Austria's natural ally was Germany, whereas Serbia looked to Russia as a big brother Slav who would back her in time of trouble.

Race and nationality must not be exaggerated when we study the causes of war. Britain and the United States certainly did not fight Germany because they liked Slavs more than Teutons. War is a complex disease, challenging humanity much as cancer challenges the scientists. In the strict sense there is no 'reason' for war, because everybody loses by it nowadays, and many intelligent people had grasped this fact long before 1914. The ordinary man ceased to benefit from war when it got beyond the stage of personal loot and the enslavement or ransoming of prisoners. Some governments went on into our own day believing that a nation could benefit from war, by acquiring territory and raw materials or by crippling its trade rivals. But if these objects could be won without fighting, so much the better.

By the twentieth century it is roughly true to say that neither kings nor cabinets deliberately sought a conflict, though individual statesmen might do so, or ambitious generals, or armament manufacturers who stood to make millions out of war, sometimes selling to both sides. Conflict came when different governments wanted certain objectives, took excessive risks, could not draw back, and had to fight.

Many road accidents offer us an exact parallel. No sane driver wants a collision. But he badly wants something else, to overtake, or to have priority at a road-junction. He misjudges the situation, does not realize that the other driver is equally determined not to give way, and there is a crash which neither intended. Emotional factors like impatience and vanity play their part.

So with the twentieth-century wars. Aggressive powers underestimated the willingness of the others to resist if they were pushed too far. Warlike attitudes were adopted which it was hard to give up without looking foolish. Policies were not made sufficiently clear and in good time. This is dangerous enough with road signs and drivers' signals; but at least a motorist can believe these when he sees them, whereas the statesmen could never be quite sure whether a warning from another country was genuine or mere bluff. It was small wonder that collisions came.

When they did, it was the ordinary man who had to fight and die. He seldom knew the complicated factors, economic, political, and strategic, that had led to the crash, nor, if he had understood them, would he have felt much enthusiasm. To persuade him to put on a uniform and leave home, to kill and be killed, the issues had to be presented in terms he could appreciate, as love of country, distrust of foreigners, hatred of injustice, and so on. This happened everywhere in 1914.   **31**

The British Fleet at Spithead, July 1914

In the years before that fatal collision various tensions were building up in Europe. It would be tedious to go into them all here. Even Britain, hitherto so secure and superior, was getting nervous of Germany. The Kaiser, when young, had been made an honorary admiral of the British Navy by his beloved Grand-mamma. This complimentary gesture had encouraged him in dreams of naval glory and caused him to yield more easily to militaristic advisers. Germany had now not only the most formidable army in Europe but was developing a fleet that worried the British Admiralty more than anything since Trafalgar. The Kaiser adored uniforms, parades and manœuvres. He made bombastic speeches about Germany's destiny. In one speech, which his ministers tried vainly to hush up, he compared his soldiers with the Huns who had beaten down the Roman Empire. The barbaric name was later used as excellent propaganda against them. History shows that the Kaiser was by no means the bogeyman he appeared, but history cannot mend past damage, only (we hope) prevent a repetition.

France and Russia had similar fears of Germany and Austria, and a network of alliances was created. King Edward, whose love of France was equalled only by his dislike of his German nephew the Kaiser, helped personally to strengthen the Entente, or 'understanding', between the British and French Governments.

In after years the British used to complain that their country had been taken completely and rather unfairly by surprise, war coming like a thunderbolt out of that cloudless sky which (they persuaded themselves) hung perpetually over Ascot and Henley and their own tennis court in the good old days. If they were surprised when war came, their government certainly was not.

32 By 1911 the War Office in London, following years of consultation with

Paris, had worked out 'Top Secret' plans for sending its small but well-trained army to take up an agreed position on the French left flank, facing a German attack. The timings of innumerable troop-trains were calculated to the minute. It was already planned where and when each unit would halt for coffee. Only one rather important question remained to be solved: how this British Expeditionary Force of about 100,000 men was to be taken safely across the Channel in the face of an ever-growing German navy. But the War Office could do nothing about this problem, for it would have meant trespassing upon the functions of the Admiralty, and until 1911 the Admiralty had made little preparation for war.

In that year, the Admiralty was taken over by Winston Churchill, then thirty-six, with instructions to put the Fleet 'into a state of instant and constant readiness for war in case we are attacked by Germany'. The veteran admiral, Lord Fisher, was by now confidently forecasting the outbreak for October 1914, and calculating that there would thus be comfortable time to get the right man installed as Commander-in-Chief of the Home Fleet. The present commander was due to retire in December 1913, and Sir John Jellicoe, a naval strategist 'with all the attributes of Nelson', could then succeed him. Churchill chose as his Private Secretary the youngest flag officer in the Fleet, David Beatty, who was later in turn to succeed Jellicoe. For the next three years Churchill tackled the reorganization of the Navy with tireless energy.

If Fisher was a few months out in his forecast, it was because of an incident far away in the Balkans, starting a chain reaction of events.

On 28 June 1914, at the little town of Sarajevo, the Austrian Emperor's nephew and heir, together with his wife, was assassinated by a Serb nationalist secret society known as the Black Hand.

The Austrians were just waiting to pick a quarrel with their small **33**

Sarajevo: the seizing of the Archduke's assassin

neighbour. Using the murder as an excuse, they sent Serbia an ultimatum so humiliating that they were sure the Serbs would reject it. To this extent the Austrian Government 'wanted' war, but they meant it to be a one-sided little affair in which their huge empire would win its objectives without serious trouble.

Today it seems obvious that a one-sided little affair was impossible. Russia was sure to help the Serbs, Germany must then aid Austria against Russia, France would come in as Russia's ally. It was uncertain what Britain would do, for she had no hard and fast alliance with France, only an understanding.

Austria sent her 48-hour ultimatum to Serbia on 23 July, skilfully choosing a moment when the French President was at sea, returning from Russia. To the fury of the Austrian Government they found that their unacceptable terms were, at the very last moment, accepted. In Berlin the Kaiser declared that 'every reason for war drops away', and his Chancellor sent frequent messages to Vienna urging caution. But other elements were equally set on war, and at the very same time the German General Staff were sending other messages to egg on their **34** fellow generals in Austria. The Austrian Foreign Minister was no less

'Frenchmen flocked to their depo

The crowd in Munich listening to Germany's declaration of war in 1914. Hitler, then an art student, is shown in the circle

determined to have his war. The Serbian acceptance was coolly ignored: the Austrian ambassador in Belgrade did not stay to read it, but caught his train home as already instructed. His Foreign Minister persuaded the aged Emperor of Austria to sign the declaration of war by telling him, quite falsely, that the Serbs had already opened fire, and then deleted the falsehood from the public announcements.

No less peculiar things happened in Berlin, where a newspaper came out with an untrue statement that the German army was mobilizing. The report was telegraphed to St Petersburg, where the Russian General **36** Staff was begging the Tsar to sign the mobilization orders. He now did so.

By the time the Berlin report was corrected, it was too late to countermand the order. Since the Russian mobilization was genuine, Germany had to follow suit: no nation dared lose a precious day at such a time. But it was a frightened and reluctant Kaiser who picked up the pen at the bidding of his ministers, for much as he adored reviewing ships and soldiers he had never meant to risk a great war. 'Gentlemen,' he said, 'you will live to rue the day when you made me do this.'

We speak now of 'push-button warfare' and the horror that could be released in moments by setting off a procedure incapable of being reversed. Yet in 1914 the procedures were just as irreversible, though **37** they spread over a week. Both Tsar and Kaiser tried to reverse them. Each Emperor was assured by his advisers that 'for technical reasons' it was impossible to halt the forces already on the move. The count-down had started that was to blast ten million soldiers into eternity.

On 28 July Austria declared war on the Serbs. Out went the telegrams and call-up papers and proclamations in the other countries. Germans, Russians, Frenchmen, flocked to their depots. The horses were commandeered from waggon and reaping-machine, crowded troop-trains rumbled across Europe, startled holiday-makers scuttled across frontiers just in time.

In London, the Government was divided. Some ministers still hoped that war could be avoided, some that at least Britain could keep out of it. Only a few, notably Churchill, were single-minded and resolute.

That summer Churchill had decided not to hold the usual naval manœuvres but had substituted a test mobilization, ending with a review at Spithead in mid-July, just when the Balkan crisis began to worsen. The review over, he did not send the men on leave. When he heard of Austria's declaration of war on Serbia, he ordered the ships to their war stations at Scapa Flow, in the north of Scotland, without waiting for Cabinet approval. Four days later, on Saturday, 1 August, Germany declared war on Russia for refusing to halt her mobilization. On Sunday Churchill went to 10 Downing Street and told the Prime Minister, Herbert Asquith, that he proposed to complete the mobilization of the Navy at once, though the Cabinet had decided against it the previous day. 'I will take full personal responsibility', he said. So, that Sunday, without any royal proclamation or authority whatever, Churchill took the steps he knew to be necessary, and his colleagues approved them the next day as he knew they must.

For by then all could see that war was certain. On Monday Germany declared war on France. The previous day, Germany had demanded from Belgium the right to march troops across her neutral territory and Belgium had refused. Both Britain and Germany had long ago guaranteed her neutrality. Britain now demanded that Germany should keep her word and withdraw the troops she had already sent swarming over the frontier. The British ultimatum to Germany expired, unanswered, just before midnight on Tuesday, 4 August, and, in the words of the disgusted German Chancellor, Britain was in the war because of 'a scrap of paper', the treaty which had guaranteed Belgian independence in 1839. She would almost certainly have joined the struggle anyhow, but the issue of 'gallant little Belgium', appealing as it did to British sentiment for the under-dog, was ideal for making the war acceptable to the people.

The Kaiser, meantime, was horrified by the turn things had taken. **38** He saw his country unexpectedly encircled by powerful enemies, victim of a plot 'woven by Edward VII and now brought to completion by George V'. His other cousin, the Tsar, was in it of course. 'Could I ever have dreamt', he cried, 'that Nicky and Georgie would deceive me? If my grandmother had been alive, she would never have allowed this!' But the real villain was Uncle Bertie. 'Edward VII is stronger after his death than I who am still alive.'

It is illuminating, and important, to see these events from another nation's point of view. This much is certain: whoever had schemed for this conflict (not foreseeing its full results) it was not the three royal cousins in Berlin, St Petersburg and London, or, for that matter, the august but deluded eighty-four-year-old emperor in Vienna. Yet it was in their names that the myriad armies now went marching to their doom.

3 The First World War

The world had seen nothing like those first August days of 1914. It would see nothing like them again.

The conscript masses of Europe's four greatest powers were on the march. So were the smaller forces of Belgium and Serbia and Britain, the latter soon to be joined by the amateur soldiers of the Territorial Army and by thousands of other eager volunteers who had never before donned uniform even for an evening drill. Conscript or volunteer, whether they sang the '*Marseillaise*' or '*Deutschland über Alles*' or 'God Save the Tsar' or music-hall ditties like 'Tipperary' which the British preferred, these millions marched with a spirit never to be recaptured. They did not know what they were in for, as their sons did in 1939. Most believed without question in simple patriotism, 'King and Country', a 'just war', and all those black and white issues which later generations found so difficult to accept. And they believed it was going to be a short war ('over by Christmas'), an adventure, a crusade, a clean affair of fighting man against fighting man.

Such, anyhow, was the mood of the British, who could please themselves (until conscription in 1916) whether they personally risked their lives or not. In those first weeks however there was no lack of volunteers. The recruiting offices had long lines of men outside, and boys too, for many a fifteen-year-old lied about his age. Parties of friends went off to enlist together as gaily as if to a football match. The landed gentry, their tenant farmers and their labourers flocked into the county regiment in a spirit of fellowship never to be caught again. Sometimes it was a cavalry regiment and they were able to stay with the horses they knew and loved. Students and public school boys pulled strings in London to get immediate commissions; for it was considered more important for an officer to be a 'gentleman' than to have military experience. Men rushed home from the farthest corners of the world, afraid that the war would be won before **40** they could take a hand. Many Americans, knowing that the United

'Thousands of eager volunteers who had never before donned uniform'

States would wish to stay neutral in this European quarrel, found ways (as the author Ernest Hemingway soon did) to join one army or another.

It is hard for those who were born later to understand the mood of 1914, the mood exultantly expressed by idealistic young poets like Rupert Brooke, who could really believe that:

> Honour has come back, as a king, to earth . . .
> And Nobleness walks in our ways again . . .

or Julian Grenfell, a six-foot regular Dragoon, destined like Brooke to die on active service in 1915, soon after writing:

> The thundering line of battle stands,
>   And in the air Death moans and sings;
> But Day shall clasp him with strong hands
>   And Night shall fold him in soft wings.

They did not know, as we know, of the poison gas and barbed wire that were to wipe out the last traces of honour and nobleness from war. We must understand them, for, unless we do, we cannot understand the terrible memories which shaped the history and literature of the 1920s and 1930s, as well as the individual lives and outlook of the young people growing up.

One thing is important to realize. Frightful as the Second World War was to be, the military casualties of the First, so far as Western Europe was concerned, were much heavier. And whereas, in 1939–45, many of **41** those killed were civilians, the air raids destroying young and old, women and babies and hospital patients and old men, in the 1914 War it was still mainly the young front line soldiers who died. Of these, from Britain at least, it was the bravest and most brilliant who, by rushing to volunteer, stood the worst chance of survival. It was selective killing. No one will ever measure what it cost civilization in terms of the first-class men who did not live to take their deserved place in managing the affairs of the world. Three young British officers who served with gallantry but came through alive rose eventually to be in turn Prime Minister: Clement Attlee, Anthony Eden, and Harold Macmillan. All were conscious, even forty years later, that they were survivors of what has been called the lost generation. They were missing all the time the outstanding men of their own age group who should have been their colleagues. Nor was it just in politics that the gap was felt. It was everywhere, in science and the arts and wherever talent was needed. It was there, too, in ordinary people's lives: there had been by 1918 such a slaughter (mainly of young men) that hundreds of thousands of girls were left without any chance of marriage.

Nobody foresaw this when the bands played that August, and the girls blew kisses and threw flowers, and the men marched singing to the railway station.

Meantime, on the Continent, the guns roared and flashed from the frontier fortresses, the cavalry patrols trotted along the poplar-lined roads, the grey-clad German infantry flowed forward in a seemingly irresistible tide.

The Kaiser's generals were operating the Schlieffen Plan, devised years before by a brilliant Prussian Field Marshal.

Von Schlieffen had planned against what would always be Germany's greatest danger, as it was again in 1939, the war on two fronts, east and west. Like a man attacked on both sides, Germany must aim to knock out one opponent with a lightning blow and then turn to deal at leisure with the other. Though Germany's position, sandwiched between France and Russia, was a handicap in one sense, it was also an advantage: with her excellent railway system she could move troops quickly from side to side. She enjoyed 'interior lines of communication'.

Russia, with her vast distances and poor organization, would be slower than France. France therefore must be knocked out first. But how? France had a powerful modern army and her frontier with Germany was defended by fortresses, supplementing the hills and rivers. Von Schlieffen's scheme was to put a minimum force along the southerly, more difficult, part of this line (near Switzerland) and to mass an overwhelming number

42 of divisions on the right wing facing north-eastern France and Belgium.

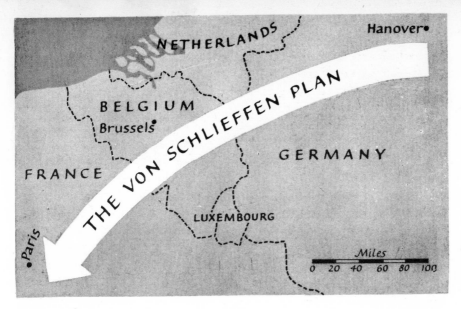

When the fighting started these divisions would sweep forward irresistibly over the flat country. They would wheel southwards as though on a giant pivot, cutting off the Channel ports from the rest of France, sweeping on anti-clockwise until they took the French border fortresses in the rear.

Von Schlieffen did not live to see his plan tried. He died in 1913 at the age of eighty, his last words being: 'It must come to a fight. Only make the right wing strong.' His successors did not obey him completely. They were afraid to leave the left wing as the light screen he had intended and in changing the proportions they robbed the right wing of the titanic thrust he had meant it to have. Even so, when those massed grey divisions poured into neutral Belgium, by-passing the prepared defence line of France and falling upon her from the north instead, it seemed as though no power on earth could stop them.

The Belgians delayed them a little. Their Liège forts commanded the easy advance route between the Ardennes (Belgium's only hills) and the Dutch frontier, which the Germans did not violate. Obsolete though these forts were, they were gallantly defended and held out until 15 August, when the Germans brought up heavy howitzers, a new development in artillery with terribly destructive power which was to have a great influence on the course of the war. The Belgian engineers had fortunately done their work well by blowing up bridges, so that it was another nine days before the Germans could run a single train beyond Liège. The last fortress, Namur, held out till the 25th. Brussels had fallen, most of the country was overrun by the invaders, but her popular and courageous king, Albert, had withdrawn most of his army intact into the port of Antwerp, turning it into a vast entrenched position. As a glance at a map will show, if the sweeping action of the Schlieffen Plan continued, it meant that the Germans were leaving an unbeaten force behind them.

43

French troops manning a ditch

These events won France and Britain a few days, badly needed because the French commanders were slow to grasp the meaning of the German moves and wasted time by futile advances of their own in the south which they could not maintain. The British Expeditionary Force was all across the Channel by 16 August; despite all the planning it had still taken eleven days. Not a man was lost by enemy attack, but this is hardly as wonderful as it seemed at the time. Not only had Churchill's energetic naval precautions made sure that no German craft could interfere but the German Navy had orders not to try. Let the small British Army come over to the Continent, it was argued, and then it would be all the easier to destroy it. The Kaiser was often quoted (perhaps falsely) as calling it 'a contemptible little army'. Whether he used the words or not, the B.E.F. (also often referred to as 'the first hundred thousand') soon adopted the title of 'the Old Contemptibles' with humorous pride. The British first encountered the enemy at Mons on 23 August, but were immediately caught up in the general retreat which carried them back 120 miles in twelve days. The French Army had lost more than half a million killed, wounded or prisoner, by the time the Germans were halted along a bulging line perilously near Paris.

Those first feverish weeks were a mixture of the past and the future. French infantrymen in red trousers charged gallantly behind white-gloved officers, looking no different from those who had faced the Russian cannon-balls in the Crimea in 1854. Cuirassiers and dragoons galloped with sabre and lance, breastplate and horsehair plume, unchanged from those who had thundered against the British squares at Waterloo. In contrast there were patrols on pedal cycles and in (to our eyes) comical little motor cars, perhaps a flat-capped German in ornately braided tunic at the wheel, while his comrade stood up in the open back, carbine in hand, spiked

44

French dragoons wearing plumed helmets and armed with lances

Early plane of the Royal Flying Corps

helmet on head. And there was the Royal Flying Corps, formed two years earlier with the backing of Churchill and a few other far-sighted enthusiasts. Navigation was still primitive. In peacetime it was not uncommon to come down and ask a farmer the way, but under war conditions this could be unwise.

So much for the lighter side of those early days; but there was nothing funny about the machine-gun, which sprayed hundreds of bullets per minute and soon ended for ever those cavalry charges which had dominated warfare for centuries. The British had despised the machine-gun until now and had very few. Luckily the regular soldier was trained to use his rifle with a speed and accuracy unequalled by the conscript armies. So rapidly could he load the cartridge-clips into his magazine and loose off his 'five rounds rapid' that the Germans imagined that they had machine-guns against them.

After a month of victories the invaders had for the moment shot their bolt. They had overrun much territory and inflicted terrible losses on the Allied armies, but they had not destroyed them. They had taken neither the Channel ports nor Paris, much less completed their dreamt-of sweep through France. The Schlieffen Plan had failed, partly because it had not been carried out as its inventor intended, partly because of mistakes and muddles on the German side as well as the Allies', but mostly perhaps because even the German Army had not the necessary mobility in 1914 to move and supply its columns. Von Schlieffen had asked for the *blitzkrieg*, or 'lightning war', which was not possible until the tank, dive-**46** bomber and paratrooper were available.

The last train to leave Antwerp before the city fell to the German assault

The second week in September saw the Battle of the Marne, after which the Germans retired fifty miles to a prepared defence line behind the River Aisne. The Allies, flushed with their first success, still deluded with hopes of early victory, found they could not break this line. One machine-gunner, well dug in, buttressed with sand-bags, and protected by a cruel maze of barbed wire, could laugh at a hundred heroes coming at him from the front with bayonets. So the Allies tried to outflank the German lines, and the Germans lengthened it to outflank the Allies, and so the process went on, week by week, until soon there were continuous entrenchments zigzagging from the North Sea to Switzerland.

Antwerp had long been isolated from help except by sea, but was still valuable as a thorn in the German side. In late September a massive assault was launched against the city. Churchill, anxious to hold it as long as possible, sent out a force of marines and sailors, and then left his desk at the Admiralty to go over in person and put fresh heart into the Belgian Government. A born fighter, he wanted to resign from his department and begged the Prime Minister, Mr Asquith, to give him a suitable military rank so that he could take command. Lord Kitchener, the Minister of War, was ready to make him a major-general, but the more conventional elements in London felt that this was rather too rapid promotion for a man who had been only a lieutenant in the Hussars. This did not prevent Churchill from dominating the defence of Antwerp, handling the Royal Naval Division (an eye-witness recorded) 'as if he were Napoleon and they were the Old Guard'. Though Churchill had to go back to London, and Antwerp inevitably fell, the siege had won more valuable **47**

time for the Allies, helped to save the Channel ports, and enabled the King of the Belgians to withdraw his army more or less intact.

Now for four years the soldiers confronted each other across 'No Man's Land'. To fire over the sandbagged parapet they had to mount a firing-step, raised above the mud and water which often filled the bottom of the trench. To 'go over the top' they used a short ladder. The British soldier carried 66 lbs of equipment and a bayonet 'charge' was usually made at a lumbering walk. There was only a narrow strip to cross (often the opposing troops could hear each other's voices) but it was a nightmare journey. Each front line had its barbed wire: if you were lucky you went through a gap snipped by someone with wire-cutters and if you were really unlucky you were wounded and fell sprawling over the wire, to hang there in agony perhaps for hours, a helpless living scarecrow whom no one could rescue. There were deep craters, too, all over No Man's Land, gouged out by shellfire. Their shelter might save your life, but they collected rain-water and churned-up mud: many a man drowned in them.

The odds were all on the defending side. Attacks were ordered and **48** made, but at an appalling cost in human lives. Thus, on 1 July 1916, began

the Battle of the Somme. The British lost 60,000 men the first day. They kept up their attack until October. In four months they pushed the Germans back seven miles, to no very remarkable advantage, and lost 420,000 killed and wounded. Next year at Passchendaele, fighting through a summer and autumn of mud and rain, they lost another 300,000 men. When it was the turn of the French to attack, the slaughter was as heavy and as pointless, so that in 1917 there were serious mutinies.

While the machine-gun dominated the battlefield, no frontal assault had much chance, and no flank attack was possible because the Western Front *had* no flanks. How could the deadlock be broken? New weapons were tried to give the attacker an advantage. The British invented the tank, using it first in small numbers at the Battle of the Somme, and thereby throwing away the benefit of surprise. The Germans used poison gas, the first large-scale occasion being at Ypres in April 1915, when they discharged a greenish-yellow fog of chlorine gas against two French divisions, wiping them out and making a four-mile gap in the line. But they had no reserves to follow up their success and they too were not able to spring so dramatic a surprise twice. Soon the Allies had gas-masks and were using **49** gas themselves. The deadlock continued.

It was all a very different war from the high adventure of the first days. The poets changed their tune as they scribbled by candlelight in their dug-outs. Wilfred Owen, who won the Military Cross and was killed in the very last week of the war, was writing his 'Anthem for Doomed Youth':

> What passing-bells for these who die as cattle?
> Only the monstrous anger of the guns.
> Only the stuttering rifles' rapid rattle . . .

The American Alan Seeger won the *Croix de Guerre* and the *Médaille Militaire* and was killed in 1916, after writing:

> I have a rendezvous with Death
> At some disputed barricade . . .

In the words of such men (including some, like Siegfried Sassoon, who survived) we catch a hint of their disillusionment and horror, their bitter rage against governments and generals gambling from a safe distance with millions of lives. Compare Rupert Brooke's 1914 sonnets with Wilfred Owen's ghastly realism when he set out to nail:

> The old Lie: *Dulce et decorum est*
> *Pro patria mori.*

('Sweet it is and fitting, to die for one's country') by describing what it was really like:

> Gas! GAS! Quick, boys! An ecstasy of fumbling
> Fitting the clumsy helmets just in time,
> But someone still was yelling out and stumbling
> And flound'ring like a man in fire or lime.
> Dim through the misty panes and thick green light,
> As under a green sea, I saw him drowning.
>
> In all my dreams before my helpless sight
> He plunges at me, guttering, choking, drowning.

Years later came the memoirs, the novels like Remarque's *All Quiet on the Western Front*, the plays like Sherriff's *Journey's End*. But none of them speaks more poignantly to us than these short poems torn from the hearts of young men at the time, feeling that they had 'a rendezvous with Death', and all too often being right.

What, it may be asked, was happening elsewhere? What of Austria and little Serbia, the excuse for this holocaust? What of the Tsar's famous 'Russian steam-roller' which (promised the armchair experts) was to clear a road to Berlin?

For a short while it seemed as though this promise was to be miraculously fulfilled.

*Trench warfare: during a lull i
the fighting men of the Irish Guard
attend to a wounded German prisone*

The Tsar's cousin, the Grand Duke Nicholas, took command of the armies and struck faster than the Germans had believed possible, not waiting for complete mobilization but trusting to the two to one superiority he already had. The Russian columns flooded into East Prussia and the Galician province of Austria, endless lines of stolid grey-green infantry in flat caps, masses of cavalry (including the famous Cossacks, who wore no spurs but carried whips), and a quite inadequate accompaniment of artillery and supply services, all of course horse-drawn. It was an army of courage and physical toughness, excellent for a seventeenth-century battle, not so suitable for a long war in the twentieth. The Minister of War boasted that he had not read a military manual for twenty-five years, but he 'believed in the bayonet'. Ironically enough, the most modern invention the Russians possessed, the radio transmitter, did them more harm than good, for they did not make sufficient use of code and the Germans could listen to their messages.

Still, the Russians struck, and struck panic into the hearts of the men in Berlin. There was, in those days, no independent Poland (that country was divided between Russia and Austria) so that the three warring empires had no neutral buffer state between. The Grand Duke showed more political sense than was common in the Romanov family: he proclaimed that this was a Slav war and that when it was won the Poles would have home rule. This earned the loyalty and support of the Russian Poles, who might otherwise have seized the chance to rebel against their masters, and helped to turn the Austrian Poles against theirs. It also stirred up the Czechs, unwilling Slav subjects of Austria, and as the war went on complete units of Czechs were formed to fight against their government. This is noteworthy, because (without going back into all the complicated earlier history of Europe) it helps to explain why Poland and Czechoslovakia, non-existent on the map of 1914, have figured there since 1919.

Thus, while the Germans were sweeping through Belgium and northern France during those first weeks, their own eastern province was overrun by the Russians. The Austrians, too, were staggering back, and were in no position to mop up the Serbs as intended.

In this crisis the Germans recalled a retired general of sixty-seven, von Hindenburg, who knew the East Prussian countryside and how best to use its lakes and marshes and road-system. For chief of staff he was given Ludendorff, who had just distinguished himself by piercing the Belgian defences at Liège. These two men had the urgent task of saving Germany from defeat in the east.

This territory was the historic battleground of the Teuton and Slav. At Tannenberg, in 1410, the Teutonic Knights of Prussia had been overwhelmed by a host of Poles, Lithuanians and Czechs. Now, on the same spot, five centuries later, the Germans took a terrible revenge. They out- **53** manœuvred the fumbling Russian forces, drove wedges between them and pinned them down with superior artillery. Three Russian army corps were routed (a corps might contain 60,000 men) and an immense number were taken prisoner, together with guns and stores which for Russia were far harder to replace. After this catastrophe every battery had to be reduced from six guns to four. The Russian commander, Samsonov, shot himself.

The 'steam-roller' was broken. Clearly the Tsar's armies would never defeat Germany, though they were still valuable because they tied down large enemy forces on the Eastern Front. Hindenburg won another crushing victory near the Masurian Lakes in February. When spring came he drove the Russians steadily back three hundred miles in five months. The Grand Duke was dismissed. He had not done badly with his inefficient, ill-equipped armies, but he had earned the hatred of the Tsarina, who dominated her husband and now persuaded him unwisely to take supreme command himself. For the next two years the miserable, though often heroic, Russians battled grimly against lengthening odds. They had blazed away so much ammunition in 1914, lost so much equipment, and replaced so little because of their inadequate factories, that men sometimes had to fight with bare hands and march on bare feet. In some sectors there was only one rifle between ten.

Once the Russians were thrown out of Austrian territory as well, Serbia's postponed day of reckoning arrived. In the early months the Serbs had been able to deal with the limited forces sent against them and even to drive them back. In October 1915 it was a different story. Austro-German armies crossed the Danube. Bulgaria, joining the war now as an Austrian ally, pounced on the Serbs from behind. Their mountainous little kingdom was overrun. In cruel wintry conditions they fell back through Albania to the Adriatic coast. The survivors were evacuated to the near-by island of Corfu, where they were re-formed to fight again as an army in exile. Serbia was wiped off the map, to reappear in due course, much enlarged after victory, as Yugoslavia.

It would be wrong to suppose that the war was now simplified into two main fronts, the Western bogged down in the Flanders mud and the Eastern strung more loosely across the woods and marshes of the Russian border. It was more complicated, because other countries had entered the fray.

Italy joined the Allies in 1915 and a new front was created in the Alps which divided her from Austria. The trench tactics of Flanders were here applied to a world of icy peaks and dizzy precipices. There were two sensational breakthroughs when the fighting became fluid, Ludendorff's **54** victory at Caporetto in October 1917 and the Italians' compensating

Italian troops moving up to the front

triumph at Vittorio Veneto a year later, but for most of the time this front was static and seemed to add only a third stalemate to the others. Unfortunately, this was not chess but war, and even stalemate meant the continual drain of human life.

Turkey came in on the German side in November 1914. If we remember all the Arab countries then subject to the Sultan of Turkey we shall see that the German alliance, or Central Powers, now stretched unbroken across Europe from the North Sea to the Bosphorus and on to the Persian Gulf. The Kaiser hoped that the Turks might be able to cut the Suez Canal, then and for long afterwards regarded as vital to British security; they might even punish faithless Georgie by robbing him of his Indian Empire. One thing was certain: with Turkey straddling the narrow waterway between the Mediterranean and the Black Sea, Georgie could not ship Nicky the military supplies he so badly needed.

This last consideration prompted the Gallipoli adventure.

Gallipoli is a hilly, shoe-shaped peninsula on the European side of the Dardanelles, the straits leading to Constantinople, now Istanbul. They are the Hellespont of legend. Troy stands opposite on the Asiatic shore.

Churchill was prime mover of a bold plan to force the Dardanelles, which were at first very feebly defended, sail through to Constantinople, knock Turkey out of the war, and establish a supply line to the warm-water ports of Russia, whose northern harbours were ice-bound and useless much of the year. Churchill however met with strong opposition from **55**

Gallipoli: The River Clyde *ran into merciless fire as the troops attempted to land*

Cabinet colleagues and Service chiefs, as well as from the French, who, having the Germans on their own soil, naturally wanted every man and gun devoted to the Western Front. Over and over again throughout these years there was constant argument between the Western Front enthusiasts and their opponents. The former, like Sir John French, the British commander-in-chief, and Sir Douglas Haig, who soon succeeded him, felt that only in France could the war be won. The others, like Churchill, were always seeking some imaginative stroke to shorten the useless butchery of the trenches.

Gallipoli might have been such a stroke if dealt swiftly. By the time Churchill gained grudging permission to try, it was too late. The original naval attack was abandoned after the loss of several ships, although (had the British realized it) the enemy forts had used up half their ammunition and there were no reserves of mines to lay. The Turks, in fact, despaired of beating off a second attack by sea. But none came. After weeks of hesitation the British landed troops instead on the Gallipoli peninsula. During those weeks the Turks had prepared defences and increased their force nearly tenfold.

The land attack was entrusted largely to the men who won immortality as the 'Anzacs', the Australian and New Zealand Army Corps, rugged, individualistic volunteers, shipped straight from their home Dominions to base camps in Egypt and thence across the Aegean. With them were United Kingdom troops of the 29th Division. In command was Sir Ian Hamilton, a popular general, whose inventive mind found plenty of scope in the plans for landing. Surprise being vital, it was decided to approach the coast under cover of darkness and attack at dawn. Several beaches **56** were chosen. The Turks were to be deceived by feints in other directions,

Australians going into attack at Anzac, named in honour of their Corps

including one by French troops on the Asiatic side. Most of the men would be towed in open boats from miles out at sea, but a large contingent would be packed inside an old collier, the *River Clyde*, rushing out through holes cut in her side, Trojan Horse fashion, when she was run aground in the shallows. The Navy played a vital part. One New Zealand officer in the Royal Naval Division swam two miles to plant guiding flares along the beach. He survived to win the Victoria Cross a year later, to be wounded nine times, to become Governor General of New Zealand. His name was Bernard Freyberg.

Some landings achieved complete surprise and the men got ashore without loss. Other parties ran into death-traps. Turkish machine-gunners, invisibly entrenched on the scrubby cliffs above, raked them as they crouched helpless in their boats or struggled like dying flies amid the barbed wire submerged beneath the shallow water. The *River Clyde* ran into a merciless fire. It was suicide to emerge. The survivors had to stay within the shelter of their plated sides until darkness returned. The carnage of that April morning was equalled a score of times on the Western front, but it is remembered with particular poignancy, especially in the two Dominions which lost so many of their finest young men.

Perhaps the whole campaign is remembered more than its strict military importance demands. Gallipoli became a word of bitter controversy, tragedy-laden, a reproach hurled at Churchill for the next twenty years. It was a good example of the conflict between the Western Fronters and their opponents, and of what happens when a plan is neither accepted nor rejected but is put into practice half-heartedly. First, time was wasted, so that when at last the expedition got ashore it had to fight desperately for every yard of a peninsula it could have walked over two months before. **57**

C

Secondly, the beach-heads won, Hamilton was not given enough reinforcements to finish the job. At the end of the year he was still doggedly hanging on, confident of final success. But the Government was determined to give up an adventure in which it had never fully believed, and Hamilton was replaced by another general who decided on evacuation. This dangerous operation was carried out brilliantly and without loss under cover of the Navy. Perhaps the only man to profit much from the campaign was an officer, Mustafa Kemal, who distinguished himself on the Turkish side and won the reputation which made him years later the popular national leader and founder of modern Turkey.

Gallipoli was not the only campaign against the Turks. A British Indian force sailed up the Persian Gulf and occupied Basra, where the Tigris joins the Euphrates. An over-optimistic advance up-river led to their heavy defeat and to their being besieged in Kut, where they had to surrender. More successful was the attempt to stir up the Arabs against their Turkish masters. This 'revolt in the desert', stimulated by a highly unorthodox Englishman, T. E. Lawrence, kept large Turkish forces guarding railways against guerilla dynamiters, and helped to shatter their decayed empire into the half-dozen states we see today.

There were other 'side-shows', as they were termed. There was fighting for instance in Tanganyika, formerly German East Africa, which like all Germany's scattered colonies was promptly assailed by the British in 1914. The Greek port of Salonika too became an Anglo-French base of operations against Bulgaria, though not much happened there until the closing weeks of the war. More important than these campaigns, however, was the war at sea and in the air.

'Jellicoe', said Churchill, 'was the only man on either side who could lose the war in an afternoon.'

One great disaster could destroy a nation's supremacy at sea and the Japanese had shown at Tsushima the danger of underrating an enemy. Without naval supremacy Britain could not transport troops and supplies to the various war zones, cover landings like those at Gallipoli, or bring in food for her population, raw materials for her factories, and armies from her Dominions. Nor, without it, could she blockade the enemy's ports and destroy their overseas trade. This was her strategy. Although the Central Powers formed one continuous territory, that territory was virtually under siege by the Allies, as the Kaiser had dreaded, and cut off from the world except for a few small neutral neighbours on land.

Jellicoe had to keep things that way. It would, of course, be splendid to sink the Kaiser's vaunted navy, but it was not essential. To keep it bottled up in harbour would do nearly as well. What he must guard against, if it **58** did come out and challenge him, was some pretended retreat which would

British seaplane escorting a convoy

lure him into a trap, such as a pack of submarines or a fresh-laid minefield.

There were, in the first six months or so, some spirited encounters at sea, though the main fleets were not engaged. Churchill's former assistant, the enterprising young Beatty, made a raid into German coastal waters near Heligoland, and sank several light cruisers. Later the Germans raided the Norfolk and Yorkshire coasts, bombarding Scarborough and other towns, but on a third visit they were caught by Beatty and badly mauled in a battle off the Dogger Bank. Further afield, the German Navy enjoyed a brief success. They had a Far Eastern squadron of five ships under Count von Spee, with a base in China. This was promptly attacked by Japan, entering the war as Britain's ally. The five German warships became out-laws. One, the *Emden*, bombarded Madras and raided merchantmen in the Indian Ocean until she was sunk by the Australian cruiser, *Sydney*. The others ranged across the Pacific, defeated a weaker British squadron off the coast of Chile, and were themselves annihilated at the Battle of the Falkland Islands.

Perhaps the most useful naval achievement early on should be credited to the Russians. A German light cruiser was sunk in the Baltic. The body of a drowned officer was picked up, clutching cipher and signal books, **59**

The Women's Forage Corps getting in the harvest

which the Russians sent to the British Admiralty. For the rest of the war it was possible to pick up and read the German naval signals in London, and pass them on instantly to Jellicoe at Scapa Flow. Even when the puzzled Germans suspected a leak and varied their codes, the Admiralty cryptographers were able to break them. Later, when radio was developed for the direct location of ships' positions, the actual reading of signals became less vital.

This directional radio played an important part in the one major sea-battle, at Jutland, on 31 May 1916, when Jellicoe and Beatty engaged the German High Seas Fleet west of Denmark. For all the new scientific aids to navigation and communication there were muddles on both sides, some of which cancelled out. Eventually the Germans slipped home to their bases under cover of mist and darkness. Jellicoe was criticized for this, but he had fought the battle correctly, if cautiously, ever mindful of a possible trap. As it was, his losses both in men and tonnage were roughly double those of the enemy, the Germans having better armour-piercing shells. Three big British ships blew up, but no German. 'There seems to be something wrong with our damned ships today', was Beatty's typical understatement, as he ordered a change of course nearer to the enemy. Altogether the British lost fourteen vessels and the Germans eleven, mostly smaller ones. Clearly the Kaiser's fleet was no laughing matter. All the same, it never engaged the British again.

The main German naval weapon was the submarine or U-boat. Early **60** in 1915, when they had only about two dozen underwater craft, the Ger-

Women of the First Aid Nursing Yeomanry worked as drivers at the front in France

mans announced that they would impose their own blockade by this means. Any ship in British waters, neutrals included, might be sunk at sight. The Cunard liner, *Lusitania*, bound for Liverpool from New York, was torpedoed off the Irish coast and went down with nearly twelve hundred passengers and crew, including 124 American citizens. This was a shock to the whole civilized world, still unused to the idea that war could involve the deliberate killing of non-combatants. It was a particular shock to the United States, and quickened the gradual swing of public opinion from neutrality towards joining the Allies. It was not till almost two years later, however, that the United States (on 6 April 1917) declared war on Germany.

That was just after the Germans had announced 'unrestricted submarine warfare'. By then they had about 150 U-boats, and Allied shipping losses had reached the appalling figure of 875,000 tons in a single month. In April 1917 one ship out of every four leaving British ports was sunk and the kingdom's food reserves fell to a six-week supply. For a time it looked as though Britain could be starved out by this submarine siege. Every possible counter-measure was put into force: decoy vessels or Q-ships, which looked helpless but suddenly revealed their guns; depth-charges; swift submarine chasers; seaplanes; and a long mine barrage, mostly laid by the United States Navy, to stop U-boats passing between Norway and the Orkneys. Most effective of all was the convoy system, whereby merchant ships were marshalled together and sailed under strict Admiralty control behind a protective screen of destroyers. Again the U.S. Navy **61**

weighed in with substantial help. Shipping losses went down. Submarines were sunk as fast as the Germans could build new ones. They were more and more hampered in their operations, their crews increasingly demoralized. By 1918 the worst was over. It had been bad enough. Ten million tons of shipping had been sent to the bottom, thousands of seamen drowned. Neutral Norway alone, an inoffensive little nation, unable to live except as a goods-carrier for other countries, lost 800 vessels.

The first aeroplanes were such lightweight ramshackle machines that the nickname of 'kite' was not unduly unfair. They were mainly for scouting. They were the bicycle of the skies. For dropping bombs the Germans used airships, named after Count Zeppelin who invented them. These long, cigar-shaped craft, their crews in cars or 'gondolas' suspended below, began night raids on Britain early in 1915, and continued for about eighteen months, until the improvement in aeroplanes and ground defences, and above all the explosive bullet, made their reception too warm to be comfortable. The total casualties and damage they inflicted were no more than those caused by a single night's medium bombing in World War II, but the psychological effect was considerable. These first few hundred civilian deaths demonstrated grimly that a new age of warfare had arrived.

Over the actual battlefields, curiously enough, it was the aviators who preserved for a year or two longer the last traditions of chivalry. They shot at each other with pistols as they sat exposed in their cockpits, their slow little machines buzzing through the air, more like gliders than the high-powered fighters of a generation later. Man was pitted against man. It was almost a sporting contest. The outstanding champions were known by name to the other side. It was a kind of combat even Homer would have understood.

Soon a light machine-gun was mounted. The propeller got in the way until Fokker, a Dutchman working for the Germans, invented an interruptor gear which so controlled the stream of bullets that they missed the whirring propeller blades. With this device, and the improved aeroplanes he built, the Germans won air superiority. The Allies regained it by organizing squadrons instead of relying on individual combat. The Germans went one better by forming special squadrons under some outstanding pilot who then recruited others, rather like a gang leader. These units were shifted from place to place, wherever the commanders on the ground specially needed air superiority, and because of this touring habit they were nicknamed 'circuses'. Such a 'circus' was headed by Baron von Richthofen, a chivalrous fighter who was shot down in 1918. His squadron was then taken over by a man destined to earn a very different reputation in later days, Hermann Göring.

This Sopwith Camel shows the marked advance in aircraft development

Meanwhile there were rapid technical advances. Engines were becoming more powerful, speeds rising, bomb-loads increasing. Slowly the Allies began once more to dominate the air. When the Zeppelin-raids stopped, the Germans began to send bombing planes over London in daylight, but the defences proved so strong that they switched their attentions to Paris. On the battlefronts, where the troops were deeply dug in, not much could be done from the air, but in the closing stages of the war, when the armies began to move about in the open again, there was scope for aerial attack on vital roads and bridges. 1918 saw the large-scale use of the new air weapon in this way, just as it saw the first development of a strategic bomber force designed to hit the German war industries. By then the aeroplane had truly come of age. The British Royal Flying Corps had started with 150 machines in 1914, its successor, the Royal Air Force, had over 22,000 in 1918, and though it was then the most powerful in the world the other major countries mustered a formidable total. And it was still only ten years since the Wright brothers had demonstrated the bare possibilities of their invention.

4 Enter America

When Woodrow Wilson ran again for President his policy was still neutrality. He was in the midst of a massive programme of social reform. Already, by the Federal Reserve Act, he had taken the control of the national finances away from the bankers and brokers of Wall Street and given it to the Federal Reserve Banks. Other Acts had lowered tariffs and strengthened the unions in their struggle (often more bitter than anything known in Britain) against the power of big business. Wilson wanted only to carry on with this progressive programme at home. His Republican opponents, except for a pro-Ally minority led by Theodore Roosevelt, were equally anxious to keep the United States out of the war.

The election was in November 1916. In January 1917 the re-elected Wilson had to summon the German Ambassador and tell him to leave the country. On 6 April the United States declared war.

How did it happen, this sudden turn-about?

For two and a half years both sides had been striving to influence the United States. The Allies wanted her to come in on their side: Germany, with no chance of getting America to fight for her, sought only to keep her out of the struggle. As that was precisely where most Americans wished to stay, Germany started with an advantage, and it was the Allies who had to do the persuading.

It was a complicated situation. The British could play on the 'common ancestry' of their 'American cousins'. But they had to reckon with millions of Irish-Americans. These hated Britain not only for bygone injustices but for what was still happening in Ireland, such as the crushing of the Easter Rising in Dublin, 1916, when a handful of idealists had risen in hopeless revolt against the British Government. Then there were all the Americans of German origin and the Poles and Jews who had emigrated to escape Russian tyranny. The Jews represented a very influential section in America, as in other countries, and special efforts were made to win **64** them over to the Allied cause. In the end Mr Balfour, the British Foreign

Woodrow Wilson

Secretary, made his historic Declaration, promising support for the Jewish plan to establish a national home in Palestine. Unfortunately, at the very same time, other Englishmen like T. E. Lawrence were quite sincerely encouraging the Arabs to suppose that they would be unchallenged masters of all those territories, once the Turks were expelled. Out of this confusion rose the conflict in later years when Palestine was partitioned into Israel and Jordan. The Balfour Declaration came about six months after America's entry into the war, but it was the climax of a long period of propaganda.

Propaganda was a new weapon. Its great exponent was Lord Northcliffe, founder of the *Daily Mail,* and the British must take the dubious credit for being best at it in those early days. Strictly speaking, 'propaganda' means only 'what-should-be-made-known', that is, the facts or beliefs that you sincerely hold to be true and wish to make public. Sincerity and truth had little chance against the wartime emotions of hatred and fear. Propaganda came to mean any story, true or false, which would influence people in a desired way—hearten one's own side, mislead or discourage the enemy, win sympathy from the neutrals. Favourite and widely believed propaganda stories were circulated about little Belgian children whose hands had been cut off by the Germans, about a Belgian boy walking round with a pail full of eyes gouged from wounded German heroes, and about Canadian soldiers crucified with bayonets. Despite careful investigations, no victim was ever found, dead or alive, with any sign of these mutilations, nor any witness of their having taken place.

Perhaps the worst consequence of propaganda was that many people found an excuse for ignoring even the truth when they found it painful **65**

A German U-Boat

or inconvenient. 'It's just propaganda!' has become a parrot-cry which is the curse of our century. It was necessary for men to learn that newspapers (and later radio and television programmes) could lie, that documents and even photographs, films and tape-recordings, could be faked. But to go to the other extreme, and pretend that nothing was true, nothing proved beyond reasonable doubt, was an attitude more worthy of ostriches.

In Woodrow Wilson's America the Allied and German propaganda organizations competed for the people's sympathy. That sympathy remained very much divided. Against the sinking of *Lusitania* could be set the British naval blockade, which stopped business men exporting goods not only to Germany but to neutrals like Holland and Sweden which might send them on to Germany overland. From across the Atlantic there did not seem much to choose between the two sides. Wilson himself wished to mediate between them and end the fighting. He did not want either to win a crushing victory.

Suddenly, all this changed. It was the moment when Germany, having built up her fleet of U-boats, decided on an all-out effort to defeat Britain by starvation. She knew that her new policy of unrestricted submarine warfare was one which a sea-trading power like the United States could not accept. Very well. The United States would probably come into the war. But she had only a small army, it would take time to create a big one, and there was the Atlantic to cross. The war could be won by Germany

66

Arab chieftains and their followers on the march

before American strength was brought into action. So the Germans took a calculated risk and the United States declared war, to be followed by every South American republic except Chile and the Argentine.

It was a grim year, 1917.

It saw the submarine siege of the British Isles. It saw the collapse of the Eastern Front following the Russian Revolution, an event dealt with in the next chapter. It saw fresh mass slaughter on the Western Front, where the Germans had withdrawn into skilfully prepared defences (the Hindenburg Line, or, as they called it themselves, the Siegfried Line) and were being reinforced by divisions no longer needed against Russia. It saw the defeat of the Italians at Caporetto.

Only in the 'side-shows' were the Allies doing well. In Mesopotamia (now Iraq) a British army avenged the surrender at Kut. A prisoner from that siege, receiving a censored letter from England with the mystifying information that 'Father's trousers have come down', was able (by mentally decoding 'trousers' into the current slang 'bags') to delight a whole camp with his interpretation, 'Baghdad has fallen'. It was true, and a serious blow to the Turks. Another British army was pushing northwards from Egypt into Palestine, with Lawrence and his Arabs playing their will-o'-the-wisp guerilla role in the desert on the right flank. Just before Christmas Jerusalem was entered by Allenby, a brilliant cavalry general who was able in that wild open country to use horsemen in a way now **67**

New York's army of conscripts parade up Fifth Avenue

impossible elsewhere. These two victories removed the threat to India and the Suez Canal and paved the way to fresh moves in the Balkans; but they did not mean much to the war-weary soldiers and civilians of France and Britain, who now had their backs against the wall, or to the Americans whose sole quarrel was with Germany.

How soon could America's man-power be thrown into the scales? Her dollars could be thrown in at a stroke of the pen. Invaluable—but no substitute for soldiers. Arms must not only be manufactured and paid for, they must be handled by trained men. Britain, like France, was scraping the barrel for troops. Immature youths, middle-aged and unfit men, were being drafted as cannon-fodder. Revolution had wiped out the soothing vision of countless Russian allies. All hopes centred on America. The most popular song of the period had a refrain:

> The Yanks are coming, the Yanks are coming . . .

But could they arrive in time?

The Germans knew they must win quickly or not at all. Their submarines had failed to administer the knock-out. Blockaded themselves, they could hardly feed their people and keep their factories in production. Innumerable commodities from the hot countries, such as coffee and chocolate, rubber and cotton, were denied to them. Their proud army **68** had suffered appalling casualties, though less than the Allies, and there

'Could they arrive in time?'

was similar war-weariness among its ranks. The fear of Russia had gone, the rosy dream of easy world-conquest had faded. The Kaiser shared his people's depression. He had long ago lost control of affairs, a figure-head, withdrawn into a world of his own, comforting himself with trivialities.

So, by 1918, the two European groups were like battered boxers, tottering from their corners to meet each other for the final round.

In February Hindenburg and Ludendorff addressed a secret session of the Reichstag, the German parliament, and promised a supreme last effort. They would strike a shattering blow against the British line where it hinged on the French. It might cost a million and a half German casualties, but it would be decisive. To raise morale the Kaiser himself would be nominally in command.

In March this attack was launched, taking the British by surprise and outnumbering them at vital points by four to one. They were particularly weak just then. They had sent help to the Italians and they had 300,000 trained men in Britain, held there by the Prime Minister (now Lloyd George) because he was afraid that his commander-in-chief, Haig, might throw them away in yet another wasteful offensive. The Americans had only just begun to arrive in France. There were about a quarter of a million of them, not enough to tip the scales.

The offensive started without warning. Instead of the usual long bombardment beforehand there was a short one of tremendous violence, including gas-filled shells. Then, covered by a 'creeping barrage' (the gunners aiming just ahead of their advancing infantry), the Germans swept over the British line. They used tactics new then but usual in the Second World War. Instead of delaying to mop up strong points which defied them, and to rally after each stage of the advance, the various groups pushed ahead, infiltrating through the defences as deeply as possible.

For some days the British position looked desperate. The Germans recovered a great tract of territory lost in previous years and in places touched their high-water mark of 1914. Sometimes success went to their heads and even Prussian discipline could not stop them from pausing to plunder. After blockaded Germany the British Army's rear zone seemed a land of plenty. The splendid British equipment, boots and waterproofs and leather jerkins, the food, the petty luxuries, even the writing-paper, emphasized the difference between Britain's shortages and the near-famine state of Germany.

It was not the Germans' occasional drunkenness and indiscipline that halted the offensive, it was the dogged resistance of the British, responding to Haig's historic order of the day: 'There is no other course open to us but to fight it out. Every position must be held to the last man. With our backs to the wall and believing in the justice of our cause, each one of us **70** must fight on to the end.'

A cartoon by Bruce Bairns-father. In the grim tragedy of war the British sense of humour was not altogether lost

SO OBVIOUS
The Young and Talkative One: 'Who made that 'ole?'
The Fed-up One: 'Mice'

The Germans were held. A joint Allied command was at last agreed to, Haig and the French general Pétain consenting to serve under the supreme control of the French general Foch. The Americans were begged to speed up the transport of their divisions. Huge liners, converted into troopships and crammed like human beehives, ran the gauntlet of the submarines. By November two million American soldiers had crossed the Atlantic.

Ludendorff's knock-out blow in March had failed, but he still had mighty forces at his disposal. He delivered another attack in April, a third in May, then rested, and started a fourth in July, with plans prepared for a fifth. It never came. The fourth offensive had just begun when, on the 18 July, Foch hit back. The French attacked at dawn with a force of light tanks leading the way, and quickly broke through on a front of twenty-seven miles. That day marked the turning of the tide. Over the next two or three months Germany's fortunes were ebbing away.

One outstanding Allied success was the British surprise attack made near Amiens on 8 August. It followed cunning preparation. Nearly 300 special trains brought up troops and ammunition sufficient to double the strength of the British Fourth Army and another 1000 guns were concentrated in the area, unsuspected by the Germans. Canadians being so often used as assault troops, their appearance in the line had become a sort of gale warning: as a ruse, therefore, two of their battalions were openly moved away, but other, and larger, Canadian forces were secretly brought up from the rear at the last moment.

The attack started with a massive onslaught by 456 tanks, the modern equivalent of a cavalry charge. Behind them came the Canadians, the **71**

American soldiers in the front line

Australians and the men of the United Kingdom, dim shapes amid the heavy ground mist of a summer dawn. An overwhelming barrage plastered the enemy positions and subdued their guns. Soon British armoured cars were speeding along the roads, turning surprise into chaos. The staff of one German army corps found itself attacked at breakfast. By the end of the day 16,000 prisoners had been taken.

The actual scale of the victory mattered less than the shock to German morale. 'August 8,' wrote Ludendorff afterwards, 'was the German Army's black day.' Realizing that he would never be able to deliver the promised knock-out, he declared that the war would have to be ended. 'I see that we must strike a balance,' the Kaiser agreed. 'We are at the end of our resources.'

To strike a balance . . . The Germans' best course now was to defend themselves resolutely and bargain for reasonable terms. They must try to deal with the idealistic President Wilson rather than the revengeful French.

Affairs were moving swiftly to their climax. With American troops pouring into the front line, Foch was able to keep up a succession of jabbing blows at the enemy. It was as though one of the exhausted boxers **72** had taken on a fresh lease of life and was sailing in with demonic fury to

The ruins of Amiens, one of the many devastated cities in northern France

finish the bout. On 12 September the American Army under Pershing won its first independent victory, advancing in difficult wooded country to wipe out the St Mihiel salient which the enemy had held since 1914. The Americans took 16,000 prisoners and 443 guns. The Germans were back on their Hindenburg Line again, but with a difference: they knew that this time they could not hold it. On 15 September they put out peace feelers to Wilson, but found that he was not prepared to deal with any government which did not truly represent the German people. The Kaiser therefore accepted the resignation of his ministers and asked a more liberal-minded statesman, Prince Max of Baden, to become Chancellor and form a democratic government acceptable to the Americans. The Prince begged the generals to fight on a little longer, so that he could stand out for favourable terms, but both Hindenburg and Ludendorff insisted that he must be quick. The actual request for an armistice was sent off on 3 October.

Meanwhile those autumn weeks saw the whole alliance of the Central Powers crumbling like a sand-castle as successive waves lick round it.

On 15 September the Allied armies on the Salonika front attacked the Bulgarians, split their army in half, and by the 29th were blotting their signatures on the surrender document. **73**

Lawrence of Arabia

October saw Turkey's turn. From Megiddo, near the Sea of Galilee, Allenby carried out a remarkable advance on Damascus and Aleppo, covering 350 miles in thirty-eight days and taking 75,000 prisoners with only 5,000 casualties. Again he made much use of cavalry, including the Australian Mounted Division and the Desert Mounted Corps. Once, to conceal from enemy observers the fact that he had moved them, he had 15,000 canvas dummies tethered in the empty horse-lines. He had aircraft, too, bombing and machine-gunning the Turkish columns to turn their retreat into rout. And on the desert flank there were the Arabs, outriding the regular cavalry and led by an incongruous figure in a Rolls Royce, a man in Arab dress, 'talking English perfectly and in the hell of a rage'. This was Lawrence, impatient as usual, but he had little cause to grumble: on 31 October Turkey surrendered.

Austria was not long behind. The aged Emperor had died in 1916 and no one believed that the Austrian Empire would hold together any longer. Bulgaria's surrender had released an army of Serbs to liberate their old country. In mid-October a bloodless revolution in Bohemia proclaimed the new republic of Czechoslovakia. On the 31st a similar revolution took place in Hungary. A few days before this the Italian Army, with British support, had launched the offensive which developed into the battle of Vittorio Veneto. Whole battalions of Czech and Polish troops serving in the Imperial army were delighted to surrender without firing a shot. The prisoners numbered half a million and 5,000 guns were captured. Austria surrendered unconditionally on 3 November. The new Emperor Charles abdicated. Vienna, long the proud capital of the great Austro-Hungarian Empire and the city from which the world catastrophe had been touched off four years earlier, was now only the top-heavy centre of a tiny landlocked republic containing 6½ million people.

Revolution, mutiny, abdication, were in the air. Russia's example was fresh in every mind. Now it was the day of reckoning for Germany. Her fleet, ordered to sea as a forlorn hope, refused to sail. Ludendorff, who had thrown up his command on 28 October, fled in disguise to Sweden. Hindenburg stayed at his post with grave dignity and eventually supervised the demobilization of his armies. On 9 November a republic was proclaimed in Berlin. A provisional government under a Socialist saddler, named Ebert, took over from Prince Max, and the Kaiser abdicated, seeking refuge in still-neutral Holland where he lived quietly as a country squire until his death in 1941.

On 11 November 1918, at five o'clock in the morning, the armistice terms were signed in a railway carriage which Foch used as his head-quarters. The Germans were to retire behind the Rhine and to surrender most of their navy. Peace terms were to be on the general lines suggested by President Wilson in a summary known as the Fourteen Points. New **75**

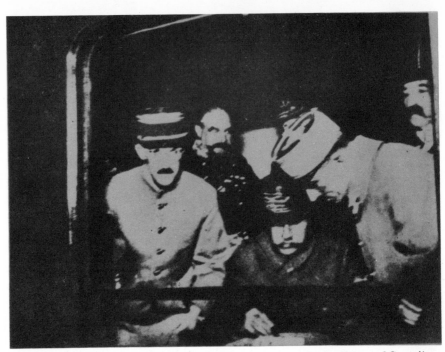

Signing the Armistice in General Foch's railway carriage in the Forest of Compiègne

frontiers were to be drawn placing people in the countries to which they wished to belong and a world organization was to be set up, called the League of Nations, to ensure that war could never happen again. Time would show that these ideas were not so easy to put into practice as they seemed. But who, at that moment, would have wished to delay the armistice with further argument?

It was signed. Six hours later it came into force, and the war was over. It had cost the lives of 10 million fighting men. The total casualties would never be accurately known.

5 Lenin and the Russian Revolution

On 8 April 1917, just two days after America's entry into the war, a moment when Germany was in the mood to try anything that would hasten victory, a Russian exile in Switzerland suddenly informed his landlord that he and his wife were leaving immediately for home, though the rent of their bed-sittingroom was paid till the end of the month.

'I hope that you won't have to work so hard in Russia as here,' said the kindly Swiss, mindful of his tenant's long hours of letter-writing and of study in the Zürich public library. The stocky little man, forty-six, bald, snub-nosed, button-eyed, with a reddish-grey beard, utterly undistinguished in his cloth cap and baggy trousers, but soon to step into world history, answered with sardonic humour: 'I think that in Petersburg I shall have even more work.'

On the following afternoon Lenin, with his wife Krupskaya and thirty other exiled revolutionaries, pushed their way through excited demonstrators and got into the train for Germany. Sympathizers waved red flags and sang the *Internationale*, already the recognized anthem of Communism. Others jeered: 'Spies! German spies!' and shouted that the Kaiser had paid for their tickets. Lenin was never a man to be moved by opposition. He was far more concerned, as a non-smoker, that his comrades' cigarettes should not annoy him during the long journey ahead. He insisted that any one wishing to smoke should retire to the lavatory. Already his personality was so dominant that he could dictate even in matters like that.

There was some justification for the hostile demonstrators. A new government had just taken control in Russia, its policy to continue the war with more vigour and efficiency. Lenin was against the war and always had been. From the German point of view he would be a most useful trouble-maker if he could be shipped back to St Petersburg. The only way was across Germany and the Baltic Sea from neutral Switzerland to neutral Sweden, and thence by train again into Finland, in those **77** days part of the Russian Empire. Since any ordinary Russian traveller entering Germany would be arrested at once as an enemy, the journey was possible only with the approval of the German Government. This had been given. Lenin had insisted on a 'sealed' train through Germany, their compartments to be given the same extra-territorial rights as a foreign embassy. He was promised that no one should be seized and taken off. Under the circumstances it was quite clear why the Germans were behaving so helpfully, though neither their General Staff nor their Foreign Office, who concocted the plan, foresaw its worldwide consequences. Lenin did. 'If the German capitalists are so stupid as to take us over to Russia,' he said, 'it's their own funeral.'

After a two-day journey, via Frankfurt and Berlin, they reached the Baltic coast and sailed across to Malmo in Sweden. Another long train journey followed, first to Stockholm and then to the frontier at the far north of the Gulf of Bothnia, just short of the Arctic Circle. Sledges took them over the frontier into Finland, where they boarded a train for St Petersburg. Their week-long odyssey was drawing to a close. Lenin wondered if he would be arrested the minute he set foot on the platform, but his sister joined him at a station just outside the city and declared that he had nothing to fear from the new government.

Even so he was hardly prepared for the reception which awaited him. As he stepped out of his second-class carriage a great bouquet was pressed into his hands, a guard of honour presented arms, a band began to play. Everywhere were banners, slogans, triumphal arches in red and gold. A committee of welcome awaited him in the ornate waiting-room that had once been the Tsar's. When he emerged into the gathering twilight the square outside was solid with cheering, singing demonstrators, their faces spot-lit by the questing beam of a searchlight, which now swung round and came to rest on the armoured car he mounted as a speaker's platform.

'Comrades,' he began, 'soldiers, sailors and workers! I greet you as the vanguard of the world-wide proletarian army. The Russian revolution accomplished by you has opened a new epoch . . .'

What had happened? And how? To understand that, we must go back a good many years.

Lenin was born in 1870 in a small city on the banks of the Volga, a place of wooden houses, like the provincial towns depicted in the classic Russian novels. His mother had been a schoolmistress, his father a physics teacher now promoted to schools inspector. Their home was one of respectable middle-class comfort, one in which ideas were discussed. Lenin and his brothers expected to go to the university.

78　At an early age, the children learnt that homes like theirs were mere

These Russian peasants were among the more fortunate as they lived on the estate of Leo Tolstoy. Their primitive homes are seen in the background

islets scattered over an ocean of poverty and ignorance. The Russian Empire was a land of illiterate peasants. Serfdom (which we associate with the England of Robin Hood) had lasted in Russia until 1861. Though the serfs were now legally free, their position was often no better than before, and sometimes worse. Millions scratched a bare living from the land. Others, landless and desperate, trekked hundreds of miles to seek work in the few industrial cities.

Industry had developed late in Russia, generations behind the West. Even now it depended on foreign capital. Foreign experts, British, French, German, Belgian, were laying the railways, starting up the mills and factories, mining the coal and iron. There were high profits to be made in Russia, for labour was cheap and not yet organized in trade unions, but there was not a sufficiently numerous and enterprising middle class to run these expanding industries without bringing in foreigners. There was an upper class, living at Court or on country estates, rather like the French aristocrats before the French Revolution, and there was the **79**

immense working class, living on the starvation line. Between them, small out of all proportion, was the middle class to which Lenin's father belonged.

As in France, it was this class (not 'the mob') that started the Revolution. They were often intelligent, well-read, widely-travelled men. They knew what went on in the outside world, they knew the poverty of their own country, they saw many obvious improvements crying to be made. And there was practically nothing, nothing legal, at least, that they could do about it.

Russia had no Parliament so they had no votes, until 1906 when, after the risings, the Tsar granted a 'Duma', an elected assembly with very limited powers. Even after 1906 the Russian Empire was an 'autocracy', under the absolute rule of a single man. The only difference between an autocracy and a dictatorship is that, whereas a dictator is normally self-made and a strong (if often evil) character, an autocrat inherited his absolute power along with his throne. The last of the Tsars was a good-natured nonentity, like Louis XVI, and like him came to a tragic end.

The Tsar took his ministers' advice or ignored it as he pleased, decreed new laws himself, distributed honours and promotions at his own sweet will. Under him was a host of timid civil servants wearing uniforms appropriate to their grades. The vast sprawling out-of-date country was controlled by policemen and police spies, with troops, especially the dreaded Cossack cavalry and their whips, ready in the background to quell strikes, hunger marches, or other symptoms of discontent. All news-papers, magazines and books were censored, but not always very intelligently: harmless publications were sometimes suppressed while far more dangerous ones slipped into circulation.

When there is no lawful way to oppose bad government men will use force. When that government is concentrated in an all-powerful individual there is a temptation to kill him. Plots to assassinate the various tsars were frequent in Russian history and sometimes successful. Young idealists were easily tempted into such schemes. When Lenin was seventeen his elder brother Alexander, a student in St Petersburg, joined a conspiracy to throw a bomb at the then-reigning Tsar. The plotters were arrested as they carried their bomb down the main street. Lenin's father had recently died and his mother had to attend the trial alone; no one in the little town dared go with her or show any friendliness to the stricken family. Alexander and four other youths were hanged. The event left a lasting scar on Lenin's character. 'No,' he said, 'that is not the way we must go.' Already he knew that throwing bombs at emperors was point-less.

Soon he went to Kazan University, only to be expelled after four months **80** for taking part in student riots. He was now a marked man. The police

Nicholas II, Tsar of Russia, and the Tsarina

watched his movements, no other university would admit him. Eventually he was allowed to take the law examinations at St Petersburg as an external candidate. He came top in every subject and won the gold medal.

One book he had studied more thoroughly than any of his legal volumes. He had inherited it from his brother and it was called *Capital*, by Karl Marx. Henceforth it was to be his Bible, and through him to become the Bible of almost half the human race.

Marx was a German Jew who had sought refuge in London after the revolutionary uprisings in Germany in 1848. There, patiently researching in the British Museum Reading Room, he had spent the rest of his life elaborating his political and economic theories into a complete philosophy of life.

Though a Jew by race and brought up as a Christian, Marx did not believe in religion, which he called 'the opium of the people', meaning that the rich used it to keep the poor quiet, promising them Heaven to make up for their ,sufferings in this world. Lenin could see that the Orthodox Church in his own country was more concerned with splendid ceremonial, vestments and choral music than with denouncing the evils around it. As the son of a science teacher he was the more ready to accept Marx's view that all life could be explained in materialist terms and that Man himself was merely an intellectual animal, motivated by self-interest and without an immortal soul. This self-interest lay behind all political effort.

All history was the record of class struggle, the never-ending fight between the 'haves' and the 'have-nots'. Who could deny that in bygone ages the slaves and serfs had been exploited by their masters? Marx argued that the modern workers were every bit as much exploited, though in a less obvious way. The capitalist employer was robbing each man by the amount of profit he made out of his product. True, the man was free to leave his job, but unless he wished to starve he would have to go to another capitalist employer. He was no more 'free' than the slave or serf, less free than the craftsman who had owned his simple tools. A miner could not own his mine or an engine-driver his railway or a cotton-spinner his mill. Under modern industrial conditions the 'tools', the 'means of production and distribution', had become too big for the individual worker to possess. The only solution was for the working-class, or proletariat, to organize and take over their 'tools' collectively.

Theories of socialism and communism had been put forward by many thinkers before Marx. But Marx brought the theories down to earth and hammered out a harsh and realistic programme for action. The 'bourgeoisie' (the capitalist class owning the factories, mines, land and so forth) would never be persuaded to hand over the means of production. In democratic countries they would use every means to prevent the workers from electing a government to make the change by law. If necessary the bourgeoisie would be ruthless in resorting to armed force to maintain its position. So the masses would never achieve power without revolution. The preparation of that revolution, by making the masses 'class-conscious' and aware of the 'class struggle', was Marx's life-work. 'Workers of the world, unite!' he wrote. 'You have nothing to lose but your chains. You have a world to win.'

Marx, who had died about four years before Lenin read *Capital*, had never put much faith in any Russian contribution to the Communist cause. The revolution, he thought, would come in the Western countries, where the workers were better educated and freer to organize political parties and trade unions. But his books were circulating in Russia (to the censors they looked too dull to be dangerous) and they were eagerly discussed by young men like Lenin. Marx, they felt, had the answer, and his way was better than throwing bombs at the Tsar.

St Petersburg: the Winter Palace of the Tsar is on the right

At twenty-three Lenin was living in St Petersburg, earning some sort of livelihood as a lawyer, though fully absorbed in politics. Here in the imperial capital (today renamed after him, Leningrad) he found more and more to confirm his Marxist views. It was a city of staggering contrasts: on the one hand the splendours of the Court, the opera, the ballet, the princely palaces; and on the other the slums and factories, the rags and hunger. It was not till some years later that the working day was fixed at a maximum of $11\frac{1}{2}$ hours with a mere 10 hours on Saturdays. Housing conditions were so bad that many people slept on the factory floor beside their machines. Others lived in common dormitories provided by their employers, men, women and children crowded together like pigs, sometimes with only two square yards of space per person. The **83** man on the night shift had to sleep in the bed just vacated by another. It was easy, in old St Petersburg, to see what Marx had meant by 'exploitation', and, when the troops turned out to shoot down strikers, to believe his warning that the ruling class would stick at nothing to retain its power.

Lenin and his friends planned to publish an uncensored (and therefore illegal) newspaper. Before the first issue could appear they were arrested. Lenin spent over a year in prison awaiting trial. He managed to do a little writing in secret, using milk instead of ink and moulding 'ink-wells' out of bread, which he could swallow if interrupted. Krupskaya, a young school-teacher also active in the revolutionary movement, used to stand outside on the pavement for hours to catch a brief glimpse of him when the prisoners were brought out for exercise. At his trial he was sentenced to three years in Siberia. This was the common Tsarist method with such offenders, to remove them out of harm's way. Exile could be harsh, according to the circumstances, or mild. When, a year later, Krupskaya herself was exiled, she was allowed to join Lenin and marry him. It was a happy marriage. Lenin might be an atheist, contemptuous of 'bourgeois morality', and unscrupulous in political matters, but his private life was of almost puritanical respectability.

Their exile ended in 1900. They left Russia, lived some time in London, and then settled in Switzerland. Lenin still wanted to produce an uncensored newspaper, but it seemed easier to print it abroad and have copies smuggled into Russia. It was called *Iskra*, 'the Spark', and it certainly helped to start the fire which grew into the Communist revolution. Lenin became more and more important among the Russian revolutionary leaders abroad.

The movement was rent by many disputes, varying from sincere differences of opinion to bitter personal intrigues. A main disagreement was about the best form of organization with which to overthrow the Tsarist government and gain power. Some, like the brilliant Jew, Leon Trotsky, wanted to build up a mass party like those of the Western democratic countries, with membership open to any sympathizer. Lenin, on the other hand, favoured a small, secret, highly-disciplined party of 'professional' revolutionaries, obeying without question the instructions of its leadership. Such a party would be like a spearhead for the working class as a whole. Trotsky thought it would lead too easily to dictatorship. At a conference held in London in 1903 the movement split on this issue. Lenin and his friends won a temporary majority and were known henceforth as the 'Bolsheviks' (or majority group), while the Trotskyist minority were called the 'Mensheviks'. The feud continued for a long time, but in the end it was Lenin's ideas which set the pattern for the Communist party not only in Russia but throughout the world, and the term 'Bolshevik' was commonly applied to the second 1917 Revolution when it came.

Shortened to 'bolshy', it passed into English slang to describe anybody or anything disapproved of by the speaker.

Lenin went back to Russia during the 1905 Revolution which followed the Russo-Japanese War, but he was not so prominent as Trotsky, who was chairman of the St Petersburg Soviet. When this revolution failed, both had to escape abroad again, and the Bolshevik-Menshevik wrangles continued in exile. At one point Lenin, who was very good at expelling people with whom he disagreed, had the weapon of expulsion used against himself, but year by year he was strengthening his hold on the movement and building up a core of faithful followers. By 1912 these were organized in a separate Bolshevik Party, the name being changed to 'Communist' in 1919.

In July 1914 Lenin happened to be in Austria and was (ironically) arrested as a Russian spy. He soon convinced his captors that he was anything but a loyal subject of the Tsar and they let him go back to Switzerland. He was there in 1917 when the German General Staff hit on the ingenious idea of sending him home to upset the reviving Russian war-effort.

But why 'reviving', if indeed it was? And why did the square in front of the Finland Station flower with red flags to welcome him when he reached St Petersburg? Once more, to understand the situation, we must go back a few years and follow another thread of the story.

Nicholas II, last of the Romanov emperors, had been Tsar since 1894, when Lenin was starting his underground activities in the capital.

In some respects Nicholas resembled Charles I of England, though in others he was less interesting. Like Charles he believed in the divine right of kings, was too much influenced by a foreign wife, and adored his children. Like Charles too he came to a tragic end.

His wife, the Tsarina, known as Alexandra Fedorovna, had been Princess Alice of Hesse-Darmstadt, and was regarded as a German with pro-German sympathies which in fact she did not possess. On her mother's side she was half English, being a grand-daughter of Queen Victoria, and she was very much of a strict, strong-willed English Victorian type, completely dominating her devoted husband. They had four daughters and then at last a son and heir, the Tsarevitch Alexis. Unfortunately the little boy had inherited the disease of haemophilia. If he suffered even a trivial cut he was liable to bleed to death, since his blood was deficient in the element needed to make it clot. Alexis was therefore always a delicate child and had to be surrounded with precautions. When he had an attack of bleeding none of the Court doctors seemed able to stop it until he was dangerously weak. The Tsarina's own health was now poor. She would have no more children, so that all hopes of the dynasty rested on **85**

86   *'A tattered figure with unkempt beard and extraordinarily hypnotic eyes'*

the only son. She had never been a highly intelligent woman. From this date she became more and more neurotic and superstitious, but she lost none of her power to influence the Tsar.

At this point a quite outlandish character takes the stage, one more appropriate to a weird folk-tale than to the sober records of the twentieth century.

Out of Siberia came a tattered figure with unkempt beard, greasy hair falling to his shoulders, and extraordinarily hypnotic eyes. He was a *starets* or 'man of God', the equivalent in old Russia of the holy men who still beg their way along the roads of India. It was said that in his native village, before turning to religion, he had been a horse-thief, a drunkard, and worse, and that he had deserted a wife and three children. He was still drunkard, beastly in his habits, shamelessly immoral. But along with these qualities he had a peasant shrewdness in summing people up and a theatrical genius for projecting his strong personality. Thus he was able to win the patronage of a superstitious grand duchess and then to gain admission to the innermost circle of the Court. Once there, Gregory Rasputin was unassailable. It did not matter that he was illiterate and uncouth, that he hardly ever washed, put his hands in the soup, and smashed furniture when fighting drunk. By some means, probably hypnotism, he could stop the Tsarevitch's bleeding as no doctor could. The Tsarina was deaf to complaints against him.

If the Tsar ruled Russia, the Tsarina ruled the Tsar, and now Rasputin, the 'man of God' or 'Our Friend', as she called him in letters, ruled the Tsarina. Gradually Rasputin extended his control over every department of government. At a word from him ministers were dismissed, his favourites promoted. To stand well with Rasputin became essential. To incur his dislike spelt ruin.

The system of Tsarist autocracy was ideal for his purpose. The Tsar and his wife lived in a closed little world of their own, no longer in their palace at Petersburg but fifteen miles away at Tsarskoe Selo. Even their imperial relatives had few chances to talk freely to them. Outwardly the charming and kindly 'Little Father' of his people, Nicholas would receive ministers and appear to agree with all they said; but when they returned to their offices they were liable to receive, within hours, written orders to the exact opposite effect, or even their own dismissal. They might indeed discover with some surprise, on opening the newspaper, that they had 'resigned'.

By 1914 Rasputin's power seemed secure. Neither the warnings of the highest nobility nor the police reports on his outrageous private life had the slightest effect upon the Tsarina and her obedient husband. Rasputin held receptions, listened to petitions, sent orders to government departments, even told Nicholas what he should write to his fellow sovereigns in **87**

The 'Little Father' blessing his troops

Greece and Serbia. When the war began he demanded advance information of the military plans, so that he could ensure their success by prayer. The response of the generals was not sympathetic: the Tsarina was regarded as a German and the 'man of God' himself was against the war. But it was not easy to withstand Rasputin. It was he who secured the dismissal of the Grand Duke Nicholas from the supreme command and encouraged the Tsar to take over his cousin's post in person. Henceforth, with the Tsar mainly at the front, the affairs of the Empire were more than ever in Rasputin's hands. When the discontent of the people became obvious even to the Tsarina, she still bombarded her husband with letters urging him to refuse the slightest concession to democracy.

'Russia loves to feel the whip,' she wrote. 'How I wish I could pour my will into your veins! Listen to me, which means Our Friend . . . Be the Tsar, be Peter the Great, Ivan the Terrible—crush them all under you . . . We have been placed on the throne by God, and we must keep it firm and hand it on intact to our son.'

The Tsarina wrote these words towards the end of 1916, when Russia was slipping into chaos with mass desertions at the front and famine behind the lines. A group of aristocratic patriots decided that Rasputin must be removed before it was too late. The conspirators included the Tsar's cousin, the Grand Duke Dimitri, and the husband of the Tsar's

niece, Prince Yusupov, a handsome and wealthy young man who had been educated at Oxford. About midnight on 29 December Rasputin was lured to the Prince's house by the hope of meeting the Princess, whose beauty was well known. A very different welcome, however, had been prepared for him in a basement room: wine and fancy cakes, chocolate and almond, containing potassium cyanide. Rasputin partook freely of the poisoned refreshments, but they seemed to have no effect upon him. The Prince grew more and more afraid that this man did indeed possess the uncanny powers attributed to him. He slipped upstairs to consult his fellow-conspirators. There was a feverish discussion. Yusupov borrowed a revolver, went back, and shot Rasputin through the heart. The others came downstairs, examined the body, and agreed that life was extinct. They retired for further discussions, but when the Prince returned once more to look at the corpse he was appalled to see Rasputin clambering to his feet. There was a struggle. Rasputin tore one of the epaulettes from the Prince's tunic. Yusupov broke away and fled upstairs in panic, the indestructible Rasputin scrambling after him on hands and knees, roaring like an animal. It was the very stuff of nightmares. Rasputin broke out into the courtyard. Another conspirator, a conservative politician, drew a revolver, fired twice and missed, then twice again. Rasputin collapsed in the snow and was dragged indoors again, where the Prince (who had just been violently sick with the horror of it all) battered him hysterically until dragged off by his servants. Before dawn the body, bound with ropes, was thrown over a bridge into the Neva. It is said that when divers recovered it they found it freed from its bonds and the post mortem certainly revealed that Rasputin had been alive when he went into the water. But he was dead now, indisputably, and the Tsarina was heart-broken. The Tsar hastened back from his army headquarters to console her.

Rasputin's death had come too late to make much difference. Greater forces were sweeping the Russian Empire to its doom. Rasputin had ruled through his influence over the Tsar, but his misuse of that influence had undermined the Tsar's authority. It was not merely that the class-conscious workmen cared nothing for the Romanov dynasty, that the soldiers were sick of dying for the 'Little Father' and that by now over a million and a half were listed as deserters. Things had come to such a pass that even the nobility forsook their loyalty to the throne. They saw that there would *be* no throne, if Nicholas was allowed to sit on it much longer.

So in March came the first of the two 1917 revolutions, known as the February Revolution because Russia was then using the old calendar. The Duma had just opened a new session. It was an assembly with little power but it gave politically-minded men an excuse to meet together. Petersburg was at boiling point. A hold-up in food supplies led to angry queues and bread riots. The police fired on the crowds. The workmen then walked out of the factories, the boys out of their schools. Everywhere **89** the streets were thronged with flag-waving demonstrators. More shooting followed a day or two later. A regiment of Guards went over to the people, followed by the greater part of the garrison. The arsenal was raided, arms distributed, the prisons broken open, the headquarters of the political police set on fire. The revolution had flared up quite spontaneously, but soon a committee of the Duma took control as a provisional government. Desperately its president telegraphed to the Tsar appealing for some democratic move. 'The last hour has come,' he warned Nicholas, 'when the destiny of the country and the dynasty is being decided.'

Nicholas made no answer. He *knew* no answer to such situations but the time-honoured method of the Tsars, repress by force. He despatched a small army to restore order in St Petersburg. They could not get through: the Provisional Government had telegraphed to all the main military commanders and they supported its policy. So did the principal Grand Dukes, the Tsar's own relatives. Nicholas started off for Tsarskoe Selo but the railway line was blocked against him. Two delegates from the Provisional Government came to meet him and he realized that there was nothing for it but abdication. As his son's disease was incurable it was agreed that he should resign the crown to his brother instead, the Grand Duke Michael.

The Provisional Government, however, was not entirely master of the situation: it had a rival in the Petersburg Soviet, an assembly composed of delegates from the factories, regiments and naval units of the capital. These men were the real power in the distracted city and they wanted no more Romanovs to rule over them. A brilliant young Socialist lawyer, Alexander Kerensky, both a member of the Provisional Government and a delegate to the Soviet, persuaded the Grand Duke to delay his acceptance until the crown could be offered to him by a democratic constituent assembly. It never was. So, with the Tsar deposed and under arrest, and the throne vacant, the rule of the Romanovs petered out. This was the confused state of affairs, with the masses determined to end the war with Germany and the Provisional Government promising to carry it on more efficiently, when the German General Staff decided to help Lenin on his homeward way.

Lenin was not the only historic personage making for St Petersburg. Stalin was there before him, a swarthy, pock-marked Georgian, who had escaped five times from Siberian exile and had been released from his sixth term by the Provisional Government, which he supported until Lenin instructed him otherwise. And from America by devious means, first held, then let go by the British, came Trotsky, shock-haired and foxy-faced, with tuft of beard and rimless pince-nez, as fierily eloquent with **90** pen as with voice, and soon to display a fresh side to his genius as a military

'Comrades, we shall now proceed to build the Socialist system.' Lenin harangues a crowd

organizer. An old rival and opponent of Lenin's he now buried the hatchet and joined the Bolshevik Party. These and many other seasoned revolutionaries, famous in their day but since forgotten, were winging like eagles to the battlefield.

The Western democracies welcomed the 'February' Revolution because it looked like replacing a harsh and corrupt government with one more like their own, which would fight better against Germany. But Lenin and his friends had no use for a new government like that. They were working for an entirely fresh system, the 'dictatorship of the proletariat', to be wielded by one party (their own) in the interests not of the whole population but of the working class. 'Peace, bread, and land', was their slogan. The war must be ended, the peasants must carve up the estates, all power must be transferred to the soviets which already had control in many districts.

Despite the banners and bouquets which had welcomed him, Lenin was still one voice in the argument. The Bolsheviks were only one party among several, and by no means all Bolsheviks agreed with Lenin. He had to fight his way along a zigzag path to victory. Then, as at all times in his **91**

Trotsky, 'as fiercely eloquent with pen as with voice'

life, he had no scruples. To the Bolshevik, bred on Karl Marx's theories, politics were not the gentlemanly sport they seemed to British members of Parliament. They were another form of war, with no holds barred, no tricks forbidden. The end justified the means. Loyalty meant loyalty to the Party, not to country or flag or personal friend, if one had to choose between them. It was the logical conclusion of the Marxist philosophy, which had no place for absolute values such as 'truth' and 'honour', but held that everything was relative to the final supreme interests of the working class. Whether this view of life be accepted or rejected, it must be studied calmly if the growth of Communism throughout the world is to be understood.

It was in this spirit that Lenin now co-operated with, now opposed, anyone who for the moment shared the political stage. Whatever he said, whatever he wrote, he never wavered in his purpose, the achievement of power. If he seemed inconsistent it was only the tacking of a yachtsman against the wind. 'If you are not ready to adapt yourselves,' he was to tell his comrades a few months later, 'if you are not prepared to crawl on your belly in the mud, you are not a revolutionary but a windbag. I propose

this action not because I like it but because we have no other course.'
Intellectual though he was, ever concerned with the hammering out of
correct theories, he was also supremely practical.

Against such implacable determination the Provisional Government
had little to set but worthy intentions and fine promises it had no power to
fulfil. Its moving spirit was not its official leader, Prince Lvov, but Kerensky, a theatrical figure with demonic energy and personal courage, who
might have made a successful statesman in easier times. In 1917 all the
circumstances were against him. He was not in the same class as Lenin.
He had no more chance than, in the French Revolution, Lafayette had
against men like Danton and Robespierre.

By July the situation had become so difficult, with the government trying simultaneously to hold a line against the German armies and to resist
the Bolshevik agitation for peace, that Kerensky was made Prime Minister
and took strong action. The Bolshevik Party was declared illegal, its
newspaper *Pravda* suppressed, Trotsky imprisoned, Lenin driven into
hiding in Finland. From there he continued to direct his comrades working underground in the capital.

In September the commander-in-chief of the Russian Army, a Siberian
Cossack named Kornilov, tried to march on Petersburg and establish a
military dictatorship. Kerensky needed every ally against this threat.
Arms were distributed to all and sundry, including the Bolshevik workers.
It was the Bolsheviks who stopped Kornilov, not as it happened by shooting but by political methods. Railwaymen hindered his troop movements,
telegraphists suppressed his messages, agitators mixed with his soldiers
and turned them against him. Kornilov never reached the barricades
outside Petersburg. Kerensky was able to arrest him and take over in
person the command of the armies at the front. But everyone knew that
it was really the Bolsheviks who had stopped the attempted coup, and their
prestige went up. Kerensky was forced to release Trotsky and other leaders.
He was unable to call in the weapons that had been issued. The Bolsheviks
now had teeth as well as tongues.

Lenin moved nearer to the Finnish border. 'The crisis is here,' he wrote,
'it is criminal to delay.' The time had come for an armed rising. Picked
squads of Bolsheviks should arrest the General Staff, occupy the telephone
exchange and all key buildings, and seize the main bridges linking the
numerous river islands which made Petersburg a little like Venice. If the
committee did not act soon, Lenin threatened that he would resign and
oppose them as a rank and file member. In late October, disguised, a wig
over his baldness and the well-known beard removed, he slipped back into
the city to meet Trotsky, Stalin, and the rest of the Party leaders. It was
Trotsky who, as head of the Military Revolutionary Committee, was
chiefly responsible for planning the seizure of the capital. He managed to **93**

Lenin in disguise, 1917. This photograph was taken for an illegal identification card. RIGHT: *Red Guards manning an armoured truck in St Petersburg*

win over most of the garrison and to get hold of another five thousand rifles for distribution to Bolshevik supporters.

Over the next week or two events moved quickly to a crisis. Public demonstrations were forbidden, Cossacks patrolled the misty rain-swept streets, troops guarded the long brownish-ochre façade of the Winter Palace where the Provisional Government was established. Some distance away the City Soviet, not yet a Bolshevik organization but more and more dominated by Bolsheviks, had its headquarters under the blue-cupolaed roof of the Smolny Institute, a former convent which had been till lately an exclusive girls' school. Here sat Trotsky, perfecting his battle plans, and here he was joined just before midnight on 6 November by Lenin, a dirty bandage wrapped round his face to hide it from the roving Cossacks. It was still October by the old calendar. Within a few hours the 'October' Revolution had begun.

While, in the early hours of that morning, the last furious arguments were raging between the Bolsheviks and their opponents in the City Soviet, Kerensky was holding an equally urgent meeting of his cabinet in the Winter Palace. Feeling that he could not rely on the soldiers and sailors in Petersburg, he decided to drive to Gatchina twenty-eight miles away, rally the Third Cavalry Corps by his personal magnetism and authority, and lead it back to suppress the threatened rising. At 3 a.m. Kerensky

drove out of Petersburg in a car disguised by an American flag. In effect, he drove out of history. For he found no troops at Gatchina, and by the time he had mustered a force a few days later it was too late. He had to escape from Russia with the help of the British agent, Bruce Lockhart. Half a century of exile lay before him in Paris and America, but never again was he to have any influence on world events.

It was a strange day, that 7 November 1917, in the city soon to be renamed Leningrad. People went to work, shops opened, little strings of streetcars jangled along, silent films flickered in the cinemas, Chaliapin sang at the opera house, Karsavina appeared in a new ballet . . . and while all this was going on as usual the Bolsheviks occupied the strategic points according to plan and tightened their net round the Winter Palace itself. As the day passed, its defenders gradually melted away: by nightfall they were scarcely 1000, mainly officer-cadets, with 130 members of a women's battalion.

The signal for action came at 9 p.m. with two blank cannon shots, one from the Fortress of St Peter and St Paul, one from the cruiser *Aurora*, which had moved up the Neva and was playing its searchlights on the riverside façade of the Palace. Soon live shells and bullets began to pepper the beautiful eighteenth-century building, but little serious damage was done, for the Palace was spread over four and a half acres and the bom- **95** bardment was intended to frighten the inmates into surrender, not blow them to pieces. There were few casualties, far fewer than in the February Revolution: the bloodshed came not with the seizure of power but in the years afterwards. Soon after midnight parties of armed Bolsheviks had broken into the mazelike building at various points and were wandering through its endless corridors. Within another hour or two the whole Palace was in their hands and the Provisional Government (except for Kerensky) under arrest.

On the following evening there was an exultant meeting at the Smolny Institute. Lenin mounted the platform and waited some minutes for the ovation to die down. 'Comrades,' he said quietly, 'we shall now proceed to build the Socialist system.'

What followed must be dealt with in a later chapter. Here there is space only to tie up a few loose ends. What happened to the war with Germany, which the Western Allies had to wage for another twelve grim months? Lenin, as he had promised, ended it so far as Russia was concerned, signed the Treaty of Brest-Litovsk on terms very favourable to Germany (he had no alternative, with his country exhausted and in a state of anarchy), and released dozens of German divisions for use against the West.

And the unfortunate Tsar, deposed and arrested by the Provisional Government? During these months he and his family were moved from place to place, to Tobolsk in Siberia and thence to Ekaterinburg (now Sverdlovsk) in the Ural Mountains. Their situation was all the more dangerous just because the Bolsheviks had not complete control of the country. Rival factions and individual army commanders were operating in different regions. There was always a strong possibility that the Tsar would be rescued and used as a figurehead to rally the forces hostile to the Revolution. That was the reason, though not a justification, for the action of the Ekaterinburg Soviet. Threatened by the advance of a counter-revolutionary column (which did in fact take the city a week afterwards), they had not only the Tsar but his wife, the little boy Alexis, and his sisters, brutally murdered in a cellar.

This atrocity was committed without the knowledge of the Bolshevik Government nearly a thousand miles away in Moscow, which they had made once more the Russian capital. Later, indeed, twenty-eight of the men responsible were arrested and five executed. But this retribution did nothing to lessen the shock to the civilized world. Henceforth all the evils of Tsarist Russia, which had once horrified liberal-minded people everywhere, were swept into oblivion. The Russian people were stigmatized as monsters who had killed their monarch. Few in France and England remembered Louis XVI and Charles I.

6 'A Land Fit for Heroes'

In London, in Trafalgar Square, the flames licked the base of Nelson's column and Australian soldiers danced singing round the fire. In Piccadilly Circus flag-waving figures clung to the roofs of the halted traffic. Strangers kissed and hugged, laughing and weeping by turns. In New York, Broadway was ankle-deep in torn paper. And in smaller places the rejoicings were no less deeply felt, if not always so hysterical.

The date was, of course, 11 November 1918, that 'Armistice Day' with which we ended Chapter 4. World War I (the 'Great War' as it was then called) was over at last. Its ending was like the reprieve not of one condemned man but of millions. It meant that the soldiers in the trenches would not now be killed, prisoners would be set free, boys in their last year at school would be spared. There was scarcely a family not closely affected by the news.

That was why the day that ended the war was (like the day that began it) different from any other day in history. The individual's chance of coming through alive had been so much less than it was to be in World War II. Three times as many British Servicemen were killed in the first conflict, seven times as many wounded. True, the United States' fatal battle casualties were only 115,660 in the first war, compared with 295,000 in the second, but that was because her forces were engaged so much longer and so much more widely in the later conflict. Had the first war continued the United States would have suffered losses like those of the European armies. When the front-line butchery was at its height a young infantry officer could expect, on average, to survive only a few weeks.

Statistics may be dull, but if later generations wish to understand modern history at all they must make the effort to project themselves into the minds of the people who shouted and danced so deliriously on that day in 1918. The mood of 1945 was entirely different. It was the first war that linked the survivors in the comradeship of great organizations like the **99**

Crowds in Trafalgar Square wait-
ing for news of the Signing of the
Armistice

A happy carload on Armistice Day. The scene is London, the car from the U.S.A.

British Legion and the American Legion; that created the symbolism of the unknown soldier's tomb in Westminster Abbey, in Arlington National Cemetery, and in other national shrines; that made the artificial 'Flanders Poppy' a badge of gratitude; and that caused the erection of countless monuments, even in small villages. All these betokened a great thankfulness, a living faith that it had been indeed, as promised, 'the war to end war'. In 1945 a less optimistic generation was content merely to add fresh dates and names to the old rolls of honour.

Once the delirium died down in 1918, the cry was 'back to normal', or 'normalcy', to use the word made popular by Republican politicians in the United States. There it seemed possible, but in Britain those who imagined that 'back to normal' meant 'back to 1914' were soon angry and confused. The country the fighting men returned to would never be the same again. The workers who had been kept at home in vital industries were now organized in far more powerful trade unions. The women had worked on farms and in munition factories, driven ambulances and done a host of jobs previously considered unsuitable for a female. They could no longer be denied the right to vote and to enter Parliament.

One way and another, there was more equality in the new Britain, though a gulf still yawned between rich and poor. True, many of the former rich were rich no longer, but new men had taken their places, astute and sometimes unscrupulous businessmen, the so-called 'profiteers' who had done well out of the war. The old aristocracy had slipped further

The Profiteer (on the subject of himself): 'As I sez, once a gentleman always a gentleman.'
The Other: 'Ah. That unique occasion must have escaped me.'

from its dominant position. Heavier taxes made it difficult to keep up the stately homes. Many such mansions were turned into boarding-schools and hospitals. If they were close to a growing city their mellow, timbered parklands might be cut up into housing estates for those who before the war had lived in slums.

In the United States also there were great changes, though the causes here were due only in part to the war: they sprang mainly from technical progress, and the development of mass-production, in which the United States henceforth was to lead the world. The cheap automobile, pioneered by Henry Ford, is a good example. In 1915 the United States contained $2\frac{1}{2}$ million cars, in 1920, 9 million, in 1925, 20 million. Only the new mass-production techniques made it possible to build all these cars and only the growing practice of 'easy payments' made it possible to sell them. By 1925 three out of four cars, new and old, were sold in this way. About the same proportion were covered against the weather: ten years earlier, forty-nine cars out of fifty were open ones.

The last fact is important. The car had not only become cheap, it had become a comfortable room on wheels, not just a means of transport. First in the United States, then in Britain and other countries, the car began to revolutionize everyday life. People no longer had to live near their work or close to a railway station. So began, in earnest, the problem which is still with us. The town centres, once full of life and sociability, began to wither; evening found them dead and deserted, nothing but bright shop windows and locked doors. In Britain car-ownership spread less rapidly (working men did not yet aspire to cars and the middle-class family dreamed of no more than one, under Father's unchallenged control), but the smallness of the country made the results more obvious. The English countryside was progressively ruined as narrow ribbons of housing crept out along each road. Town planning, as now understood, was unknown. In both countries the car brought many far-reaching conse- **101** quences and it was blamed, rightly or wrongly, for the decline in church-going and the increase in immorality. More certainly it meant the virtual end of horse-drawn transport and a growing threat to the supremacy of the railroad.

The car marked only one field of technical progress. There is no space here to deal with the other mass-production industries that now developed, giving the United States an increased economic leadership in the world and transforming the lives and habits of her citizens. As similar methods spread to other industrial countries, if only on a smaller scale, everyday life began to alter there as well. One great American social experiment was not imitated elsewhere, the introduction in 1920 of Prohibition (the complete banning of alcoholic liquor), a well-meant Puritan reform that transformed social life in a way very different from what had been intended. Instead of making the United States more sober and law-abiding, this ban produced new varieties of gangsterism and crime, since vast sums could be made by the sale of illegal drink. Prohibition ended in 1933.

But we have run too far ahead, and we must return to other events that followed the end of the war in 1918.

In the General Election which he won sweepingly within a few weeks of the Armistice, Lloyd George defined the nation's new task, 'to make Britain a fit country for heroes to live in'. Those words are often quoted unfairly as a promise. War-weary, the average citizen felt that he had 'done his bit' and it was up to 'them' (the politicians) to do the rest. But no politician, not even the clever little Welsh lawyer, could provide Heaven on a plate. Effort would be needed. 'Don't let us waste this victory', he had continued, 'merely in ringing joy-bells'. Once the bells died away, however, people were chiefly concerned with their own interests. They had had enough of national unity and patriotism. They went back to the old wrangle between the political parties, the trade unions and the employers. It grew bitter when, after a year or two of trade boom, there came a slump and mass unemployment. That Britain did not become 'fit for heroes' was not the fault of any one section.

Another popular legend is that 'the soldiers won the war and the politicians lost the peace'; that if 'they', the politicians, had been less stupid or less wicked, 'we' should all have lived happily ever after. It is well worth studying what happened and asking ourselves honestly how much better we could have done.

Thirty Allied nations took part in the Paris conference to decide the peace terms, the British Dominions counting as separate states. But Russia's chair was empty. The Allies did not recognize the Bolshevik government and had been doing their best to upset it by sending troops and

supplies to various Tsarist generals attempting counter-revolution: this

Clemenceau, Wilson and Lloyd George after signing the Peace Treaty at Versailles

intervention, for which Churchill as Britain's Minister of War was largely responsible, merely embittered the Russians and left a legacy of suspicion between them and the Western democracies.

With Russia absent, the conference was run by an inner group of the Big Four: Woodrow Wilson, the idealist President of the United States; Clemenceau, well nicknamed the 'Tiger', France's veteran statesman whose distrust of Germany stemmed from vivid memories of the 1870 war; Lloyd George for Great Britain; and the Italian Prime Minister, Orlando. Orlando could not speak English, Wilson and Lloyd George could not speak French. Clemenceau, who had long ago studied in Connecticut and married an American, alone needed no interpreter.

There was an even more serious sense in which the quartet did not 'speak the same language'. Wilson's idea of a just peace was based on his earlier proposals: he had no interest in revenge or conquest; he wanted the map re-drawn to suit the wishes of the peoples, not the ambitions of their rulers, and he visualized a League of Nations to prevent future wars. Clemenceau, having twice seen his country devastated by Germany, wanted the frontiers re-drawn so that it could never happen again. He also demanded that Germany should pay 'reparations' for the damage she had done. Lloyd George supported this: he had promised during the election to 'squeeze Germany till the pips squeaked'. Neither he nor Orlando liked Wilson's demand that the victors should not help themselves to slices of enemy territory. Orlando finally walked out when Italy was denied the Austro-Hungarian port of Fiume, which went to Yugoslavia. Lloyd George was interested in the German African colonies, such as Tanganyika and South-West Africa, and those parts of the Turkish Empire, such as Palestine and Iraq, which Britain had occupied. A solution was found by making such territories 'mandates' of the League of **103**

This Punch *cartoon illustrates differing views on Reparations.*

THE WORLD'S PREMIER DUETTISTS

The Welsh Harp: 'You won't take this piece too *furioso*, will you, dear boy?'

The French Horn: 'Certainly not, *mon brave*, not if you don't take it too *moderato*.'

Nations, like wards under a guardian. Thus, Iraq was not to be added to the British Empire but merely controlled and protected by Britain until sufficiently developed to govern herself. Other nations would have similar mandates, France taking over Syria, for instance, and some West African colonies. Clemenceau agreed to Wilson's League of Nations but the shrewd old Frenchman wanted it to have a strong army with which to enforce its decisions.

For months the argument raged. At one point Clemenceau called Wilson 'pro-German' and stormed out of the room. 'How can I talk to a fellow,' he complained, 'who thinks himself the first man in two thousand years to know anything about peace on earth?' While the Allied statesmen wrangled in Paris, people in the defeated countries died of hunger, notably the children in Vienna, for the blockade was still in force. This may have been logical in a cold-blooded legal way, since the war was not 'over' until a treaty could be signed, but it was unnecessarily inhuman. Europe had enough bitter memories without that.

At last, in the early summer of 1919, the terms were settled. They covered 300 pages. 'Well, now,' said someone, 'have we forgotten anything?' 'Yes!' said the Tiger. 'We have omitted to ask for the Kaiser's breeches!'

Apart from the Kaiser, still wearing his breeches in the safety of Holland, the victors' demands went far enough. Germany was to return the Alsace-Lorraine provinces taken away from France in 1870, the Rhineland to be occupied by Allied troops. Other territory went to the newly-formed states of Poland and Czechoslovakia. This much-reduced Germany was forbidden to make an *Anschluss* or union with Austria, her even more reduced Teutonic neighbour. All these points crop up again when we come to Hitler. It is easy to see now that the Treaty contained the seeds of future wars, not so easy to say what its conditions should have been.

It was signed in the Hall of Mirrors at Versailles, a superb gallery decorated with the painted victories of Louis XIV, where (after the surrender of Paris in 1871) the Kaiser's grandfather had been proclaimed emperor of the new Germany. It was a sweet moment for the Tiger, but one of unforgettable humiliation for the German delegates. As one of their newspapers commented on the scene, 'Never has murder been committed with more formal courtesy or more cynical equanimity.'

Yet the victors were equally dissatisfied. Each morning the *Daily Mail* attacked Lloyd George for his softness, repeating: 'They will cheat you yet, those Junkers! Having won half the world by bloody murder they are going to win the other half with tears in their eyes, crying for mercy.' Clemenceau's latest nickname, *Père la Victoire,* was mockingly changed to *Perd la Victoire.* The worst reaction was reserved for Wilson. A rather cold, rigid man, he lacked the political flexibility required to manage Congress and the common touch needed to make his high idealism acceptable to the ordinary man. The people of the United States were suspicious of becoming involved in the future troubles of the outside world. Now the war was over there was an instinct to shut the door and mind their own business. A less stubborn and self-righteous leader might have won them over and defeated the opposition forces marshalled in Congress by the elder Senator Henry Cabot Lodge. As it was, though ironically Wilson was awarded the Nobel Peace Prize, his own people rejected his policies, would not join the League that was his brain-child, and retired into the old 'isolationism', thereby leaving the road clear to World War II. Wilson suffered a stroke, but finished his term as President, jealously guarded by his wife, who successfully concealed from the nation the knowledge that it was being 'led' by a helpless invalid, incapable of making decisions. He died in 1924. The rest of the Big Four lived on, but with little further influence on affairs. Lloyd George (defeated in the 1922 Election) was the last to head a government.

If we compare the maps of 1914 and 1919 we can quickly appreciate the transformation made by the peace settlement. New names abound, old shapes are altered. If we know the history of the 1930s we detect the shadows of a dozen problems soon to come.

The ancient state of Poland was re-created. As an outlet to the sea she was granted a strip of territory, the 'Polish Corridor', which had the effect of dividing East Prussia from the rest of Germany. Russia, still racked by civil war, was in no position to defend her old western frontiers. She lost land to Rumania as well as Poland. Her Baltic coastline split off into three tiny republics, Estonia, Latvia and Lithuania.

If Czechoslovakia's western boundary had been drawn on Wilson's **105** principle (to include only Czechs) it would have been impossible to defend. So, to provide a defensible mountainous frontier Czechoslovakia was allotted the Sudetenland, inhabited by people of German speech and ancestry, though they had never lived in Germany. This we shall have cause to remember when we consider the Munich crisis of 1938.

But why point out every alteration on the map and its consequences, which became all too plain in the next two decades? The Turkish Empire was split up, the former German colonies shared out under the mandate system. Britain took the lion's share. Here too some problems were laid up for future statesmen to cope with. German South-West Africa, for example, was mandated to the neighbouring Union of South Africa, nobody foreseeing the latter's racialist policy of *apartheid* ('segregation') destined to make her so unpopular in years to come. Britain herself was to find Palestine a thankless responsibility, with endless strife between Jew and Arab, continuing long after the partition of the country between Israel and Jordan. It is easy enough to rub out lines on a map and draw new ones. Historic problems cannot be erased so quickly.

The decade following the Great War has been labelled 'the Gay Twenties', the era of the 'bright young things' portrayed in the comedies of Noel Coward and the novels of F. Scott Fitzgerald and Evelyn Waugh. The label is partly true, partly misleading. Certainly in Britain and the United States, where there were no shell-wrecked cities to rebuild, no fields to clear of skeletons and rusty weapons, it was easier to forget the war and natural enough (for those who could afford it) to plunge into a feverish quest for the gaiety so long denied.

Jazz crossed the Atlantic in 1919. The new syncopated rhythms spread infectiously throughout Britain, from the smart London hotels and the newly-invented 'night clubs' to the ornate dance halls or *'palais de danse'* that sprang up, along with luxurious cinemas, in every town of size. A wave of violent, almost hysterical dancing often follows periods of war and revolution, and jazz was still primarily music to be danced to, not listened to.

The jazz craze of the 1920s was also part of the Americanization of Britain, along with the films (nearly all from Hollywood), mass-production methods, chain-stores and hire-purchase or instalment-buying, the 'never-never' system. The dancing itself involved a degree of physical contact shocking to the older generation and underlined the new free and easy relationship between the sexes. In both countries the war had destroyed many of the rules of etiquette, though not all. A respectable girl could now go out unchaperoned and dance repeatedly with the same young man, but most parents still imposed conditions as to late hours and latchkeys.

106 Such restrictions did not worry the real 'bright young things' who made

Europe 1919

the newspaper headlines with their bottle-parties and other goings-on, but these were never more than a tiny minority.

Most young people had too little money and too much sense for these extremes, but bright and gay they often were, and as always they managed to upset some of their elders. Skirts had become very short, partly through wartime scarcity of cloth, partly because girls now worked and played more strenuously, and partly because the invention of 'art' (artificial) silk stockings enabled them to display their legs attractively. Their elders had been taught that little should be seen above the ankle; that short sleeves, let alone no sleeves, were immodest; and that no real lady wore noticeable make-up or smoked in public. They had to get used to the girls of the 1920s doing all these things. Oddly enough, the girls sometimes played down their most feminine attractions and were also blamed for **107**

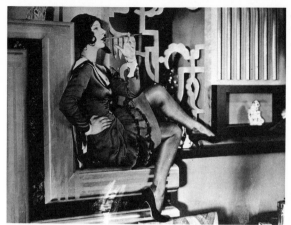

looking like boys. They cut their hair short and flattened their figures until they resembled not boys so much as herrings. The young men's appearance changed less drastically, but after the years of uniform there was a swing towards more casual, brighter clothes. Many older men went on wearing stiff collars, hats and formal suits, and often the young ones had to conform in business hours, remaining literally 'black-coated' and 'white-collared' workers.

In Britain children could leave school at fourteen, though those of the middle class usually stayed until at least sixteen. The compulsory minimum age in the United States varied between fourteen and sixteen according to state. Except for those who went on to a university (a small minority, especially in Britain, where universities were few and small and there was not the widespread system of grants operating today), most boys and girls took jobs in their own locality and lived with their parents until they married. Obviously some were forced, by their careers, to travel and live in lodgings or hostels, but living at home was the norm. Though the population was becoming more mobile, particularly in the United States, millions still passed their whole lives within the same square mile of grimy streets.

Existence was not necessarily duller just because people moved about less. Towns then had more individuality, more sense of community. They had not achieved their present sameness, every shopping centre just a reshuffle of the usual multiple stores with standardized fronts and equally standardized goods. In a big English city like Nottingham normal business was still disrupted for three days each October so that the market square could be crammed with merry-go-rounds and swing-boats, freak shows, a menagerie, and all the fun of the fair. Twice weekly throughout the year those same cobblestones were occupied by rows of canvas-covered stalls, lit by lurid naphtha flares until late evening, selling farm produce, cheap clothes and drapery, patent medicines and junk of every kind. It was so in many towns until arguments of traffic congestion and hygiene banished most markets to covered buildings in the back streets and most fairs to waste ground on the outskirts.

Towns usually had a theatre, perhaps more than one. In Britain the shorter distances favoured the touring company, which could tour for a year, a week in each place, before returning to the same town. Repertory theatres were fewer—it was in the United States that they flourished in a semi-amateur form through the Little Theatre Movement. But whether from road show or local repertory even the smaller cities could enjoy their 'live' theatre and all the pleasurable excitement of an evening out. The standard of performance might be mediocre compared with today's, but there was as yet no television to bring the greatest actors into the home.

Television was still only an inventor's dream (J. L. Baird, a Scotsman, demonstrated it to the Royal Institution in 1926) but radio entertainment started in 1920 in the United States and was taken up two years later by the British Broadcasting Company, later transformed into the present Corporation under public control. To older listeners the 'wireless' was a mystery and a miracle: the then Archbishop of Canterbury, hearing it for the first time, wondered whether to open the window, the better to hear the music from so far away. Schoolboys saw no mystery at all. They learnt to construct simple crystal sets from the wood of a cigar box and a few cheap accessories. To hear with such sets it was necessary to wear headphones. It was common in homes lacking the more expensive models with loud speakers to see Father and Mother sharing one pair of head-phones, each listening with a single ear.

From now onwards people relied more and more on mechanized entertainment. The piano, once the focal point of social life, became in many living-rooms a space-wasting encumbrance, a mute display stand for family photographs. Amateurs grew shy when the world's finest performers could be switched on. In that pre-television age the sports commentaries on radio could not replace the excitement of attending the actual event, but more and more people preferred watching to playing themselves. Professional sport became bigger and bigger business.

On the other hand there was a new enthusiasm for camping and the open-air life. In the United States the emphasis was on the week-end cabin by the lake, easily reached by car, and the organized summer camps. In Britain the smallness of the country and its abundance of pleasant footpaths encouraged the hiker, carrying his own lightweight tent or sleeping inexpensively in youth hostels. These hostels started in Britain only in 1930 (though known in Germany for twenty years before) but thousands of farms and cottages offered bed and breakfast for a small sum. Hitch-hiking came a little later. The first young wanderers were more independent, satisfied to cover shorter distances, riding bicycles if **109**

they did not wish to walk. Using their new freedom the girls entered into these pastimes on equal terms. Annual holidays and weekends were both, however, shorter than they are today.

These were just some of the changes obvious in everyday life. Under the surface there were deeper changes in the way people thought and felt, changes which set up a violent conflict between old and young.

Particularly there was the influence of Freud, the Viennese professor who evolved the technique of psycho-analysis. He had been propagating his ideas for many years, but only now were they penetrating beyond medical circles. Freud taught that only one part of our mind is 'conscious'; that, like an iceberg, it has much larger areas, submerged and unsuspected, full of forgotten experiences and repressed impulses which largely determine our behaviour. Thus, we may think we know why we decide on a certain action, yet the 'reason' we give, quite honestly, may not be the real reason but a 'rationalization', an excuse invented by the mind to cover the genuine one. A simple Freudian process which we can all recognize is that of forgetting an unpleasant duty which, unconsciously, we do not wish to remember.

Freud's theories applied to everyone, not just to the mentally sick people who came to him for treatment. A moment's reflection will show why they had such a revolutionary effect. As a pioneer thinker Freud could be bracketed with the two nineteenth-century giants: Darwin, whose theory of evolution had shattered the religious faith of millions, and Marx, whose political doctrine had helped to destroy the Russian Empire and still threatened the other capitalist governments. Both these earlier thinkers had relied upon evidence and argument. Freud too used evidence and argument, but to prove that they were not everything. Man was *not* an entirely rational being. Even the finest intellect must always allow for the hidden influences, some planted in infancy, others even present at birth.

110

The application of Freud's theories (and sometimes their misapplication), together with later theories sponsored by disciples who broke away and became his bitter opponents, began from the 1920s onwards to affect education, the treatment of criminals, art, literature, even advertising and salesmanship. Only a minority read his books or mastered his teaching, but at second or third hand everyone was influenced to some degree. His theories were falsified in popular notions such as: 'Everything comes back to Sex, really', and, 'It's very bad for you to repress things', and, 'There's no such thing as will-power. I'm just like this, and you can't expect me to do anything about it'. Freud himself was intensely moral and believed in self-discipline. He deeply regretted that his teachings were used as an excuse for uncontrolled and immoral behaviour, as they frequently were.

In literature the older writers like Shaw and Wells continued to appeal to men's reason, but others (outstandingly D. H. Lawrence) concerned themselves with the emotions and instincts whose importance Freud had revealed. Often they wrote with a frankness that shocked the more conventional. Others, however, like Virginia Woolf, who followed James Joyce in using the 'stream of consciousness' technique in her novels, combined the new psychological insight with a subtle and delicate use of language.

All in all, it was an exciting decade for the arts. In 1923 T. S. Eliot, an American settled in Britain, wrote *The Waste Land*. This started a new trend in poetry towards a more austere, intellectual and 'difficult' form of expression contrasting strongly with the easy lyricism of the pre-war writers, who had been absorbed by beauty but had sometimes achieved only the 'pretty-pretty' and sentimental. Lytton Strachey's witty biographies, *Eminent Victorians* and *Queen Victoria*, were so different from the old pompous and over-respectful type that they started a cult of 'debunking' traditional heroes and institutions. In lesser hands than Strachey's this became cheap and nasty. Like Freud, Strachey indirectly influenced many who never read his books or even knew his name. The cynical idea common today, that no well-known figure alive or dead is really deserving of admiration, owes much to Strachey's demolition of the Victorian idols.

Painting and sculpture saw the usual time-lag between the creation of new styles and their acceptance by the public. It was still mostly the forward-looking young people who began to adorn their bed-sittingrooms with reproductions of the Post-Impressionist painters like Cézanne, Gauguin and Van Gogh, though they were really nineteenth-century artists. Matisse and Picasso were very much alive, and violently discussed. So was Epstein, who was horrifying the man in the street by departing from the classical conception of sculpture. His memorial to the naturalist, W. H. Hudson, erected in a London park in 1925, was tarred and **111**

feathered. Few could have foreseen then that Epstein would finish with a knighthood and a commission to adorn Coventry cathedral.

After the stirring events of the preceding years the 1920s in Britain and the United States seem lacking in major historical drama. Elsewhere, Lenin and his colleagues were grappling with the gigantic problems of Russia, Mussolini was establishing Fascism in Italy, Hitler was planning to imitate him in Germany, Gandhi and Nehru were struggling for the independence of India. But these topics can be handled better in their separate chapters. Here let us pause only briefly to see how the first fragment of the British Empire broke away into independence as the Irish Free State.

Civil war in Ireland had been prevented in 1914 only by the outbreak of a much bigger war. In 1916 there had been the Easter Rising in Dublin, a tragic farce put on by a handful of idealistic rebels, promised arms from Germany which never arrived. The leaders were nearly all captured and executed. One whose death sentence was commuted was Eamon De Valera, who, though born in America of a Spanish father, always regarded his mother's country as his own. He was one day to head the Government of a free Ireland, to preside over the League of Nations, and to be recognized as one of the world's senior statesmen. All this, however, lay ahead. When, in 1921, Lloyd George offered to make Southern (mainly Catholic) Ireland a dominion within the Empire, like Canada, De Valera and the extreme republicans refused to agree that half a loaf was better than no bread. They demanded a republic, which Ireland is today, that republic to include the Six Counties of Protestant Ulster, which have remained however with Britain. De Valera's faction was overruled. Other leaders accepted the British offer and signed a treaty. Then followed a guerilla war between the Free Staters, forming the new government, and De Valera's illegal I.R.A., the Irish Republican Army, a struggle as murderous as any previously waged against the British. There were ambushes, cold-blooded shootings from behind, burnings and dynamitings, before the Free Staters won the day. But the eventual victory was De Valera's, for early in the 1930s he came to power by democratic means

Street barricade in Dublin during the Irish Civil War

and began inch by inch to lever Southern Ireland out of the Empire. When World War II came in 1939 the Republic of 'Eire' was a fact. Eire was completely independent and neutral, treating Britain and Germany so impartially that many individual Irishmen boiled with frustrated emotion.

Ireland apart, Britain was chiefly concerned with home affairs. Many people were learning for the first time that the new-fangled science of economics, like psychology, was something which touched everyone and needed to be understood. Only economics could explain why the gold sovereign had vanished in 1914, never to return, and why the pound note which had replaced this coin was worth less than half its pre-war value; why income-tax, one shilling and twopence in the pound before, now wavered between four and six shillings; and why unemployment now threatened not only the manual worker but the ex-officer and the university graduate. One placard seen in the streets, worn by a respectably-dressed man, read as follows:

I KNOW 3 TRADES
I SPEAK 3 LANGUAGES
FOUGHT FOR 3 YEARS
HAVE 3 CHILDREN
AND NO WORK FOR
3 MONTHS
BUT I ONLY WANT
ONE JOB

113

Unemployment was never below the million mark during this decade: at times it rose above 2½ million. All nations had spent immense sums on the war. Britain had lent money to her European allies and borrowed it herself from the United States, as well as selling many of her foreign investments. Now she could recover nothing from her allies: one big borrower, the Russian Empire, had vanished from the map, and the new Union of Socialist Soviet Republics refused to take over the debt. Nor could anything be got out of the defeated enemy, despite Lloyd George's promises, though the French did their best to apply the screw by marching troops into Germany's industrial area.

In 1871 a victorious Germany had made France pay reparations in gold. In 1945 a victorious Russia was to strip a defeated Germany of her industrial plant and other capital equipment. But the 1919 victors tried to obtain reparations out of Germany's current production, an idea condemned from the start by the far-sighted British economist, J. M. Keynes. Such massive transfers of wealth from one nation to another could not be made without causing unemployment in the receiving country. It was for this very reason, to keep out foreign goods, that the United States maintained high tariffs.

Nevertheless, persistent efforts were made throughout the 1920s to obtain reparations and the repayment of war debts between the Allies. An immense sum was fixed for Germany. She paid one instalment in 1921, and then could not continue. The main effect of the demand for reparations was inflation: the German Government printed more and more paper money until by 1923 it was valueless. In 1914 the mark stood at twenty to the pound sterling: nine years later it stood at 200,000. The United States, as the great creditor nation, was owed money by everybody and tried hard to work out a solution. In 1922 Congress set up the World War Foreign Debt Commission to seek ways of recovering American loans without accepting goods that would compete with American business: France and Britain sent some gold, but that was all. They complained that they could get nothing out of Germany.

In 1924 an international committee was formed under the Vice-President of the United States, Charles G. Dawes, to investigate Germany's capacity to pay. A reduced scale was fixed, known as the Dawes Plan, superseded in 1930 by the Young Plan, but this soon proved unworkable, and with the rise of Hitler all hopes of payment finally disappeared. Britain, though unable to recover anything from friend or foe, struggled to honour her own debt to the United States, but could not continue after 1933. This failure was a lasting cause of misunderstanding and ill-will between the two countries.

As a result of the war and of the rapid progress achieved by the United **114** States, the City of London lost much of its former pre-eminence as the financial centre of the world. Wall Street, in New York, took its place. But Britain, for all her difficulties, escaped the chaos of inflation such as Germany suffered. Money was worth less, but it was worth something. Cigarettes were twenty for a shilling, five shillings admitted one to a *thé dansant* at a luxury hotel, and for fourteen pounds one could travel to Lugano and enjoy a seventeen-day inclusive holiday with a balcony overlooking the lake. A man's tweed suit cost four guineas. In the United States (where at this time the dollar was worth 4s 1½d) twenty cigarettes cost about sixteen cents, a good seat for a Broadway show about three dollars, and a two-week luxury trip to Florida one hundred and sixty-six dollars. A good tweed suit could be bought for forty dollars.

Few politicians had much grasp of economic principles. The British were nurtured on the ancient classics, the Americans favoured legal studies as the best preparation for government. Neither was equipped to cope with the problems looming in the modern world. Neither saw that the running of a nation's business might be essentially different from the housekeeping of a family. Thus, when the British Government was alarmed by its heavy expenditure, a slashing economy drive was launched (called 'the Geddes Axe', after the minister responsible) which merely increased unemployment and made matters worse all round.

Lloyd George fell in 1922 when (largely because of the Irish Treaty) the Conservatives refused to stay in his coalition. Liberalism went into a decline. The Conservatives governed for almost the entire period until 1945, though in times of crisis, as in 1940, they invited other parties into the Cabinet and gave it a national basis. Only for two short periods, however, did they lose control of Parliament. The rapidly-growing Labour Party governed in 1924 and again in 1929–31, but although it had won more seats than the Conservatives it did not have a clear majority, because of the Liberals, whose votes could bring down the new Government as soon as it tried any of its Socialist theories. It was a frustrating period for idealists in all parties. The working class, disappointed by the emptiness of its victory in Parliament, put most of its fighting effort into strikes and demonstrations.

The great event was the General Strike of May 1926, when foreign newspaper readers who did not know Britain imagined for a few days that the country was on the brink of revolution. Were not the troops out? Were there not armoured cars and Grenadiers escorting food-convoys from the London Docks? Was not Hyde Park turned into a vast encampment? All this was true, but, stirring as it was, it never developed into a revolutionary situation.

Far from being the diabolical Bolshevik plot pictured by some, the General Strike was a well-meaning if muddled demonstration of sympathy with the miners into which the men of other industries stumbled at **115** a word from trade union leaders who had themselves no clear programme. It began when the Government stopped paying a subsidy to the coal-mining industry, then privately owned. The mine-owners announced a wage cut but no plans for reorganization and improvement. When the miners refused the new terms they were locked out. The 'strike' began only when the Trades Union Congress brought out other workers in sympathy, hoping that the Government would be forced to help the miners.

The idea of a general strike had been discussed for a century. This was the first and last time it was tried in Britain. Railways, buses, factories, came to a standstill. Ships lay with untouched cargoes at the wharves. There was an unwonted quiet. The air over the industrial towns hung smokeless and pure, and distant hills came back into view which had not been seen within living memory.

No government however could tolerate a paralysis of the nation's life. Action had been long prepared. Posters went up everywhere, calling for volunteers, as though a war had broken out. The middle class abandoned their office-work, their studies or their sports, and rushed into action as enthusiastic (if often unskilful) manual workers. Amateur bus drivers and conductors ran a limited service with boarded-up windows and barbed wire to prevent interference by the strikers. Students hastened to the docks and soon learnt the difference between Rugby football and humping sacks of flour. The headmaster of Eton and all his staff were sworn in as special constables. A few trains ran, though at some risk of giving a double meaning to the phrase 'skeleton service'. There was little desire to go down into the mines. As the printers were on strike the only news available was that broadcast by the B.B.C. or contained in miniature sheets published by emergency methods. Winston Churchill, now back in the Conservative Party and Chancellor of the Exchequer, edited the official *British Gazette* with characteristic pugnacity. He was answered by the Trades Union Congress in its *British Worker*.

Despite all the armoured cars, the Grenadiers and the special constables, there was little high drama. Stones were thrown, cars overturned, banners waved. There were small riots and scuffles, no barricades or machine-guns. Meetings sang the 'Red Flag', that doleful ditty which Bernard Shaw (being not only a Socialist but a music critic) contemptuously described as 'the funeral march of a fried eel'. But few really wanted the red flag to fly as it flew over the Kremlin, and the Government was careful not to goad its opponents into angry action. As Stalin said to H. G. Wells later, admiring the cleverness of the British ruling class, 'The first thing any other bourgeoisie would have done would have been to arrest the trade union leaders.' The Prime Minister, Stanley Baldwin,

116 knew as well as the Russian dictator that this would have been the one

The General Strike: armoured cars convoy food lorries from the London docks

way to rouse the British working class. So the eight days of the General Strike passed calmly, with friendly football matches between police and strikers and long negotiations between Government and T.U.C. Finally the latter, alarmed by the situation into which they had slipped, clutched at an excuse to call off the strike. The miners remained locked out and (as many felt) betrayed by their comrades. It was six months before hunger forced them to accept the longer hours and lower wages offered.

Labour disputes were not lacking in the United States as well. Wages and conditions had improved during the war and the subsequent boom in American industry. The American Federation of Labor had strengthened its organization of skilled workers in 'craft' unions and fought any attempt to worsen their position. It was prominent in the campaign to reduce immigration, so that its members should not suffer from the competition of foreign labour entering the country with lower standards. Some union leaders, notably the forceful John L. Lewis, President of the United Mine Workers' Union, sought to mobilize the less skilled men of the mass-production industries who could not claim to have a 'craft'. Later Lewis was to found a rival body, the C.I.O. (Congress of Industrial Organizations), which conducted a lengthy feud with the A.F.L. until the two groups eventually amalgamated in 1955. If the 1920s witnessed no single conflict quite as dramatic as the British General Strike, those years did not pass without incident in the United States. Lewis's miners, for example, were on strike in both 1923 and 1925, staying out on the second occasion for 170 days.

Far worse things were in store. The 'Gay Twenties' closed with a bang in 1929, the famous Wall Street crash which echoed round the world.

America had been enjoying a remarkable trade boom. The Republican President Calvin Coolidge had followed the policy of free capitalist **117**

An anxious crowd waiting opposite the New York Stock Exchange as the nation plunges towards its worst depression

enterprise which was the ideal of American business: public debts and expenditure were cut down, income-tax reduced, government interference eliminated. At first prospects seemed rosy, and people who had never in their lives owned stocks and shares began to buy them. Prices climbed. Some people sold again and were dazzled by their profits. Others held and were even more dazzled by the mushroom-like growth of their paper fortunes. Any working man with a few hundred dollars saved had the chance to become wealthy, and many did. The continual rise depended solely on confidence, confidence that the boom would last for ever. Stocks and shares have no exact permanent 'value', only a day-to-day 'price', just as high or as low as other people will pay. Millions of hapless Americans learnt these hard elementary facts on a single autumn day in 1929, when several large blocks of shares were offered on the market, starting a loss of confidence and a whispering that grew to a panic-stricken roar. Others started selling. Prices fell like the water level in an emptying bath tub. The telephone lines were jammed as every frightened investor tried to reach his broker.

In one day 19 million shares changed hands. It was bad enough for people who had lost their life-savings. It was worse for those who had borrowed money, mortgaging houses and farms so that they could
speculate, and for those who (versed in Stock Exchange procedure) had

juggled with capital they had never possessed. As the horror of the situation dawned upon them some reached for the pistols in their desk drawers and blew their brains out. Others jumped from the upper windows of skyscrapers.

The Wall Street crash affected everyone. Millions of Americans who had never taken part in the stampede to make money were overwhelmed in the ruin of those who had. Hundreds of banks failed, countless firms went out of business, millions lost their jobs. Workless ex-soldiers marched on Washington and had to be dispersed by troops. Farmers stood at bay with rifle and shot-gun against the bailiffs who arrived to foreclose their mortgages. Schools were shut or went without heating. For a whole year Chicago could not pay its teachers.

Soon other nations felt the back-wash of the economic tidal wave which had demolished American prosperity. We have seen how New York had replaced London as financial centre of the world. Now, as the Stock Exchanges of London and other capitals reacted to the catastrophe, unemployment and bankruptcy came to their countries too. That story belongs however to the 1930s.

The General Strike: volunteer bus driver
in London with police protection

7 'A Spectre is Haunting Europe'

'Russia, the land where there is no unemployment . . .'

It was a favourite slogan in the 1930s. Banners carried it, hoarse orators declaimed it on street corners, multitudes accepted it as a gospel. In a sense it was true, though Russia perhaps had worse troubles of her own. What caught the imagination of the shabby millions queueing for relief was that a country existed where the Wall Street collapse caused not an answering tremor; where stocks, shares and the whole complicated paraphernalia of capitalism no longer existed. Things might be grim in Russia. How grim, nobody was sure. Most of the adverse newspaper reports were fiercely rejected as mere hostile propaganda. Anyhow (argued the unemployed) things were now getting better in Russia instead of worse. The Russians had hope, they had the much-discussed five-year plan launched in 1928.

'Comrades,' we left Lenin saying in 1917, 'we shall now proceed to build the Socialist system.' For sheer optimism, in the face of a thousand deterrent factors pointing to the impossibility of doing any such thing, these words rank high among the political promises of history.

Off the platform, away from the red banners and the radiant faces, the Bolshevik leaders sat in shabby rooms under feeble light bulbs, grappling with realities. The outlook was as bleak as the weather outside.

Russia was falling to pieces. Like the ice floes that drifted down the Neva every spring, the old empire was splitting, melting away. The Germans were still hammering at its western side, its soldiers were deserting in hordes. Generals loyal to the captive Tsar were longing for a chance to strike at the Revolution. In the depths of the vast country, remote from the capital, different parties were taking control of their own districts. In St Petersburg itself the Bolsheviks were in a minority in the Constituent Assembly, the Parliament set up earlier by the Provisional Government.

Was the situation hopeless? Lenin looked round at his colleagues. Most were men like himself, intellectuals, professional conspirators who had

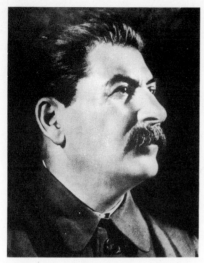

Josef Stalin

spent their lives in prison or in exile. Kamenev and Zinoviev had been with him for years; they had often disagreed with him frankly and fiercely, but they were veteran Bolsheviks and he trusted them. They were, like Trotsky, of Jewish origin. Trotsky himself was a brilliant fellow, perhaps not wholly reliable: he had a theatrical streak that might lead him into trouble, a biting tongue that made enemies. Also, he had only recently joined the Bolsheviks. In contrast there was Stalin, the dour pock-marked Georgian, who said little but listened thoughtfully. Lenin had little personal acquaintance with him: while he had been in Switzerland, Stalin had been working underground in Russia or enduring exile in Siberia. But he had always found Stalin dependable, loyally carrying out instructions sent from abroad. These men, and a few others, formed the inner circle. Only one, Krasin, had had any experience of running even a business: he had been managing director of an engineering firm. Yet with them Lenin proposed to take over the bankrupt Russian Empire.

At first they called themselves the Provisional Workers' and Peasants' Government. All kinds of sweeping changes were immediately decreed, mainly because they had been in the revolutionary programme for years and nobody dared to point out that they were not at the moment convenient. Banks were abolished, private trade declared illegal: all shops closed and food shortages developed into famine. Factories were handed over to the workers to run: confusion resulted and output fell to almost nothing. The land was nationalized: few peasants knew what that word meant, but they drove out their landlords and seized the fields for themselves. Church property was confiscated, though the deliberate persecution of religion did not begin for some time. What the new Government did now was only a development of what western rulers like Henry VIII had started centuries before.

121

E

An armistice with Germany was vital. The fighting must stop. When someone objected that the people had not had the chance to vote for peace, Lenin answered with his usual blunt humour: 'They have voted with their legs.' It was true. Already war-weary, more and more soldiers made tracks for their native villages when they heard that the land was being shared out.

Lenin's strength lay in this: for all his theories, for all his years abroad, he could feel with the people. He might not always agree with everything they demanded, but he knew when to go with them. At this time he was like a man shooting the rapids in a canoe: he could not go against the stream of events, but with skill and luck he might steer between the rocks and reach his objective.

He also knew when to take charge, when it was safe to break the rules and act toughly. The Bolsheviks were outvoted in the Constituent Assembly? All right, but what did the people care about the Constituent Assembly? The people wanted results. Lenin did as Cromwell had done three centuries before, he dissolved the Constituent Assembly under the threat of force. The government would now be 'the dictatorship of the proletariat'. While the class struggle lasted it would not pretend to represent all the population but only the wage earners and peasants who elected the soviets, and in practice things were so rigged that the industrial worker's vote was worth five cast by the backward and illiterate peasants. The former nobility, priests, traders, and so forth must watch their step or be denounced as 'class enemies'. They had always been superior beings before, now they would be inferior. Individuals could work out their own salvation by joining the proletariat (Lenin and his friends were themselves from the middle class) but equal human rights would not be granted to all until the last traces of capitalism vanished in the classless society which was the Communist aim.

The dictatorship could not be wielded by the proletariat itself. It must be wielded *for* them by a disciplined and declared Communist Party, hand-picked, restricted to about half a million members, setting an example and taking the lead in every town soviet, trade union committee and co-operative society. Party members would explain Government policies. To help them, the Government took control of the newspapers with a thoroughness that went beyond the Tsarist censorship. Lenin early realized that the cinema offered wonderful scope for political education. The Moscow State School of Cinematography was started in 1919 and soon directors like Eisenstein and Pudovkin were making films which, for all their propaganda, were recognized in the West as supreme artistic achievements. But in the very first years the Communists had to rely on older means of persuasion, mass-meetings, newspapers, leaflets, and the secret police.

Russia had always been a police state. The new Russia could not do without the same apparatus of spies and informers. In those years it was called the Cheka or 'the Extraordinary Commission'. In 1922 it became the G.P.U., in 1934 the N.K.V.D. Always, under whatever change of name, it remained an important part of the Soviet system. Lenin never meant it to become as permanent or as powerful as it did. But it was one of the far-reaching consequences of his policy during the chaotic period after the Bolsheviks seized power.

Many Bolsheviks never believed they could hold power. The odds against them were too heavy. Either they would go down with the red flag flying, an example to inspire the next generation, or they would be saved at the eleventh hour by other Communist risings in Germany, Britain and elsewhere. It was not as absurd a dream as it may now appear. Those years saw the proclamation of short-lived Soviet Republics in Hungary and Bavaria, while mutinies in the French Army, unrest in Italy, and other symptoms seemed to threaten capitalism in the West. 'A spectre is haunting Europe, the spectre of Communism.' Marx had written those words in 1848. Now they had a fresher, more intense significance.

Trotsky was one who put his faith in the 'permanent' (or world) revolution which, once started, would roll on through country after country. As Commissar of Foreign Affairs (the Bolsheviks disliked the word 'Minister' or any word which reminded them of Tsarism) he went to discuss peace terms with the Germans. He was horrified at their demands, which were considerable since they held Russia at their mercy. He kept them talking as long as he could, hoping that the Bolshevik triumph in St Petersburg would stimulate the German workers to overthrow the Kaiser. But nothing happened. The German generals smiled at the fiery little man's threats of the coming world revolution. Finally Trotsky resigned rather than accept their terms. The Germans broke off the talks and marched deeper into Russian territory. Lenin shrugged his shoulders and signed on even more humiliating conditions than Trotsky had just refused. 'Let us give way in space,' he said, 'but gain time.' The Treaty of Brest-Litovsk was waste paper before the end of the year. Germany had herself surrendered to the western allies.

In that short interval new blows fell upon the Communists. No sooner had they ceased fighting the Germans than they were attacked by their former allies. For to Britain and France, still hard pressed on the Western Front, Russia's dropping out of the war seemed a monstrous act of treachery. They did not recognize the Communists as the true government. Since they could not deal with the Tsar (still alive, but a prisoner) they supported the various anti-Communist groups that sprang up all over Russia and claimed to be exercising his authority. **123**

From 1918 to 1921 was the nightmare period of 'War Communism', the Civil War and the Allied 'Intervention'. The Communists moved their government to Moscow, the ancient capital which Peter the Great had forsaken when he built St Petersburg. Petersburg was now too dangerously exposed, almost within gun-range of hostile territory. Nearly all the proud empire of the Tsars was gone and the country controlled by the Bolsheviks had shrunk to something more like the 'Muscovy' of long ago. Studying their maps inside the temporary safety of the Kremlin ramparts, Lenin and his companions saw their state crumbling like a sandcastle at high tide.

The Kremlin

Finland and Poland had gone. The Baltic lands had broken off as Estonia, Latvia, and Lithuania. There was a breakaway movement in the Ukraine, another in Stalin's homeland, the Transcaucasus. Siberia had proclaimed a separate government.

The situation there was especially remarkable. That vast, then partly unexplored, sub-continent of swamp, forest and mountain was held together by the steel thread of the Trans-Siberian railway, the longest in the world, running 4,388 miles from the Urals to the Pacific. In 1918 that thread was held by (of all people) the Czechs.

These Czechs were former prisoners-of-war from the Austrian Army. They had volunteered to fight against their old masters and had been formed into a Czechoslovak Legion. When the war ended on the Eastern Front they bargained with the Bolsheviks that they should be allowed to transfer themselves to the Western. The only way to do this was to go round the world. Undaunted, the Czechs set forth in troop-trains on an **124** adventure rather like a modernized version of Xenophon's 'March of the

The Union of Socialist Soviet Republics

Ten Thousand'. Soon disputes broke out with the local soviets through whose territories they passed. Fighting developed. The Czech trains were strung out at intervals along the line. In driving off all who threatened their passage they found themselves waging a private campaign against the Bolsheviks. It was the Czechs who seized the Russian gold reserves, previously evacuated to Kazan, and took them eastwards into Siberia. It was the Czechs who battered their way into Ekaterinburg just a week too late to save the Tsar and his family.

It was a time of atrocities, not all on one side. The armies roved the country, towns changed hands repeatedly, and changes were marked by pitiless executions. There were the Red Guards and the White Guards. So far as the terrified population were concerned they might as well have been Roundheads and Cavaliers. Most people cared little who governed them. They wanted peace and bread.

Perhaps 1919 was Lenin's blackest year. Enemies converged from every side. One, Admiral Kolchak, already master of Siberia and dubbed 'Supreme Ruler of Russia', advanced against the Volga. Another Tsarist commander, General Denikin, held the fertile 'black earth' region of the south and threatened Moscow. A third, General Yudenich, struck at St Petersburg from Estonia. Far to the north, at Murmansk beyond the Arctic Circle and at Archangel, thousands of British, American, French and Italian troops were supporting the local anti-Communists. Halfway across the world, at Vladivostok, the Japanese were making their own intervention.

How were these myriad enemies to be defeated? This was Trotsky's great period. He had become Commissar for War and thrown his dynamic **125** genius into the task of creating the Red Army. A complete amateur in military matters, a writer, journalist and politician, Trotsky had proved his ability in the seizure of St Petersburg. Now he demonstrated it again on a vaster scale, speeding from battle front to battle front in an armoured train, exhorting, directing, galvanizing his makeshift forces to ever greater efforts.

It was then that he fell foul of Stalin. Trotsky believed that the Red Army must use the services of former Tsarist officers like General Tukhachevsky if they volunteered. It was risky, but their qualifications were too valuable to waste. They must be watched carefully, shot if they turned traitor, otherwise given their chance. Stalin trusted only the commanders thrown up from the ranks, like Voroshilov and Budienny. Voroshilov was one of his old associates in the underground movement, a metal-worker who now commanded an army of 50,000 men. Budienny was an ex-sergeant-major with a bold suggestion that a massive striking force of cavalry should be raised. Trotsky's professional experts were contemptuous, but Trotsky at last agreed. The exploits of Budienny's Red Cavalry became one of the legends on which future Russian children were brought up.

Both Trotsky and Stalin were partly right. The army needed experienced officers *and* self-made generals. But the hatred of the two Commissars was too deep for compromise. It reached its climax over the defence of Tsaritsin, a key town on the Volga, later world-famous during a second siege as 'Stalingrad', now once more renamed 'Volgograd'. On one occasion Stalin, as the man on the spot, scribbled 'to be disregarded' on one of Trotsky's telegrams. Trotsky in turn clamoured for Stalin's recall and threatened Voroshilov with court martial. Lenin tried to keep the peace between them, but the feud between the Commissars and their supporters could end only with death. So it was to be with Trotsky and Stalin, so with Tukhachevsky, whose death warrant Voroshilov and Budienny signed nearly twenty years later.

One may wonder how, with these quarrels added to their difficulties, the Communists nevertheless won the Civil War. Yet win it they did. By 1921 they were masters of the country, though they did not march into Vladivostok till the following year and there was sporadic resistance in remote corners of Central Asia even after that. Those years left Russia scarred and devastated. To later Soviet citizens they were represented in countless films, novels and paintings as a splendid heroic period. The outside world remembered them rather as a time of appalling horror and brutality. There was truth in both pictures. The great Russian writer, Maxim Gorki, recorded what Lenin said to him in conversation. 'The young people,' said Lenin, 'will have much happier lives than we had.

126 They will not experience much that we have lived through. There will not

In Russia famine increased and starving people queued for bread

be so much cruelty in their lives . . . And yet I don't envy them. Our generation achieved something of amazing significance for history. The cruelty, which the conditions of our life made necessary, will be understood and vindicated. Everything will be understood, everything.'

In 1921 began a new phase which lasted until 1927, and was called the New Economic Policy. Lenin saw the ruin of his country, produced not only by the continual fighting but by the over-hasty changes decreed in the first flush of the Revolution. Communist theory had brought ordinary life to a standstill. At one point the population of St Petersburg fell to a third of its normal size. Hunger drove people to the countryside where food was produced, but they met with disappointment because less and less food was being produced. The peasants looked after themselves, but with their old markets closed they were not going to grow anything extra merely to have it taken by the State. When the Government tried to occupy tracts of the nationalized land and turn them into State farms, the indignant peasants rose in revolt. Famine increased, made worse by a severe drought. In places there were grim whispers of cannibalism. Malaria and other diseases added to the misery. Infections were spread by millions of homeless people who had taken to the roads. Among these were countless children, war orphans, wandering across the country, jumping trains, making dens amid the shells of burnt-out houses, and often forming delinquent gangs which did not stop short of murder. **127**

Herbert Hoover

Not only in Russia were conditions like this after the Great War. Twenty-three devastated countries were helped by the American Relief Administration, headed by a Quaker engineer, Herbert Hoover, who in 1928 was to follow Coolidge as President of the United States. Hoover's organization dealt with a terrible typhus epidemic in Poland and Rumania and brought help to 6 million starving children. In 1922 it delivered a million tons of food to the stricken areas of Russia.

Such help was welcome, but Lenin knew that Russia must help herself, and quickly. The New Economic Policy shocked many of his followers because it looked like a shameful admission that Communism would not work. Private trade was allowed again. Factories were taken out of the hands of the workers and put under the control of trusts or even individuals, any one indeed who could get production moving. Shops and cafés took down their shutters. The peasants were allowed to have their fields on lease, to hire labour, and to sell their produce, so long as they paid a proportion to the tax-collector. By such inducements the Government managed by 1927 to raise production to the 1913 level, no wonderful achievement (mocked the West) but, all things considered, not to be despised.

It took all Lenin's personality to force these common-sense measures upon the theorists in the Party. He was no spell-binding orator like Trotsky, his words (said Gorki) had 'the cold glitter of steel shavings', but when it came to persuasion, as the British agent Bruce Lockhart once reported, Trotsky 'was as incapable of standing against Lenin as a flea would be against an elephant'. Lenin got the Party to adopt the New Economic Policy. He got agreement to send trade missions abroad and make commercial treaties with capitalist governments, which by this time seemed unlikely to be overthrown by their working class populations. The call to World Revolution was played a little more softly but not allowed to die away. A distinction was made between the Soviet Government and the Communist Party which controlled it. The Government behaved 'correctly', was in time recognized by other nations, exchanged ambassadors, and dealt with kings and capitalists as though they were normal human beings. The Party, in close association with foreign parties through the Comintern (Communist International) centred in Moscow, denounced these same rulers in virulent terms and incited their subjects to rise against them. It was a noteworthy example of not letting one's right hand know what one's left hand was doing.

Lenin was now one of the most powerful men in the world, his influence extending into every continent. In character he was quite unchanged. He slept on a plain iron bedstead in an uncarpeted room in the Kremlin, surrounded by all the dazzling magnificence of the empire he had helped to destroy. When admirers sent him food parcels during the worst of the shortages, he gave them away. He was no saint who believed in self-denial for the good of the soul, but he was too much absorbed in his work to spend time on personal enjoyment. He was certainly aware of the good things in life, but he was more concerned to win them for everyone in the future. After listening to a Beethoven sonata he remarked wistfully: 'I can't listen to music too often. It affects your nerves, makes you want to say stupid, nice things, and stroke the heads of people who could create such beauty while living in this vile hell. And now you mustn't stroke anyone's head, or you might get your hand bitten off. You have to hit them on the head, without mercy, though our ideal is not to use force against anyone. Yes . . . our duty is infernally hard.'

There had been an attempt to kill Lenin just after the October Revolution. In August 1918 he was shot and seriously wounded by a woman, Dora Kaplan, no patriotic Tsarist but a fanatical member of the Socialist Revolutionaries, a left-wing party at odds with the Bolsheviks. 'Everyone acts according to his lights,' said Lenin afterwards, but the incident spurred his fellows to even severer treatment of their enemies. If Lenin had died, it is hard to say how the history of Russia would have developed.

Lenin lived. He steered his country through the Civil War into the calmer waters of the New Economic Policy. But late in 1921 his health began to show the strain. He suffered a stroke and left the Kremlin to con- **129** valesce in the country. He struggled back to work, but two more strokes followed. His right hand and leg were paralysed, his speech became difficult. His brain remained active but he could no longer take the lead in the day to day work of the Government.

Stalin came to visit him regularly, to keep him up to date and to ask his opinion. Stalin was Commissar of Nationalities, the hundred and one non-Russian peoples, like the Ukrainians, Uzbeks, Turcomans, Mongols, Armenians and his own Georgians, who had been subject to the Tsars. Some of these peoples had tried to break away when the Empire collapsed. Some, like the Finns and Poles, had succeeded. It was Stalin's achievement that he held most of them together, and, a non-Russian himself, persuaded them to accept partnership with their ancient conquerors. The Russian Empire became the Union of Socialist Soviet Republics. Each nationality was encouraged to develop its own language and culture. Some of the smaller and more primitive groups were provided with the first alphabet they had ever had. They had their own theatres, newspapers, films and radio stations. Russian became in these regions merely a compulsory second language, a common link between them. Just as a Scot resents the use of the name 'England' when the 'United Kingdom' is meant, so the Communists took pains to speak not of 'Russia' but of 'the Soviet Union' or 'the U.S.S.R.'

Stalin's other achievement was less admirable. He saw that the way to wield power under the new system was not to deliver brilliant speeches as Trotsky did but stealthily to manipulate the complex Party organization so as to plant one's own supporters in the key positions. Then, when it came to a vital decision, one was sure of the votes. The orators could declaim until they were blue in the face. The man who controlled the Party machine would get his way. This method suited Stalin's nature. He had no great intellectual gifts, he was a dull speaker, but he excelled at crafty intrigue.

Lenin had always thought him reliable. He had never opposed Lenin as most of the others had at one time or another. Probably he had no wish to. But when Lenin went, Stalin did not mean to play second fiddle to any one else. He laid his plans now for the struggle ahead.

Lenin also was looking ahead, not for himself but for the future of the Communist venture. He was only fifty-three but he had to face the cruel fact that his days were numbered. One by one he considered the half-dozen men who formed with him the Politburo, the core of power. They laid down the 'Party line' which the lesser officials, the local secretaries and the rank and file, loyally followed and explained to the populace at large. Which of the half-dozen would be able to hold the Politburo together as he had done?

There were his old Bolshevik comrades, Kamenev and Zinoviev: he

Lenin's funeral. In spite of a temperature of 30° below zero, one-and-a-half million people passed by the coffin

could not forget that they had once opposed him at a most vital moment, and if their view had prevailed there would have been no armed rising in St Petersburg. There was Trotsky: a 'weathercock', Lenin called him, but also 'the most able man in the present Central Committee'. Tomsky, head of the trade unions, was not in the running. Nor was young Bukharin, 'the darling of the Party', author of *The ABC of Communism*, but for all his popularity a little too scholarly. That left only the Party Secretary, Stalin.

On 25 December 1922 (that it was Christmas Day in the rest of the world meant nothing in Lenin's home) he dictated a testament summing up the situation for his comrades' guidance. He weighed his words with painful care, giving his personal estimate of the various leaders in guarded terms. Recently he had begun to feel less happy about Stalin. He said: 'Comrade Stalin, having become General Secretary, has concentrated an enormous power in his hands, and I am not sure that he always knows how to use that power with sufficient caution.' His doubts grew in the weeks that followed. He foresaw a split that might wreck the Party and endanger the Revolution. He dictated a postscript to his testament. 'Stalin is too rude, and this fault becomes unbearable in the office of General Secretary. Therefore I propose to the comrades to find a way to remove Stalin from that position and appoint another man.' Two months later he suffered another stroke which put an end to all further efforts, though he lingered on through that year and died on 21 January 1924. **131**

Lenin's own comments on what happened next would have been acid indeed. For he, who in his lifetime had been so unassuming and down to earth a character, was now treated at Stalin's suggestion as though he had been an Egyptian Pharaoh. Pompous ceremonies were organized. Trotsky missed the funeral, being away from Moscow and unwell, but he declared afterwards that Stalin had deceived him about the date. Despite protests from Lenin's widow the body was embalmed and placed in the ugly red and black granite mausoleum outside the Kremlin, to attract long lines of pilgrims ever afterwards. Relics were collected for a Lenin Institute. An 'Oath to Lenin', worded in almost religious language, was read to the Party congress. Again and again the heavy phrases were repeated: 'In leaving us, Comrade Lenin ordained—' and the unvarying answer: 'We vow to thee, Comrade Lenin, that we shall honourably fulfill this thy commandment too.' Stalin knew the simple masses. They had been brought up to honour God and the Tsar, to make pilgrimages, to venerate holy relics and icons. They would be easier to handle if they were given something in place of the old faith they had lost. So he built up the cult of Lenin. Lenin's books should henceforth be as sacred as those of Marx, like the New Testament and the Old.

The actual 'Testament of Lenin', however, with its outspoken criticisms of Stalin, was hushed up. Zinoviev and Kamenev were as anxious as Stalin to block Trotsky's road to power. In spite of the widow's renewed protests, the advice which the dying leader had so painfully dictated was kept from his followers. Stalin breathed again. He was round the most dangerous corner, but he was not yet home.

For the next few years the struggle for the leadership was bitterly contested, sometimes in open meeting, more often in secret. Officially it was an argument about policy, between Trotsky's theory of permanent revolution and Stalin's of 'Socialism in one country', which Trotsky said was impossible in the midst of a hostile capitalist world, especially if the one country was poor and backward like the Soviet Union. Interwoven with these conflicting lines of thought were the personal feuds, the basic human lust for power.

Stalin, Kamenev and Zinoviev started as a triumvirate. They managed to get Trotsky moved from the Commissarship of War, where he was most dangerous, as it gave him a hold on the army. Soon Stalin fell out with his partners. They attacked him at the 1925 Congress, but his control of the Party membership swung the vote against them. Six months later came the collapse of the British General Strike. In Moscow it seemed quite reasonable to blame Zinoviev, as head of the Communist International, for failing to produce a successful revolution in Britain. Stalin got him removed from his key position.

132   Stalin excelled at playing off one man against another. First he used

Kamenev and Zinoviev against Trotsky, then Bukharin against the pair of them, gradually levering his enemies out of their strong positions and their seats on the Politburo, sometimes getting them expelled from the Party itself. Trotsky still fought back. In 1927 he denounced Stalin with all his old eloquence. It was useless against Stalin's crafty chess-playing technique. Trotsky turned from open criticism to underground conspiracy. He was expelled from the Party and sent to Alma Ata, remote in Central Asia. At this stage it was still impossible to execute a former leader, even when in disgrace. The most Stalin dared attempt was Trotsky's exile. Trotsky went to Turkey and later to Mexico, where he spent the rest of his life preaching the World Revolution, virulently attacking Stalin, and writing his own monumental history of the events in which he had taken part. The year of his expulsion from Russia, 1929, saw a final opposition move against Stalin, this time by Bukharin, his latest ally, by Tomsky, and by Rykov.

It failed, as all such moves had failed. Lenin's old team-mates never learnt in time, were always too late, always outmanœuvred by the dour Georgian. It is instructive to look over the list and see what happened to them in the end. Kamenev and Zinoviev were executed for treason in 1936, Bukharin and Rykov in 1938. Tomsky escaped sentence only by committing suicide before trial. Trotsky was harder to reach. He turned his house in Mexico into a miniature fortress and all strangers were carefully scrutinized. Yet somehow, in 1940, a mysterious visitor, almost certainly an emissary of Stalin's Secret Police, managed to reach his room and batter him to death with an ice-axe. The account was closed at last.

That was just a tidying-up operation. For ten years Stalin had been unchallenged master of the Soviet Union. By the end of the 1920s he was ready to abandon the New Economic Policy and apply his own plan for building, at whatever cost in human suffering, 'Socialism in one country'. He saw to it that there was indeed no unemployment in Russia. What did it matter if foreign critics complained that there was slavery instead?

8 Mussolini and the Fascists

On 30 October 1922 an historic scene was enacted at the railway station in Rome curiously similar to one at St Petersburg five and a half years before. An excited multitude crammed the square outside. A man of destiny stepped from the train. But this time it was the overnight express from Milan, and the stocky figure that emerged, oddly attired in bowler hat, black shirt, black trousers and white spats, was Benito Mussolini.

It was the climax in a dramatic sequence of events which were to pass into legend as 'the March on Rome'. Like most legends, this grew further and further from the facts as the years went by. Mussolini, the strong man, had marched on the city with his legions, risking everything for the good of his distracted country, like Julius Caesar when he crossed the Rubicon: that was the story. Few Italians knew or cared to recall what had actually happened. Though Mussolini had toyed with the idea of the march he had then become nervous and shied away from it, until one of his lieutenants threatened him, 'We shall carry out the March on Rome without you'. He had not left Milan until he had received a telegram from the King of Italy 'requesting' him to proceed to Rome for consultations. The King, by rejecting the Prime Minister's advice to proclaim martial law and use troops against the Fascists, had ensured that the march would be a walk-over. Mussolini himself had made it in a sleeping compartment.

These discrepancies between fact and fiction do not lessen the importance of what had occurred: Mussolini had come to power, and with him the Fascist movement, a movement soon to be imitated in Germany and thereby to dominate history for the second quarter of our century.

What *was* Fascism? And, before we answer that, what sort of a man was its founder?

Mussolini had been born thirty-nine years earlier, in 1883, in a hill-top village in northern Italy, his father a blacksmith with a taste for reading and an enthusiasm for Socialist theories, his mother a school-teacher and **134** devoutly Catholic. He followed his father by growing up as an unbeliever with violent revolutionary views and his mother by going to a teachers' training college. His violence was not confined to his opinions. He was expelled from two schools for stabbing other boys. When, at eighteen, he began his brief career as a teacher, he used his knife (luckily without fatal results) on a girl to whom he had been making love. As might be imagined he had a chequered career, sometimes as a labourer or unemployed, sometimes giving Italian lessons or writing articles. He fled to Switzerland to avoid the call-up, but later did military service in the Bersaglieri, or Alpine riflemen. He had several short stretches in prison for political agitation. He had innumerable love-affairs, threatened suicide more than once, and on at least one occasion coupled it with a threat of murder.

The Italy of Mussolini's youth was racked with strikes and lock-outs, riots and police raids. He was sincere in his hatred of the poverty that gripped his country: he never forgot seeing, as a boy, nine local families going off together as emigrants to South America, because there was no livelihood at home. He was muddle-headed in seeking the solution: he lacked Lenin's hard intellect, he was swayed by whatever book he had most recently read, and even more by his own sense of insecurity. Years later he liked to boast of his working class origins and call himself 'a man of the people', exaggerating his brief spells as a labourer. At the time, however, he preferred to call himself an 'intellectual'. Like Lenin, he spoke scathingly of the 'bourgeoisie' but for a different reason: he wanted to be accepted as one of them, but, with his rough manners, his slackness in shaving and taking baths, and his ignorance of the conventions in dress and behaviour, he remained an outsider.

By 1914 Mussolini was editor of the Socialist paper, *Avanti* ('Forward'). He was against the war, like many Socialists elsewhere, but in 1915 he broke with his comrades and joined in the popular outcry to take Italy into it. He himself served as a corporal but was wounded in a trench-mortar accident, so that he was discharged and was able to edit a new paper, *Il Popolo d'Italia*. He made himself the spokesman of the men in the ranks, who had little use for the old ruling caste of Italy but even less for the Bolsheviks. 'We, the returned soldiers,' he declared, 'shall urge our claims to govern Italy.'

After the war came several years of confusion and depression. For the Italians the victory seemed a hollow one. Their Prime Minister had walked out of the peace talks in disgust. The final triumph had not wiped out the humiliation of their rout at Caporetto in 1917. Italy, united for only half a century, was divided again by political controversy. Prices rocketed, strike followed strike. Workers occupied the factories, flew the red flag, and collected arms. The Government seemed unable to impose its authority. Frightened people asked if Italy was about to follow Russia.

Italy, however, had no Lenin, backed by a disciplined party, to exploit **135** the situation. Leadership and discipline were on the other side, improvised by Mussolini and the Fascists, since Parliament seemed unable to provide them.

The movement sprang from a small meeting early in 1919 at a business men's club, to form the Milan Fighters' Fascio, the last word meaning a group and being derived from the ancient Roman *fasces*, the bundle of rods and axes symbolizing power. Ancient Rome was Mussolini's inspiration: it was his dream to revive her glories. As the movement spread it adopted the old Roman salute of the outstretched arm, the old Roman organization of 'legions' and 'centurions'. It was not merely a political party, it was an unofficial army. Nor was it content with salutes, parades, and a black-shirt uniform. It fought the Socialists and Communists in countless street-scuffles. Mussolini's newspaper office was an armoury in itself: a Colt revolver, a dagger, and several hand grenades lay ready on his desk beside the ink-pot, and the glass of milk which was his customary drink; more bombs filled the bookcase, and some were even stored in the stove, which once (it is said) the office boy was prevented from lighting in the nick of time. Mussolini's lifelong taste for violence found satisfaction in all this. 'Obedience, not discussion,' was the Fascist motto.

It is hard to say exactly what Fascism stood for (except that it was, emphatically, 'for' Mussolini), easier to say what it was against. It was against Communism. It was against democracy, free speech and individual liberty. To attract the unemployed and some at least of the working class, it made a show of being against capitalism. As things turned out, capitalism survived fairly comfortably the twenty-two years of Fascist government, though the wealthier classes had to accept a good deal of State interference. The Communists defined Fascism as an extreme form of resistance to the working class, the bourgeoisie's resort to naked force which Marx had prophesied, when no longer able to keep power by legal methods. Certainly it was the fear of Communism and the blind instinct of self-preservation that sent all manner of people flocking to enroll.

Fascism grew swiftly. Mussolini stood for Parliament in 1919 and was hopelessly defeated, but two years later he was elected with twenty-two followers. By August 1922 the workers were so alarmed by his strength that they declared a general strike, which it is interesting to contrast with the British one of 1926. Mussolini's disciplined legions took over all the essential services and the strike was broken in twenty-four hours. This convincing demonstration brought many waverers to join what looked likely to be the winning side. In October the Party rally at Naples clamoured for a 'March on Rome' to take over power from the nerveless hands of the ever-changing prime ministers. Mussolini was doubtful about the adventure. He went back to Milan.

King Victor Emmanuel and Benito Mussolini, 1929   **137**

Meantime his more determined lieutenants got moving. Fascist squads were ordered into action in selected cities like Pisa and Cremona, to create the impression that Italy was on the brink of civil war and that only Fascism could save her. Mussolini sat in his office, barricaded behind giant drums of newsprint, a rifle handy, telephoning frantically in all directions, afraid of being trapped into some false move. He would not accept the King's invitation to Rome until it was confirmed in writing.

Then he drove to the station and began his 'march', leaving orders that an attack should be made that night on the offices of *Avanti*, the Socialist paper he had once edited. 'It must not come out tomorrow,' he said, 'or I shall have a general strike on my hands.' The next morning there was no *Avanti* on the news-stands and Mussolini was bowing before the diminutive Victor Emmanuel. He apologized for his black shirt. 'Excuse my appearance, Your Majesty, but I come from the battlefield.'

When he returned to the palace with the list of names for the Government the King had invited him to form, he had changed into top hat and morning dress, each item borrowed from a different owner, the sleeves too short, the trousers too long and tight. Only with difficulty was he persuaded not to wear his spats. He was devoted to these spats, conspicuous white ones, bought earlier that year in France as a convenient means of hiding the shabbiness of his shoes.

It is easy to smile at *Il Duce* ('the Leader'), as he soon preferred to be called, or the 'sawdust Caesar', as one biographer has scornfully termed him. But if Mussolini was too often overrated in his lifetime, by people who had not the nerve or desire to call his bluff, it would be a mistake for us to go to the other extreme. Now the records are open for all to read we can see that he was clown and coward by turns, braggart and bully. Yet, if he had been nothing more, he would not have survived so long. He kept the leadership of a party in which there were cleverer men and greater rogues than himself. He gave Italy a semblance of unity unknown since ancient days. He made world statesmen treat him seriously, even fear him. The white spats were not important. The black shirt, with all it symbolized, was.

To begin with, Mussolini worked inside the parliamentary framework. He chose a mixed team of ministers, combining Catholics and Liberals with his supporters. Two departments, Foreign Affairs and Home Affairs, he kept in his own hands. He had to go carefully, for it would never do to frighten or offend the powerful interests that had put him where he was. He treated the King with respect, while sneering at him in private as 'too small a man for an Italy on the road to greatness'. The King took too much interest in State business. He was 'as inquisitive as a monkey' and 'a tremendous bore'. But King and Duce needed each other

Il Duce entered the *1930s in a glow of general approval both at home and abroad*

for self-preservation, and for a long time they could not afford to fall out.

In April 1924 the Fascists won a clear majority. There was still opposition, but they could now move more boldly to stifle it. One of their critics was the Socialist deputy, Matteotti. He disappeared and his murdered body was found a few days later in the country outside Rome. Whether or not Mussolini had approved the murder in advance, his enemies always held him guilty of it. Usually he was satisfied to order the beating up of his opponents by gangs of Blackshirts. Once he telegraphed the Prefect of Turin: 'Gobetti's damaging campaign against Fascism continues. Please take steps to make life impossible for this foolish opponent.' Gobetti was duly attacked and several of his ribs broken.

By one method or another all opponents were silenced, except those who escaped abroad, like the Communist leader, Togliatti, who spent these years in Moscow, and the veteran statesman, Count Sforza, who went to America. Those who remained in Italy were either cowed into submission, driven underground, or imprisoned, often in the rocky sun-grilled Lipari Islands. Censorship controlled the newspapers. Despite an army of police spies and informers it was impossible to suppress the Italian love of scandal and jokes against authority, so that Mussolini never achieved the complete domination of thought and word which is the aim **139** of the totalitarian state. In Italy, too, there were always some forces retaining a strong element of independence, like the royal family and the Catholic Church, some people he must treat carefully, some directions in which he could move only so far. And, well below the top level at which he himself operated, the whole Fascist organization was permeated with corruption. Many things could be bought: particular favours and 'protection' in the gangster sense, but not of course the freedom to speak out against Fascism.

The darker side was not obvious to foreigners. Tourists were delighted that the trains ran on time and the postal services were reliable. They felt that the leisurely happy-go-lucky Italian people had been shaken up by this dynamic new régime. They were impressed by public works, such as the draining of the Pontine Marshes and the lavish archaeological scheme that uncovered the Forum. They were not interested in the disappearance of a free press and free trade unions. Indeed, many a foreign visitor wished that his government at home would imitate Mussolini's firm line with the unruly workers. Fascism had its admirers in most western countries. There was a little group in Britain long before Sir Oswald Mosley (after being in succession a Conservative M.P., an Independent M.P., and a minister in the Labour Government) started his British Union of Fascists in the 1930s.

Diplomats and statesmen saw deeper (though not always much deeper) than the tourists. But whether they liked all Mussolini's methods or not, they preferred them to Communism. They did not want him to go. In this lay his luck: at first the western powers saw him as a counterbalance to Russia and later, when Hitler seized power, they deluded themselves that they could play off Italy against Germany. That is another story. In 1927 Winston Churchill was 'charmed' by Mussolini and declared that his movement had 'rendered a service to the whole world'. It was 'the necessary antidote to the Russian poison'.

One of the Duce's undoubted successes was to end the dispute between the Kingdom of Italy and the Popes, which had lasted since the unification of the country in 1870. Ever since that date each Pope in turn had remained a voluntary prisoner within the Vatican, refusing to recognize the State's authority over the territories formerly ruled by the Church. Mussolini, the unbeliever, seemed scarcely the ideal man to heal the old wound. Nor did the Church like the Fascist attempt to dominate every department of life, especially the schools and the youth movements. The Pope himself had denounced 'this pagan worship of the State'. Mussolini, however, was changing. His old atheism had shredded away along with his Socialism. What now absorbed him was the vision of reviving the Roman Empire, an empire which in its last days had been Christian. **140** Though far from becoming an orthodox Catholic he sometimes allowed

Blackshirts marching in London

himself to be represented as one, was occasionally persuaded to take Easter communion, and went through a religious marriage ceremony. All this facilitated his treaty with the Church in 1929. The Pope gave up his ancient territorial claims, except the few acres of the Vatican, and the Italian Government paid compensation in cash and securities. For Mussolini it was a good bargain: he won the support of many Italians whose loyalty had previously been divided, and of many foreign Catholics, who now vaguely felt that Fascism had the blessing of the Church.

Mussolini entered the 1930s in a glow of general approval, both at home and abroad. There were no menacing shadows yet of his future policies, but they were soon to come.

His hope was to make Italy self-sufficient. She was poor in natural resources, however, and had never been able to support her population. Millions of Italians had always had to emigrate, like those neighbours he remembered from his boyhood. The Great War and the 1929 economic crisis made emigration more difficult. In any case, to one of Mussolini's patriotic fervour, it seemed disgraceful that Italians should have to go and live under a foreign flag. Italy needed an empire like the British or French, providing land for colonists and raw materials for her factories. Unfortunately Italy had started late in the nineteenth-century race for colonies. She had only the barren 'left-overs'. Not even the Duce could rebuild the majesty of imperial Rome on such poor foundations.

What then was to be done? Mussolini's answer to that was to add considerably to the troubles of the 1930s.

9 China: The Awakening Giant

It is time to look east and see what the twentieth century had brought to the world's biggest population, the Chinese.

In 1900 a Western visitor would scarcely have felt that he was *in* the twentieth century, or even the nineteenth, once he had left his port of entry. Inland, little had changed in hundreds of years. The Imperial Government had grudgingly permitted a few railways to be built by the 'foreign devils' and some telegraph wires had recently been strung from city to city. That was about all. Immemorial China spread in all directions to the horizon, with its rice fields and canals and water-buffaloes, its pagodas and tea-houses, its porcelain elegance and its pigsty poverty. China was not interested in progress.

Visit, in imagination, the nerve-centre of this empire. Look for the people (the one person, actually) directing the destiny of a nation even then approaching the 400 million mark. A gateway set in a fifty-foot wall gives entrance to the Inner, or Tartar, City of Peking. Within that again, as in a nest of boxes, lies the Imperial City behind its purplish ramparts. And there is still a forty-foot moat carpeted with water-lilies, a grey brick wall forty feet high and forty feet thick, enclosing the innermost square mile, the Forbidden City, where the Son of Heaven, the Lord of Ten Thousand Years, sits upon the Dragon Throne, one man alone in a cloistered community of 3,000 women and eunuchs.

No wonder the Western visitor in 1900 found it hard to remember that he was on the threshold of the twentieth century, and not stepping into a scene from *Aladdin*. Yet the more he learnt of the ugly realities hidden behind the lacquered pavilions and the lotus pools, the less he would have felt that he was living in an Oriental fairy-tale. There was a closer resemblance to the Roman Empire at its most cruel and corrupt.

For all his high-sounding titles, the young Emperor Kwang Hsü had no power. The Head Eunuch, Li Lien-ying, had so much that he was slyly referred to as the Lord of Nine Thousand Years. But anyone wishing to **143**

The Dowager Empress of China. Long finger-nails, deliberately grown, were a sign of high rank

see the real ruler must seek an interview with Kwang Hsü's aunt, the Dowager Empress Tzü Hsi. This could be arranged with Li. A five-minute audience might cost 100,000 taels, £10,000 or $50,000. The bribe would be split between Empress and eunuch. The daughter of a minor official, then the concubine of an earlier emperor, Tzü knew just how government should be conducted. It was the old Chinese way and she saw no reason to alter it. She hated the 'foreign devils' and their ideas. They had conquered the rest of the world. They should not conquer China.

We must remember that in 1900 nearly all Asia was governed by white men. The Union Jack flew over India and what is now Pakistan, over Ceylon, Burma, and Malaya; the French tricolour over Indochina (now Laos, Cambodia and Viet Nam); the horizontal red white and blue of Holland over the tropical islands of Indonesia. The Portuguese had scraps of territory, small but profitable as business centres, and Spain had just lost the Philippines to America. Siberia and Central Asia were governed from St Petersburg, the Arab countries from Constantinople. Asia, in fact, was a field of giant allotment gardens, cropped by distant occupiers, a system which the Communists were soon to denounce as 'colonialism' and 'imperialistic exploitation'. In contrast to the numerous Asian members of the United Nations today, there were only five truly independent countries. Afghanistan, Persia (now Iran) and Siam (now Thailand), kept this independence by playing off Britain against Russia or France against Britain. Japan, newly modernized at great speed, was about to defy the power of Russia. And China, the Empress would have said, was—China.

There were, of course, misguided Chinese who wanted, like the Japanese, to copy the foreign devils. There were eminent and respectable persons who pleaded for reform by imperial decree. And there were those who plotted revolution.

Among these, specially hated by the Empress, was Dr Sun Yat-sen. Son of a farmer near Canton, he had been a rebel even in the village school. He had persistently challenged the traditional method of Chinese education, by which the pupil recited everything parrot-fashion to his teacher. 'What is the use,' he demanded, 'of learning by heart something I do not understand?' At twelve years old he was sent off to his brother, who had emigrated to Hawaii like so many Chinese who could not scratch a living in their own country. On his brother's little farm near Pearl Harbor, Sun saw that even working people could enjoy a reasonable standard of life. He went to a boarding school run by the Anglican Bishop of Honolulu, so that he could learn English and become a bank clerk. He was stirred by English history: his own country had not reached the stage of Magna Carta, much less Cromwell. But when he announced that he wished to be baptized, his family was horrified and he was **145** ordered home. 'I'll take this Jesus nonsense out of him when he gets back,' his father promised.

Sun, however would never again accept the traditional standards of China. Before long he had entered Queen's College in the near-by British colony of Hong Kong and become a Christian. When a medical college was started there (there were none within the imperial territories) he immediately enrolled. Again he learnt more than the mere syllabus. In Hong Kong discussion was free. The students talked incessantly of China's need to abolish her old government, wake up and come into the modern world. 'When we weren't discussing revolution,' Sun recalled in later years, 'we didn't feel happy.'

Once qualified, he tried to practise in the Portuguese colony of Macao near by, but the jealousy of the Portuguese doctors made it impossible. Then, hearing that a progressive governor was going to start a hospital in north China, he and another young man walked the whole way across the country, hoping to interest the governor in their ideas of reform. They were snubbed, but their long journey gave Sun a fuller picture of his country's poverty.

Thereafter he was a professional revolutionary. In Honolulu he founded the Society for the Restoration of China. He put great faith in the Chinese abroad. Though forced to emigrate, they had never lost their devotion to their own country. They had seen how foreigners did things, they knew the changes needed in China. Many of them, having prospered, could afford money for the cause.

The Empress was soon aware of his activities. After taking part in an unsuccessful revolt in Canton, Sun escaped (lowered in a basket from the city ramparts like St Paul at Damascus) and travelled through the United States and Europe, recruiting Chinese for his secret society. He was shadowed by the Empress's agents. When he reached London the Chinese Legation there had precise instructions.

On Sunday morning he started for St Martin's-in-the-Fields, first calling for Dr Cantlie, his old friend and benefactor in Hong Kong. On the way he met two amiable Chinese who invited him to see where they lodged. As they chatted on the threshold the door suddenly opened and Sun was dragged inside. He then discovered to his horror that he was, legally speaking, in China: it was the Chinese Legation which he had entered unwittingly through a side door. For nearly two weeks he was held prisoner while the Legation planned to ship him home in the guise of a mental patient. Once in China, he could be interrogated under torture and then beheaded. Meanwhile Dr Cantlie, living close by, was utterly mystified by his disappearance until he received an anonymous warning from an English employee at the Legation. Cantlie went to

Scotland Yard. Nobody would believe him. In any case, nothing could be done. The Legation ranked as Chinese territory: no English policeman could enter it. Cantlie went from lawyer to lawyer, official to official, until he convinced the Foreign Office. There was still a risk that Sun would be spirited away to the docks before the slow-moving diplomatic procedure could save him, so a private detective was posted in a hansom cab to watch the building. The Chinese Minister then saw that the game was up, for once the prisoner was brought out on to the pavement he could claim the same protection as any Londoner; nor could he be kept for ever inside the Legation, now that the Prime Minister himself, Lord Salisbury, was asking awkward questions. Sun was freed, much to the annoyance of the Empress.

She soon had other opposition to deal with. Her nephew Kwang Hsü tried to assert himself as Emperor, encouraged by his old tutor and his favourite concubine Pearl. He signed a rapid succession of edicts for the modernization of China. The antiquated examination system which determined posts and promotions was to be abolished. There were to be schools and colleges on Western lines. The army was to be reorganized, roads and railways built, foreign technicians engaged, and an end put to the universal practice of 'squeeze', the bribing of officials at every level. All these decrees were published in a brief period known as 'the Hundred Days of Reform'.

The Empress's reactions could be foreseen. With a long record of murders behind her, she would stick at nothing to prevent the overthrow of her power and everything she believed in. Kwang Hsü therefore instructed a general, Yüan Shih-kai, to surround her palace with troops. Yüan however was a man with far-reaching ambitions of his own. He betrayed the plan to the Empress who immediately took control, backed by all who had a vested interest in the bad old (but extremely profitable) ways. Six of the leading reformers were beheaded, others banished. As the Emperor could not be executed, he was handed over to the Chief Eunuch, Li, and held on an islet in one of the lakes in the Forbidden City. Pearl was kept for two years in solitary confinement and then thrown living down a deep well before the eyes of her lover. This was the year in which China, according to the Western calendar if nothing else, entered the twentieth century. It was the year, too, of the Boxer Rising, the Boxers being an anti-foreigner secret society whose bloodthirsty attacks on missionaries and others were favoured by the all-powerful Empress.

She ruled until 1908. The captive Kwang Hsü, never a very prudent man, let it be known that if he outlived her he would settle old scores with the Chief Eunuch and the faithless general. It was felt best, particularly by Li and Yüan, that this should not happen. When the Empress made herself ill by overeating at a picnic on her seventy-third birthday (at which she had appeared in fancy dress as the Goddess of Mercy), they pretended to suspect that Kwang Hsü had poisoned her, and in righteous **147**

*Within the Forbidden City: this photograph is thought to have been taken during the
lying-in-state of the Empress, 1908*

indignation put him to death—by poison. By this time his aunt was
feeling much better and she was able to appoint his three-year-old nephew
Pu-yi as his successor. Within another twenty-four hours she herself was
dead. With her died the old China, though for a few years longer the out-
ward forms survived.

Sun Yat-sen continued to travel the world, wherever there were
Chinese immigrants to organize, preaching his famous Three Principles
of the People. These were Nationalism, Democracy, and Economic
Justice, the last of which in time was made more definite as 'Socialism'.
Nationalism meant two things: the Chinese must unite against the
imperial family, the Manchu dynasty, who (though they had ruled since
1644) were originally alien conquerors; equally they must unite against
those foreigners, European, American or Japanese, who had taken
advantage of China's weakness to seize territories and privileges, such as
the control of great ports like Shanghai.

Sun was not a brilliant original thinker or an effective revolutionary
leader like Lenin. But, by his tireless travelling and teaching, he laid
foundations on which other men could build. Later, the Chinese Communists were to point out his limitations and play down his role in the
development of modern China, but millions of simple people would long
revere his name and speak of his 'Three Principles' as something sacred.

Sun was far away in the United States when, on 10 October 1911, the
148 long-awaited Chinese Revolution began with an accidental bomb

explosion at Hankow. Disorder broke out. Conspirators who had begun by fighting to save their necks soon found to their surprise that they were winning. Troops mutinied. Cities fell like ripe fruit into the lap of the Revolution. One of Sun's followers who particularly distinguished himself was the twenty-four-year-old Chiang Kai-shek. With a small band using hand grenades he captured a provincial governor in his palace and took over the whole area.

Prince Chun, father of the little Emperor, had previously dismissed the ambitious Yüan, but had to recall him as the only general who could put down the revolt. Yüan was given full powers and used them with characteristic disloyalty in his own interests. He quickly indicated that he would change sides if it was made worth his while, and persuaded the imperial family (who now had not much choice) to let a National Convention decide China's future. The Convention voted for a republic. The six-year-old Emperor Pu-yi abdicated, but kept his title, a handsome allowance, and the Summer Palace at Peking. Sun arrived from America to find that sixteen out of the seventeen provinces wished him to be President. Yüan, however, had the military power and had made his own bargain with the revolutionary leaders. To avoid civil war, Sun withdrew and Yüan became President.

The revolutionaries had paid a high price for their peaceful settlement. Yüan was not interested in their aims. To make sure that these were not lost sight of, the various movements formed the Kuomintang, or People's National Party. Yüan, determined to stand no opposition, fought it with every weapon from bribery to murder. He enlisted several thousand thugs in a 'Citizens' Society' and posted them round the Parliament building so that no one could leave until he had secured the vote he wanted. The Kuomintang was made illegal, its representatives expelled from Parliament. Sun found himself in exile again, working for another revolution.

Yüan was more popular with foreign governments, for they saw in him a strong man who would keep China moving along the old lines so satisfactory from their point of view. Anxious to make his future even more secure, he asked his American constitutional adviser whether a republic or a monarchy would best suit China. Goodnow gave the advice desired, in favour of monarchy. Yüan planned to proclaim himself Emperor on New Year's Day, 1916. Though the scheme was unpopular with the masses he managed (not surprisingly) to produce petitions and ballots in overwhelming support of it, and as he dared not risk Japan's disapproval he tried to buy her favour by secretly agreeing to a long list of her demands. At the last moment, however, Japan vetoed the idea. Yüan was bitterly humiliated, he had 'lost face', and less than six months later he died.

Confusion followed, with rival governments, one in the north at Peking, another led by Sun at Canton in the south. In some provinces the military commander or a bandit chief set up as local dictator. This was the era of the 'war lords', like the break-up of the Roman Empire in the Dark Ages.

Sometimes in office, sometimes in exile, Sun never gave up hope. Whatever his shortcomings he had always had a wonderful gift for inspiring people with his own dream of a better China. Among those who gave him this life-long hero-worship was the daughter of an Americanized Chinese banker, Charles Soong. Her name was Ching-ling and she was (as someone described her) 'a pale, slender, exquisite fragment of humanity'. The family were Christians and in sympathy with Sun's politics, but her parents were alarmed when at twenty she revealed her love for a man of forty-eight. They locked her in her room, but she climbed out of the window, and fled to join her hero in Japan. They were married the next day. She became his secretary, devoted herself entirely to him for the last ten years of his life, and fearlessly championed his ideas after his death. Madame Sun Yat-sen has her own niche of honour in Chinese history.

Sun had always admired Western democracy. He had hoped to reform **150** China on that model, but Britain and America were not helpful. As so often, they were slow to understand the new forces of revolution and nationalism, and to recognize that the old regime would never return. So, disappointed, Sun turned to the Russians, who were eager to make friends abroad. He envied Lenin his disciplined party, so much more effective than the Kuomintang. He wanted the 'Party' without the 'Communist'. Russian advisers came to organize his followers. Chiang Kai-shek, who had been steadily rising in influence, went to study the Red Army. Far from making Chiang a Communist, however, this Moscow visit probably influenced him in the opposite way.

Other Chinese meanwhile formed their own Communist cells inside the Kuomintang, permeating its key positions. The Chinese abroad started other cells and through these several of their most able members entered the Communist movement. Chu Teh, later commander-in-chief of Soviet China, joined in Germany while studying military science in the early 1920s. Chou En-lai, later Prime Minister and Foreign Minister, joined in Paris. But the destined leader, Mao Tse-tung, was an assistant librarian at Peking University. An avid reader and restless thinker, he adopted the Marxist philosophy after trying Buddhism, pacifism, and several other -isms.

Note these men. They were not conspicuous at that moment, but the future lay with them. They represented different social levels in the population.

Chu Teh came from a family typical of millions barely existing in the appalling poverty of the Chinese countryside. Five of the other children were drowned at birth so that there should be enough food for the rest.

Chou En-lai, by contrast, was the son of an official and his grandfather had been a distinguished public servant. He went to the university and learnt English, French and German.

Mao Tse-tung was socially between the two. His father, a rich peasant, used to beat him unmercifully and tried to make him marry, at thirteen, a girl of nineteen who was a good match. Mao ran away from home. Later he went to Peking University. He had been brought up on the classical literature of his country and wrote poetry himself, but his mind was wide open to ideas of every kind. In vacations he worked or begged his way about the country, talking to people and deepening his insight into the problems of China. He covered some 10,000 miles. He learnt with his own eyes and ears what mere printed statistics might not have impressed upon him, that 80 or 90 per cent of the Chinese were struggling peasants. 'Whoever wins the peasants will win China,' he once said. 'Whoever solves the land question will win the peasants.' The land question was how to keep an ever-growing population on tiny farms, tilled by ancient methods, without capital or modern aids, yet somehow expected to yield regular payments to the landlord, tax-collector, and money-lender. Mao knew, **151** as vividly as Chu Teh, what it meant when a farmer's only water-buffalo died or a bad harvest forced the family to eat even the seed corn they needed for the next season.

Could Sun have solved the land question? He cared about it, but had he sufficient intellectual grasp of the problem, let alone the ruthless will to batter down all opposition? He never had the chance to try. In 1925 he died. Like Lenin he was buried in an ugly mausoleum which became a place of pilgrimage. Like Lenin's widow, Madame Sun lived on to see her husband's memory revered while his ideas were distorted by his successor.

This successor was General Chiang Kai-shek. To strengthen his position, he asked Madame Sun to marry him. When she refused, he began a two-year courtship of her younger sister, Mei-ling. Again the Soong family opposed the marriage, since Chiang was not a Christian, but on his promising at least to read the Bible they consented.

In 1926 Chiang led the famous 'Northern Expedition', planned before Sun's death, against the war lords who defied the Kuomintang. There was heavy fighting but the modern equipment and methods of the Kuomintang won the day. Chu Teh commanded one of its armies, Mao went along as an expert in land reform and Chou En-lai as a political commissar, his function being (as in Russia where the idea originated) to supervise the education, propaganda, and general political behaviour of the troops. It was Chou who slipped into Shanghai ahead of the expedition to prepare the city workers for an armed rising against the war lords.

Though pleased with the military success of the Northern Expedition, Chiang was less pleased with what was happening behind his advancing armies. The peasants were taking over their land, much as the Russians had done in 1917. Chiang himself, though not rich, came from the landed gentry, and so did many of his supporters. They were alarmed at the way things were developing. Many Communists even, both in China and in Russia, were alarmed also. These fully intended the peasants to seize the land eventually, but they thought it dangerous to skip a stage in the proper sequence of a revolution. The bourgeois elements in the Kuomintang must have power for long enough to show that their policies were useless, then they must be overthrown by the proletariat. 'October' must follow 'February'.

This was in line with Stalin's theory, and in 1927 Stalin was just consolidating his own power. He sent word to the Kuomintang's Russian advisers to put the brake on. But Stalin was too late. Chiang saw that he must choose between Russian and Western help. If the Communists continued their permeation of his party he would lose all capitalist sympathy. From what he had seen in Russia he probably foresaw that he would also lose his position and even his life.

What followed may have been patriotism, or self-preservation, or (as

Chiang Kai-shek and Madame Chiang, younger sister of Madame Sun

Madame Sun called it) the betrayal of the Revolution. It depends on the point of view. And Chiang's methods must be judged by the conditions of the place and the time. In Western democracies it was possible for a coalition of parties to break up without bloodshed, by orderly votes and resignations. China had no such tradition. To lay down power meant to lay one's head on the block. Nobody, Chiang, Communist or war lord, dared trust his opponents.

So Chiang struck without warning at his Communist supporters. Chou En-lai was sentenced to death. Luckily for him, the firing squad was commanded by one of his old pupils from the Military Academy, who let him escape. Many other Communists were killed. The Party was outlawed and went underground, with headquarters in Shanghai. It was easy to hide there in a port of several million people, especially in the large area of the International Settlement, jointly controlled by the foreign nations trading there.

Chu Teh and Mao Tse-tung found refuge in the mountains of the southeast, where a mutinous army had set up a local Soviet Government. This was Mao's chance to try the policy he had been advising for some time, to develop a mass movement among the poor peasants he knew so well rather than to imitate the Russian method of building up a small disciplined party among the city workers.

For a year or two Mao's little Soviet Republic existed in the mountains **153**

F

Street scene in Peking

unnoticed by the Communist Central Committee hiding in Shanghai, by the Comintern in Moscow, or by the world in general. Its regime was hard. Its opponents (and that often meant anyone who was not a poor peasant, whether he opened his mouth or not) were mercilessly liquidated and almost every village had its execution-ground. Chiang, meanwhile, became more and more the dictator, less and less the disciple of Sun Yat-sen. Madame Sun blamed him for all the atrocities committed by the Kuomintang, as when, for instance, six young writers guilty of 'dangerous thinking' were compelled to dig their own graves and were then buried alive in them. The old Dowager Empress would have found little to teach China's new rulers.

Chiang could not catch Mao, though he put a price of $250,000 on his head. Six times he sent his armies against the 'bandits' as he scornfully termed the Communists. Five times the expeditions withdrew unsuccessfully; once the whole force went over to the Communists. The latter became expert guerillas, wearing down the Kuomintang troops with ambushes, stealthy retreats, and night attacks. The peasants helped, warning them of hostile movements and misdirecting the enemy columns.

Even so, it looked as though Chiang would win in the end. He had unlimited resources. The Communists could get arms only by capturing them. When Chiang began to build a network of blockhouses to dominate **154** their territories and marshalled an army of a million, it was clear that the days of the mountain republic were numbered. Mao and Chu decided to break out before the net closed and join another Communist group in the north. It was a bold enough idea, to cross so vast a country, running the gauntlet of innumerable enemies, but for three reasons it was far bolder even than the map suggests.

First, though the distance from point to point was sufficiently daunting, they could not follow a straight line, but a curve sweeping inland, far from the Kuomintang bases. Secondly, that route involved staggering difficulties: wide rivers, high passes, tracts of barren plateau to test an explorer's endurance. Lastly, not only the army must make the journey, but women and children, old and ailing, the whole community in a mass migration, for no one dared stay to face the vengeance of Chiang's soldiers.

So, from 1934 to 1935, the Chinese Communists enacted the epic of 'The Long March', an extraordinary achievement unheard of in the outside world for some time afterwards. Their trek took them through eleven provinces. They crossed twenty-four rivers, sometimes under fire. They toiled over eighteen mountains, hungry, cold, lashed by wind, rain and snow. They had to occupy over sixty cities on the way and beat off one enemy army after another. Their sufferings were appalling. Only about one in ten completed the journey. Mao's wife died; their child was left with some friendly peasants and never heard of again. Only about 20,000 fighting men were left out of 100,000. But the march had been made. The nucleus of Soviet China began a new life in the little town of Yenan, not far south of the Great Wall and the deserts of Mongolia. Life was still hard. Many lived in caves dug out of the hillside. Chiang continued to send expeditions against them. But now he had other troubles to contend with.

Chiang's other troubles sprang from Japan, beginning with the Manchurian incident in 1931, regarded by some as the real beginning of World War II, which did not start officially until eight years later.

Long ago the Japanese had plunged enthusiastically into the task of modernizing their country, modelling their navy on the British, their army on the German. They had used Englishmen in their railway and telegraph services, Americans in their post offices, Frenchmen and Germans in their courts, schools and hospitals. They wanted the best teachers and they learnt fast, despite opposition from the old feudal nobility. Neither assassinations nor ceremonial suicides (*hara-kiri*) halted the march of progress. It was nearly all done in the forty-five-year reign of the great Emperor Meiji, who died in 1912.

Like Germany and Italy Japan had started late in the race for colonies. However, in 1895 she fought a war with China and took the island of Formosa. At the same time she deprived China of Korea, the peninsula curving out so temptingly close to Japan. Korea became nominally inde- **155**

A shrimper at work on the Chinese coast

pendent, but in a few years was incorporated into the Japanese Empire.

To the north lay Manchuria, an outlying region of China beyond the Great Wall, once a foreign land, whose conquering princes, the Manchu dynasty, had ruled the Chinese Empire for its last three centuries. Now the region was mainly inhabited by people from China proper, but its modern development, its railways, mines and manufactures, sprang from the enterprise of Japanese business men. In 1931 the Japanese Government resolved to take over the country completely. Chiang Kai-shek was powerless to defend this distant territory. Foreign states which once would have blocked the Japanese scheme had their own problems: America and Britain were reeling under the impact of the Wall Street crash, and Russia was struggling to fulfil her first Five-Year Plan. Nobody wanted trouble in the Far East.

Japan took Manchuria with contemptuous ease. Though outnumbered twenty to one by the defending forces, her small expedition overran the country in a few months. There were eloquent speeches of protest at the League of Nations in Geneva, Japan's action was unanimously condemned, but nothing practical was done. For the look of the thing, the Japanese turned Manchuria into a nominally independent state called Manchukuo, with a puppet emperor of the ancient Manchu dynasty. **156** This was young Pu-yi, deposed from the Dragon Throne twenty years earlier, and now brought out of cold storage to serve Japan's purposes.

She had committed open aggression—and got away with it. Mussolini and Hitler noted what could be done if one had sufficient nerve. The democratic countries clearly had no nerve, only nerves. Japan's success encouraged the European dictators during the next few years, until Hitler went too far and the world was plunged into its second universal war. That is the historical significance of the Manchurian 'incident'.

Soon the Japanese began to nibble at more Chinese territory, at Inner Mongolia and the northern provinces. To sap resistance they deliberately smuggled opium and heroin, so that more and more Chinese became drug addicts, interested only in obtaining their regular supplies. Opium smoking is not a Chinese tradition. Even the old imperial government was against it. Opium was introduced into China by the British as a profitable export from India. Now, for more subtle reasons, it was carried in by a secret army of Japanese and Korean drug pedlars.

How would it all end? Patriotic Chinese implored Chiang to check the foreign intruders. There had been no official declaration of war, but the continuing 'incident' was war in everything but name. Every week there was guerilla fighting in the Japanese-occupied provinces. Who knew when another wave of aggression would sweep forward?

Chiang stubbornly insisted that he must deal with the Communists first. Once he controlled a united country, he could stop the Japanese. Some retorted that if he and the Communists spent much more time disputing who should rule China there would be no China left for either of them.

The Communists themselves were now demanding a united front against the Japanese. In this they were being prodded by Stalin. The Soviet Union had large Far Eastern territories sparsely populated, hard to defend, dangerously near Japan. She wanted Japan checked. So 'the Party line' was laid down in Moscow. Whether they liked it or not, Mao and his friends must show a united front with Chiang.

By 1936 serious fighting had died down between the Communists and the armies sent against them. Chiang hurried to headquarters at Sian to take over the command himself from his deputy, Chang Hsueh-liang, often known as 'the young Marshal', an independent-minded man who had for some time been pleading with him for the united front. Chiang meant to restore the situation by wholesale arrests and courts martial. To his surprise, he found himself arrested in a midnight coup. For some time he expected to be shot. He was, however, treated with all the elaborate courtesy demanded by Chinese convention, his captors humbly apologizing for the regrettable interference with his liberty. Along with the polite phrases there was some plain talking. Chiang had to listen to the views not only of his own supporters but of emissaries from the Communist **157**

This group was taken shortly before Chiang's arrest at Sian. He is seen eighth from the left. Ninth from left is his future captor, Marshal Chang Hsueh-liang

territories. Finally he yielded with dignity. The united front was to be formed, the campaign against Mao called off, political prisoners released, the 'Red Army' incorporated into the national defence as 'the Eighth Route Army'. Chiang was then released.

It was very much a forced marriage, this united front. Neither side could forget the past. Chiang schemed to split up the Red forces and eventually liquidate them, Mao to strengthen and spread the Communist movement. Fighting the Japanese, he frankly admitted long afterwards, was no more than 'ten per cent' of his programme. The agreement could easily have become a dead letter. The Japanese, by their own misjudgment, made it a living reality.

Six months after the famous 'kidnapping' at Sian, Japan's military leaders announced that China must be brought to her senses and liberated from Communist oppression. It was Japan's mission to do this and establish a 'New Order in East Asia', an ominous phrase repeated frequently during **158** the next decade. Still without any formal declaration of war, the Japanese

A Chinese defence line awaiting a Japanese attack

launched a full-scale invasion of China proper, no longer just the disputed northern provinces. Chiang had no choice left. He had to treat Japan as the main enemy and co-operate with the detested Communists as best he could.

This struggle continued, Japan steadily conquering the coastal areas and the Chinese doggedly retreating inland, until (after the Japanese surprise attack on the American naval base at Pearl Harbor in 1941) it merged into the Second World War.

10 Poverty in Plenty

'Hands off Manchuria!' and 'Down with Japanese imperialism!' cried some of the banners carried in the London May Day procession in 1932, and only some vigorous police charges prevented the marchers from reaching the Japanese Embassy. But most of that shabby underfed multitude were far more indignant about the Means Test, a new measure which was intensifying the misery of the British unemployed. London, New York and the other great Western cities had so many troubles of their own that they spared hardly a glance for the storm-clouds gathering in the East.

The Wall Street crash had ended the prosperity of the 'Gay Twenties' and sent shock waves radiating out from America to strike all the countries whose trade had become interlocked in the one great capitalist system. The decade which now opened has been called the 'Anxious Thirties'. At first men feared for their jobs; then they began to fear Fascism and war.

'Depression', 'recession', 'slump', 'economic crisis': these are deadly dull words. They conjure up little more than figures on a printed page, the sort of page that many readers skip. In the years following 1929 those words meant a great deal more. They meant children who never tasted fresh milk or eggs and would not have known how to eat a banana if given one, children who grew up with rickety legs and tubercular lungs, children who could not go to school because they had no shoes. They meant postponed marriages and engagements broken for ever, because young men could find no jobs. They meant family separations, when the father took to the roads and went hundreds of miles in quest of work. In Britain they also meant homes stripped of pianos and anything which, classed as a luxury under the Means Test, must be sold before further relief money could be paid. They meant misery and degradation for millions, and, if those are abstract words again, let us say bluntly that they sometimes meant bodies in the river, heads in the gas oven, prisoners in cells, and patients in mental hospitals. Nor was all this confined to the so-called working class, the miners and mill-hands and weavers and day labourers.

160

An applicant for assistance undergoing a means test

Brilliant young men and women coming out of the universities found no use for their services. So few people worried about the trouble in China. It is surprising that anybody worried at all.

Let us see first what happened in America, where the depression started, and then how Britain suffered, remembering that this 'economic blizzard', as someone called it, was raging through many other countries as well.

President Coolidge had been succeeded in 1928 by his fellow Republican, the Quaker Herbert Hoover, whose American Relief Administration had done such good work in the war-wrecked countries of Europe. When disaster struck his own people, he thought that charity was the answer. There had been booms and slumps before. They were part of the natural pendulum action of a free-enterprise system. Time would put things right. Prosperity was 'just around the corner'. Meanwhile, of course, human suffering must be relieved. If private charity could not cope with so huge a need local government might help, but the central, or Federal, Government must not interfere.

It was a good example (or rather perhaps a terrible example) of what happens when kindly men try to solve problems they have not grasped. Kindness is no substitute for clear thinking.

This crisis was utterly different. Hoover had previously dealt with famine and shortages. There were no shortages in 1929. Farmers were **161**

Ploughing cotton back into the ground

producing more food than they could sell, shops were full of goods which people wanted but could not buy, factories were silent because it was useless to make more goods until some had been sold. It was poverty in the midst of plenty. The farm-hand shivered without the coat he could not afford, which the unemployed garment-worker would gladly have made, so that *he* could buy farm produce for his hungry family. In bygone centuries, when life was simpler, such men could have bartered among themselves. In the complicated modern world they were helpless.

That was the general predicament everywhere, not shortage but surplus, production beyond the point at which crops and goods could be sold at a profit. Men had worked so efficiently that they had worked themselves out of their jobs. A popular song summed it up poignantly:

'Once I built a railroad. Now it's done.
Buddy, can you spare a dime?'

Some American farmers had other problems. The land had been ploughed year after year until its fertility was exhausted by successive crops and it was reduced to a fine dust which the wind blew away, leaving the useless sub-soil exposed. Too many trees had been cut down. There was nothing to break the force of the wind or to hold the soil together on the hillsides. The rain rushed straight down, carrying away the good earth and leaving rock behind. This soil erosion had been increasing for years **162** before 1929, as in many other countries since. Now that it coincided with

Dust storm, Oklahoma 1936

the universal crisis, and there was no one to help the ruined farmers of the
'dust bowl' area, their plight became desperate. It is unforgettably pictured in John Steinbeck's novel, *The Grapes of Wrath*, about a family trek-
king from Oklahoma to California in search of a livelihood.

Such problems demanded large-scale Government action. The Republican tradition was against 'interference' as many Americans saw it. If
public money had to be spent, let it be done on a local or State basis, not
by distant officials in Washington. Then people could see that it was not
being wasted.

It was all very plausible. State boundaries meant much in terms of law,
custom and tradition. But State boundaries could not stop winds, dust
storms, or floods. Increasingly Americans began to feel that stronger overall government from Washington must be accepted.

There was no chance to change Presidents before 1932 but the Congres-
sional elections of 1930 were won by the Democrats. This produced a
situation not uncommon in America but quite different from anything
possible in Britain: a President of one party was trying to govern while the
opposition party had a majority in the body making the laws and on all
kinds of important committees.

Conditions got worse. By 1932 there were more than 12 million unemployed, 5000 banks had closed their doors, the nation's income had been
halved. Depression gripped the country. It was a time of breadlines and **163**

soup kitchens, silent factories and shuttered stores, men trying to sell surplus apples on every other street corner. Against this grim background Franklin Delano Roosevelt opened his campaign as Democratic candidate, demanding 'a new deal for the American people'.

A distant kinsman of Theodore Roosevelt, the Republican, he had married Theodore's niece, Eleanor, a woman of warm charm and indomitable character. Franklin Roosevelt became a lawyer, entered the New York Senate, and was appointed Assistant Secretary of the Navy. In 1921 he was struck down by infantile paralysis and it looked as though his career was at an end.

Both husband and wife, however, had other views. He himself had immense will-power and courage. Mrs Roosevelt helped him tirelessly to keep in touch with affairs, so that people should not forget him. The disease was little understood at that time. Roosevelt was never again able to stand or walk without support, but he made men forget his disability. It is said that he had the best radio voice in America. It heartened millions when, in later years, he broadcast his famous fireside chats. He had a flair for phrases, some of which, like 'the New Deal', 'the Four Freedoms', and 'the century of the common man', have passed into history. His faith in the common man was one of his salient characteristics. His own manner was simple and unassuming. He was described as 'a great gentleman', because, though coming (like many American statesmen) from the upper strata of society, he showed no signs of thinking himself superior. In fairness let it be added that his simple manner concealed a good deal of cunning. Some accused him of being foxy. But there is a sad truth which all of us have to learn: no democracy can be governed without first winning an election and there is no record in history of any election having been won by a saint.

Throughout the boom years, when everything favoured the 'rugged individual' philosophy of the Republicans, the crippled Roosevelt prepared for the day when the Democrats would win power again. He spent much time in writing letters and seeing people, keeping his friendships in repair and making fresh ones. He read American history and learnt to see. things in ever clearer perspective. By 1928 he was fit enough to win the governorship of New York State, often a stepping-stone to the Presidency. In 1932 the Democrats nominated him against Hoover. Hoover had won by an immense majority in 1928, but life had been turned upside down in those four years, and so now were the voting figures. Roosevelt's fighting campaign for his 'New Deal' brought him 7 million more votes than Hoover. In the electoral college, that makes the actual choice of a new President, he received 472 votes out of a possible 531.

This triumph was nearly destroyed by tragedy. During the short period **164** before his taking office, a madman tried to assassinate him in Florida. The

Depression gripped the United States. 'It was a time of breadlines and soup kitchens': queueing up receive food and assistance

LEFT: *Franklin Delano Roosevelt.* ABOVE: *Mrs Roosevelt serving soup to unemployed women*

Mayor of Chicago was killed, but Roosevelt escaped. On 4 March 1933, he was sworn in as President and moved into the White House, which he was to occupy until his death. 'We have nothing to fear but fear itself,' he said. 'I am prepared to recommend the measures that a stricken nation in the midst of a stricken world may require'. If his powers were not enough, he would ask Congress for more, power 'to wage a war against the emergency as great as the power that would be given me if we were in fact invaded by a foreign foe.'

These were not empty words. He went into action. He surrounded himself with men who believed fervently in the New Deal. Whereas a British Government is normally recruited from men in Parliament, an American President can choose his team from the ablest in the country, whether or not they have ever been in politics. Roosevelt needed intellectuals. The original 'Brains Trust' was a group of brilliant men whom he enlisted, mainly from universities, as a kind of general staff in his war on poverty.

Not all their ideas were necessarily new. Some had been under discussion for years. Action had been delayed by the war, then by the long supremacy of the Republicans with their dislike of Government interference. Now it was as though dynamite had broken up a log-jam on the river. A flood of change was released, startling new measures jostling with schemes obvious but long overdue.

Most spectacular, perhaps, was the Tennessee Valley Authority, an example of regional planning such as America, indeed the world, had **167**

Hunger marchers in the United States listening to Communist speakers

never seen before. Here was a distressed area of 45,000 square miles, spread over Alabama, Kentucky, Missouri, Virginia, Georgia and North Carolina. Early settlers had cut down the woods and overworked the soil, creating a barren land in which 3 million people lived below the poverty line, malaria was rife, and the rivers (no longer filtered and slowed by forests) rushed down and brought periodical catastrophe. To cure this meant interfering with nature and with the local affairs of the half-dozen States affected. Roosevelt did both.

Twenty-seven dams were built. They provided cheap electric power, checked the floods which used to wreak havoc along the lower Mississippi, and made the Tennessee River navigable for over 600 miles. Along with dam building went the planting of new forests, soil regeneration and malaria control. The cost was prodigious, but the idea of the New Deal was to fight poverty by spending more money, not less. By 1940 the Roosevelt administration had spent altogether 7 billion dollars on public works and more than twice that sum on direct relief. Such figures horrified many Americans. Income-tax went up and tax evasion was more strictly watched. Roosevelt offended big business by breaking up the combines and controlling the stock market. There must be no more panics. When **168** the banks began to re-open the Government guaranteed that deposits

Washington, D.C.: army veterans outside the Capitol, determined to stay until their service compensation is paid

would be repaid. This guarantee could not be given without some super-vision.

Projects of every kind sprang from the fertile brains of Roosevelt and his followers. There were loans for housing schemes, roads, bridges, and similar improvements. New National Parks were established, tourist facilities developed. Nor, in their care for the 'common man', did the New Dealers forget the uncommon man: they remembered, as governments do not always remember, that the artist, actor, writer and musician, had to eat also. Cultural enterprises were sponsored to give them employment.

America had always lagged behind Europe in compulsory schemes of social security, like old age pensions and unemployment insurance. The New Deal produced a rush of such schemes. Laws fixed a forty-hour week as the norm, banned child labour in industry, and recognized trade unions.

Roosevelt's opponents fought tooth and nail. Their last stronghold was always the Supreme Court, nine eminent judges who decided whether any Government measure broke the Constitution. Time after time these men threw out Roosevelt's novel schemes as illegal. Time after time he returned to the attack, reshaping his proposals to get them through. Finally, as some judges retired and were replaced by men of Roosevelt's choice, the Supreme Court ceased to be a barrier to progress. **169**

President Roosevelt addressing a joint session of the two houses of Congress

Except in special areas like the Tennessee Valley, America was suffering because she had produced too much, not too little. Roosevelt tried to find the farmers new markets for their produce abroad, but he was working within the profit system, so he had also to raise prices to keep the farmer in business at all. The way to raise prices was to grow less. In its first year the Agricultural Adjustment Administration contracted to pay farmers a subsidy if they would reduce their sowing of wheat, or slaughter many of their piglets before they were big enough to sell. This deliberate restriction of production was copied by other nations. A world as hungry and ragged as ours today witnessed crops being ploughed back into the ground, burnt, or dumped into the ocean with Government approval. Thus Brazil in 1936 paid her coffee growers for every bag of coffee destroyed and reduced the crop by over $6\frac{1}{2}$ million sacks, 30% of the total. In Britain the surplus was one of unsaleable manufactured goods, so an Act of Parliament provided for the destruction of 10 million Lancashire cotton spindles, about a quarter of the industry's capacity.

The New Deal was immensely expensive, widely criticized, but remarkably successful, thanks largely to the stimulus given to industry by rearmament. It did not abolish unemployment but it reduced it by many millions. America got to her feet again, ready to face the terrible challenges of the 1940s.

Construction of the Boulder Da

Britain had elected her second Labour Government just before the Wall Street crash, again a government with no clear majority and therefore unable to apply its Socialist theories.

The 1929 Election was a narrow defeat for the Conservative leader, Stanley Baldwin, who for nearly five years had held the premiership, with Churchill as Chancellor of the Exchequer and Neville Chamberlain as Minister of Health. Baldwin was an amiable, rather sluggish gentleman, with an old-fashioned taste for Latin verse and a deep love of everything traditionally English. Though in fact a wealthy manufacturer, he appeared in the public mind as a pipe-smoking squire, never so happy as when leaning over a gate and ruminating. Baldwin was not so simple as he looked, for he had a vein of the industrialist's hardness as well as country kindliness, but, as the British voter had always distrusted cleverness, it paid to encourage the legend of 'Honest Stan'. And honest he was, by the standards of the English public school system, with a sincere regard for decent behaviour and fair play. The election results showed that the Conservatives had polled slightly more votes than Labour but won twenty-seven fewer seats. The once mighty Liberal Party, though still winning 5 million votes (the other parties had about 8½ million each) would have less than sixty members of Parliament. That was the illogical consequence of a voting system designed for two parties, not three. Even so, Lloyd George's few dozen Liberals held the balance. George V urged Baldwin to stay in office and see if the Liberals would side with him against the Socialists. 'Honest Stan' felt it more gentlemanly to resign at once.

The King sent for Ramsay MacDonald, who had led the brief Labour Government in 1924, to become Prime Minister again. MacDonald was an eloquent, emotional Highlander who had been a teacher, a clerk and a journalist. One of the Labour pioneers, he had become Party leader in 1911. He had a fatal streak of vanity. This led him to despise (not without reason) the mental equipment of some of his comrades and gradually corrupted his democratic idealism when success brought him inside the charmed circle of the society he had so often denounced. MacDonald relished the summons to Buckingham Palace, and not only because it meant a victory for the working class.

His Cabinet was a mixed team. There were veterans of the Labour Party and trade union movement, included rather because they were popular than because they had talent for running a Government department. There were intellectuals like Sidney Webb, whose Fabian Society (helped by Shaw, Wells, and others) had done so much to spread Socialist ideas early in the century. There was even a young ex-Conservative, Sir Oswald Mosley, soon to become equally disenchanted with the Labour Party and to found his own Fascist movement. And there was Margaret Bondfield, **172** the first woman ever to serve in a British Cabinet just as Frances Perkins,

Ramsay MacDonald

Roosevelt's Secretary of Labor four years later, was the first in a United States administration. Miss Bondfield similarly was Minister of Labour, but as unemployment was even now (before the Wall Street crash) a very serious problem it was made the special responsibility of J. H. Thomas, a perky, rather vulgar railway union leader, who curiously enough got on better with the King than any of the others. Thomas was given one of those traditional, meaningless titles so useful in British politics because they carry no duties and leave the holder free to tackle any work assigned to him. Thomas was Lord Privy Seal, a minister so designated because, as a wit once said, he is 'neither a lord nor a privy nor a seal'. A similar, but junior, office was that of Chancellor of the Duchy of Lancaster, given to Mosley. His real task was to help Thomas deal with unemployment. MacDonald's own interest was in foreign affairs, especially Anglo-American relations, and in naval disarmament, but his achievements were soon swept away by the tide of events. They are less remembered now than the admirable if minor activities of George Lansbury, a genial bewhiskered old idealist, who made himself immensely popular as First Commissioner for Works, brightening up London with outdoor restaurants, mixed bath- **173**

ing in Hyde Park, and beach facilities ('Lansbury's Lido') on the Thames-side frontage of the Tower.

It was not by such things, though, that the Government were to be judged. What mattered was the economic position. But the world had become such a complex interlocking organization that there was a limit to what any nation could do by itself, especially one like Britain so dependent on foreign trade. The Socialist leaders were in a particularly difficult position. They did not believe in the capitalist system, which they had spent their lives denouncing, yet they had to go on working under it. Liberal support would be taken away the moment they began to introduce Socialism.

Trade had been difficult enough throughout the 1920s, what with war debts, reparations and tariff barriers put up by other countries, while Britain still clung to the Free Trade policy that had made her prosperous in Victorian times. When MacDonald took office there were well over a million unemployed. Soon came the Wall Street crash. This immediately ended the lavish American loans to Europe, Germany in particular, which had kept business moving there. Germany's unemployment was worse than Britain's. It was nearly 2 million in 1929 and in two years it shot up to more than $4\frac{1}{2}$. Britain's went up by roughly a million per year, passing 3 million in 1931. That meant more than 22 per cent of the working population. (In the 1960s it wavered between 1 and 2 per cent.) French unemployment in 1932 was thirty times what it had been in 1929. Whether a government was Conservative or Socialist, British, French, German or American, the economic blizzard was the same.

Britain's blackest year was 1931. The rising unemployment meant a steady drain of public money, since the so-called 'dole' was only partly covered by insurance contributions. As prosperity declined, less money flowed in from Income Tax and other revenue. Philip Snowden, a dour little Yorkshireman, was Chancellor of the Exchequer. He set up a committee of experts to study how the nation's finances could be balanced.

Before they could report, alarming news came from Vienna, where the principal bank closed its doors on 18 June. Knowing how the troubles of one country could affect another, the Bank of England at once went to the rescue, offering the Austrian Government an advance of £5¼ million. The Bank of England was not then publicly owned but worked closely with the Government: Socialists complained that the Bank told the Government what to do, rather than the other way about. Despite this prompt assistance, the panic spread to the main banks in Berlin. Again London went to the rescue, supplying the German State Bank with a large credit. On 20 June the American President (still Hoover, at this date) tried to stop the rot by suggesting a moratorium, or postponement, of all war debt and reparation payments. The French, who (after the Americans) held the

Drawing the dole at Shoreditch, London

world's biggest gold reserves, delayed their agreement for two weeks and the chance was lost. By then Britain herself was in difficulties. Foreign investors, afraid of losing their money, were drawing it out of London. The time-honoured phrase, 'safe as the Bank of England', became for the first time a grim joke. Millions of pounds of foreign deposits were whisked away from London during the latter half of July. The Bank of England had to ask New York for dollars and Paris for francs, £50 million in all, to save the pound sterling from collapse.

Unemployment is something anyone can understand. Inflation is harder. It sounds like another dull abstraction, a term in economics affecting only financiers. Yet inflation can make the price tags in the shop windows meaningless between one day and the next, and turn a man's life-savings into something not worth the paper and ink of his deposit book. It had happened in Germany and Austria less than ten years earlier. Was it going to happen in Britain and America now?

The value of the pound could be kept up only with credits from France and America. Bankers in those countries would not risk their money so long as the British Government was spending beyond its income. It was as simple as that.

On 31 July Snowden climbed painfully to his feet (like Roosevelt he was a cripple) and told an anxious House of Commons that his committee had reported and that their report would come as a shock. It did.

The committee forecast that the Government would face a deficit of **175**

£120 million. To balance the budget there must be slashing economies. Every public servant, from Ministers to Whitehall typists, must take a cut in salary. (Nothing was said about the King, but within a month he had himself insisted on giving up a substantial part of the Civil List, the sovereign's official income.) There were to be pay cuts for all ranks in the armed Services, 12½ per cent for policemen, 20 per cent for teachers, 20 per cent for the unemployed, who would now receive 24/- per week instead of 30/-. All this would save about £100 million. The other £20 million must be found by taxation.

The report certainly came as a shock. Another followed when Snowden found that the committee had underestimated: the deficit was going to be £170 million and they would have to save another £50 million. The Cabinet argued for days. How far could the economy proposals be accepted? Why not save money by abandoning Free Trade and clapping a 10 per cent duty on manufactured goods? Snowden and four other fanatical Free Traders threatened to resign rather than agree to a tariff. Others were equally determined that no Labour Government should take a penny from the unemployed. It was then that the afterwards notorious Means Test was first discussed. Men would draw benefit only for the first twenty-six weeks of unemployment. After that the benefit would depend on what savings or possessions they had, or what help they could reasonably get from relatives. It was the next Government that incurred all the hatred for bringing in this regulation.

Something had to be decided, and quickly. The King, with his usual conscientiousness, had hurried back from his holiday at Balmoral in case he was needed to receive resignations. Baldwin hastened home from Aix-les-Bains. Lloyd George was recovering from an operation, but the acting Liberal leader, Sir Herbert Samuel, was watching the situation. There was no time to summon Parliament. A question had been put to the American bankers, J. P. Morgan and Co.: if the Government imposed such and such economies, such and such new taxes, could they borrow £100 million? When the answering cablegram came, it put a counter-question: had the Government's proposals the full approval of the City of London? To Socialists in 1931 this was the final humiliation. It was like asking them if they had the blessing of Satan. There was a stormy discussion: it was nine o'clock on a humid Sunday night and nerves were already frayed, for they, the British Government, had been kept hanging about, strolling aimlessly round the garden of 10 Downing Street, waiting for the reply from Morgan's. They debated a little longer, could not agree, and told MacDonald that they would resign. Just after ten o'clock he rushed out of the Cabinet room, exclaiming emotionally: 'I am off to the Palace to throw in my hand.' The others went home, assuming that the

next day would see Baldwin at the head of a Conservative Government.

King George V, Princess (later Queen) Elizabeth, and Queen Mary

George V, however, had had other ideas. Though a modern sovereign often seems little more than a rubber-stamp for the decisions of his ministers, there have been a few occasions like this, when one has felt compelled to take the initiative. Earlier that day the King told his Private Secretary to summon the Conservative and Liberal leaders. By chance Baldwin could not immediately be found and Sir Herbert Samuel arrived before him. The King thus got Samuel's opinion first and was much impressed by it. Samuel thought it would be best for MacDonald to stay on as head of a National Government drawn from all parties. When Baldwin appeared, he assured the King that he would do anything to help. So, when MacDonald arrived that night, looking 'scared and unbalanced' as the King's Private Secretary noted, he was surprised and flattered to learn that in His Majesty's opinion he was 'the only man to lead the country through this crisis', and that the Conservatives and Liberals had already promised to back him. At noon the next day MacDonald was able to walk **177** jauntily into the Cabinet room, fresh from a conference with the King, Baldwin, and Samuel, and tell his old comrades that he himself was not resigning after all. He was going to form a new 'Cabinet of Individuals'. Who would support him? He put the question to them one by one around the table. Thomas volunteered, Snowden most reluctantly, and one other. The rest eyed their old leader as though he were Judas Iscariot. In a few minutes the meeting was over.

The new National Government had one urgent job, to rush through economy measures sufficient to reassure bankers abroad and save the pound. Snowden, continuing as Chancellor, proposed to do this by pay cuts of £70 million and by raising another £100 million in taxes and other ways. The announcement of pay cuts produced the first naval mutiny since 1797: at Invergordon the men refused to sail on manœuvres. There was no violence, no disrespect shown to officers, no one hanged from the yard-arm, and the authorities tried to explain away the whole incident as the work of a few Communists. But to investors abroad the mere thought of mutiny in the British Navy came as a paralysing shock. They remembered the mutinies in the Russian and German fleets which had heralded the collapse of empires. There was a renewed 'run on the pound'. Within a week the Government had to do the very thing it had been formed to prevent: it suspended the gold standard under which Britain had to pay out gold on demand in exchange for sterling. Abroad, the pound dropped to 70 per cent of its value the day before. This was hard on firms importing foreign commodities, hard too on people taking late holidays on the Continent, but helped exporters by making their prices cheaper.

The worst had happened, and it had not meant complete catastrophe. The patient was still alive, if very sick. What next? The three parties in the National Government could not agree on one clear policy, so at the General Election they simply asked the voters for 'a doctor's mandate', or a free hand to do whatever seemed best. Each candidate fought under his own label. The Conservatives were solidly 'National' and hardly needed the extra word, but MacDonald's group and Samuel's had to call themselves 'National Labour' and 'National Liberal' to avoid confusion. Just as the main body of the Labour Party was now fighting its old leader, so Lloyd George, risen from his sick bed to resume control, was rallying the remnants of the Liberal Party to denounce Samuel's entry into the new alliance.

It was a venomously-fought election, with many accusations of treachery and much play on the fears of everybody with a few savings to lose. These ensured a high poll but probably persuaded few voters to change their usual political sympathies. British elections are decided by the swing, right or left, of a mere million or two citizens in the middle.

Certain seats are always safe for one party, because the local class structure

Unemployed men from Jarrow, marching to London

and traditions give it a supremacy which would take a generation to whittle away. Everything depends on what happens in the 'marginal' constituencies where only a few thousand votes separated the candidates last time. Here, if one person in twenty can be won over, it may change the result, and it will not matter if the other nineteen remain rooted in their prejudices.

So it was in 1931. The Labour Party, bereft of its leader and jeered at from all sides, still managed to hold together its supporters to a remarkable extent, but the result looked as though they had been utterly discredited. They lost 200 seats to the Conservatives and went back with a mere 52 members. Lloyd George's anti-Government Liberals were reduced to a family group of four. The National Government had a clear majority of about 500. Whereas MacDonald, Snowden and Thomas were returned in triumph as National Labour members (helped for once in their lives by Conservative votes), all their life-long comrades in the recent Cabinet were defeated at the polls except the much-beloved Lansbury. Now, at seventy-two, he found himself leader of the Parliamentary Labour Party.

Two junior members of the late Government had scraped into Parliament and helped him rebuild the shattered organization. Both were extremely able, both destined for high office: one was the former Postmaster General, Clement Attlee; the other, an eminent barrister, Sir Stafford Cripps, had been Solicitor General. Both were of the type that was more and more to provide the leadership of British Socialism, middle class, university-educated intellectuals with a strong social conscience who had never themselves suffered poverty but fought it with no less fervour than the trade union veterans and the street-corner revolutionaries.

Some promising juniors appeared also on the more crowded Government benches. One future Prime Minister, the handsome Anthony Eden, was soon promoted Lord Privy Seal with special League of Nations responsibilities. Another, Harold Macmillan, had just won back a seat after two years. Of the seniors who did *not* figure in the National Government quite the most outstanding was Churchill. For eight years he was to remain a private member, supporting the Government but not hesitating to oppose its policies in India or to criticize its blindness to German rearmament. Many people wrote him off as a spent force, an unreliable fellow who had changed sides too often and made too many wrong decisions. It seemed unlikely that he would ever enter the Cabinet room at Downing Street again.

So the Government got down to work, first under MacDonald and after his retirement under Baldwin, who won another election in 1935, though many Labour men regained their old seats. Long before then another Conservative, Neville Chamberlain, had replaced Snowden as Chancellor. The Government's cure for the depression was very different from the

Some 2,000 'hunger marchers' have arrived in London from all parts of Britain, and more than 5,000 police are on duty in case of disturbances

New Deal a year or so later. Roosevelt spent lavishly, creating work and causing money to circulate, which in turn created more work. In Britain the idea was to cut expenditure, so that people had even less wages to spend, thus reducing the demand for goods and causing more unemployment. It remained very high until 1934. When the position improved it was due not so much to the economic wisdom of the Government as to the fear of Germany, which stimulated the iron and steel industry and others affected by rearmament. Money could always be found for war. But in the early 1930s there seemed precious little money for peace.

In the South Welsh valleys there were sometimes nine pits idle for one producing coal. The railway sidings lay silent, the shops were shuttered. Grass grew in the shipyards of the Tyne, the Clyde and the Mersey. Many ships were laid up, rusting and derelict, in estuaries that looked like an elephants' graveyard. All over industrial Britain the smokeless factory chimneys stood up like warning fingers against the sky. Parts of the countryside began to look equally desolate, as weeds sprang up, land went **181** sour and boggy, and fences and buildings fell into disrepair. Again, it was to take a war and the fear of starvation to make the British farm prosperous and the landworker a hero.

It was a dark time. In the first dramatic days there were angry demonstrations in Parliament Square and other places, stone-throwing, police charges, arrests and imprisonments. Later came a mood of dogged resistance or sullen despair. Hunger Marches brought men from the depressed areas of Scotland, Wales and the North to show their grim faces to the still comfortable-looking crowds of the London West End. The sight of these Hunger Marchers, tramping through cities like Oxford and Cambridge with their home-made banners, their pathetic kettle-drums and penny whistles, roused the sympathy of many students and drew them into active political agitation against the economic system which seemed to blame. Some intellectuals joined the Communist Party, but usually left it after a short time. Many more were in vague sympathy. Most of the younger poets, novelists, and other writers ranged themselves on the Left wing at this time. The news from Europe pushed them even more definitely towards the Left as Hitler began to figure in the headlines.

11 Hitler's Rise to Power

By 1932 German unemployment had risen to 5,703,088. This was one factor, but only one, that helped to sweep Hitler into power and began an age of terror in which Europe was to tremble for the next twelve years. The ever-mounting fear of what this man would do next made the late 1930s a period of constant anxiety and tension. The 1940s, for all their horrors, brought a kind of relief, because at last the dreaded worst had happened and there was something for ordinary men to do.

Adolf Hitler was an Austrian, born in 1889, of peasant stock, his mother a maid, his father a Customs officer, who died when the boy was fourteen. Mother and son moved to Vienna. There was an optimistic idea of making Adolf an architect.

It was optimistic because he had neither money nor influence and his education was sketchy. He was a morose boy (*mondsüchtig,* his mother called him, 'moon-struck') and he would study only what interested him. He did well at geography and world history. Many years later one of his old schoolfellows recalled how they had teased him for poring so long over his atlas and how he had come out of his dreams to answer them, with a glassy stare, 'I am wiping out Germany's boundaries and making them larger—larger!' This habit of romantic day dreams characterized his whole life. Unfortunately they became nightmares for everybody else.

Unable to become an architect, he tried to sell sketches, but he had no real artistic talent, only a certain skill, and he had to turn to house-painting. That poverty-stricken period in Vienna developed several traits in his character. He came to hate both the working class and the Jews, then so numerous and influential in Austria and Germany. Though he never seems to have suffered any particular injustice, he believed that he deserved a better place in the world and that others were to blame for denying it to him. Long afterwards, when the whole German nation was in the same resentful mood, he was their natural leader.

Hitler was a tangle of psychological kinks which became worse under **183**

Hitler at school, aged 14. He is on the extreme right

the strains and stimuli of his last years, when he wielded so much power that nobody dared to cross his will. But they were there, increasingly evident, from the start. He was incapable of a normal love-affair and so of all the satisfactions, in marriage and family life, that may follow. He felt romantic attractions and sometimes made himself ridiculous, but was unable to develop a real relationship. In a sense he could not achieve a real relationship with anyone, man or woman, for there was no give and take in his attitude. He was not interested in them, their interests, or what *they* had to tell *him*, unless it directly tied up with his own obsessive schemes. Talk, yes, and the company of those who agreed with him, but a genuine exchange of ideas, no. He had no desire to see foreign countries, only to drive into their capitals as conqueror. He was terrified of meeting people who were his intellectual superiors and might question his dogmatic assertions. Early in the 1930s his future antagonist Churchill visited Munich and was anxious to meet this man who by then had emerged as a leader of an unusually powerful movement. Hitler was invited to dinner. He shilly-shallied like a coy girl, but his press adviser begged him at least to drop in for coffee. In the end he never plucked up courage to meet Churchill, though he was seen hanging about in the hotel in the green hat and dirty white macintosh he used to wear.

Hitler's substitute for a natural relationship with another human individual was his relationship with a mass audience. He was a superb orator, especially before the use of microphones took the special magic out of his voice. For him a public meeting was a love-affair. He charmed, then mastered, his listeners in an extraordinary fashion. Speaker and crowd merged as one. The very rhythms were those of a physical experience, the hammer-blow phrases alternating with the concerted yells of '*Sieg Heil! Sieg Heil!*' Violence and cruelty gave him another substitute for the satisfactions of love.

All this lay in the future as the disgruntled youth worked with paint-brush and ladder in Vienna. In the same city at the same time, by coincidence, Freud was patiently uncovering just such shadowy corners of the human mind. And thirty years later, because he was a Jew, the old scientist would have to flee from home when the house-painter returned in triumph.

In 1912 Hitler crossed into Germany. Munich, the third largest city in the Kaiser's empire, became his adopted home, the base of his political career. It was an easy change. The language, history and culture were much the same. He felt no pride in being an Austrian. He considered himself one of the German 'folk', whose blood made them all one family wherever they lived.

Probably he had by this time met the writings of Houston Stewart Chamberlain, a learned English crank not connected with the Chamberlains in Parliament. This man, a lecturer at Vienna University, had evolved a theory of a German master-race destined to save the world by putting the Jews in their proper place. He was a neurotic who wrote in a feverish trance-like state, believing himself to be spurred on by demons. But he was widely read and could marshal facts to support the most preposterous theories (one being that Christ had not been a Jew), and he impressed many Germans, including the Kaiser. In 1909 he settled in Bayreuth, the Bavarian town especially associated with Wagner, to whose music he was devoted and whose daughter he had married. Hitler too was immoderately moved by Wagner's music and cared little for any other. Its stormy barbaric splendour and the old Teutonic myths it glorified ideally matched Chamberlain's racial theories. During the 1914 War Chamberlain became virulently anti-British, took German citizenship, and was awarded the Iron Cross for his propaganda. He met Hitler in 1923 at Bayreuth and was much struck by him. 'You have great things to do,' he wrote. 'It proves Germany's vitality that, in her hour of deepest need, she produces a Hitler.'

What had happened to the young painter during the preceding years? He had fought as a lance-corporal, won medals, been wounded in the Battle of the Somme, and gassed a month before the Armistice. In hospital he heard of the mutinies and revolution, the Kaiser's flight, Germany's humiliating surrender. 'It was on 9 November 1918,' he used to recall, 'that I decided to become a politician.'

There were plenty of openings. The new Republic soon had over thirty parties, many quite obscure. He joined a small Munich group, the German Workers' Party. His burning eloquence soon won him the leadership. He changed the name to the National Socialist German Workers' Party. Gradually the idea of 'Workers' and 'Socialists' was dropped in favour of the 'Nationalism'. It is as the 'Nazis' that his followers will be remembered.

Those were already violent days in German politics. Street fights were common, murder not unknown. It was an atmosphere in which Hitler enjoyed himself. The figure which history has made familiar begins to emerge from the shadows into the lamplight: staring hypnotic eyes under a slanting quiff of hair, comic little Charlie Chaplin moustache above a mouth opened wide to roar and howl, arm stiffly upflung in the Nazi **185**

G

salute. Hitler, who could not ride and disliked horses, carried a whip for self-defence as well as a revolver. His followers formed a private army, the S.A. (*Sturmabteilung*, or 'Storm Troops'), not to be confused with the S.S. *(Schutzstaffel)*, the more select 'Black Guards' who originated as his personal protectors. The S.A. men wore brown shirts, breeches and jack-boots. Their badge was the ancient swastika, already used by other anti-Jewish movements. Added to the old red, white and black imperial flag (disused since the Republic) it made a distinctive Party banner.

In November 1923 Hitler supported an armed rising or *putsch* in Munich, designed to set up a dictatorship under the popular wartime general, Ludendorff. With the general himself, the famous aviator Her-mann Göring and others, he led a march of 3,000 armed Brownshirts through the streets. They were stopped by a detachment of 100 policemen, carrying carbines. There was brisk shooting for about a minute. Three policemen were killed and sixteen Nazis. The rest of the rebels fled. Only Ludendorff stalked on, a grim figure whom no policeman wished to harm. Hitler picked himself up from the roadway, shaken but untouched by the bullets, and ran after the others. Two days later he was arrested, given five years for treason, and put in the Landsberg fortress. There he was kindly treated and allowed visitors, one being his faithful disciple and fellow-prisoner, Rudolf Hess. Hess took down at his dictation the first half of *Mein Kampf* ('My Struggle'), destined to become the Nazi equiva-lent of the Communists' *Capital*, though the works of Hitler and Marx could hardly have been more dissimilar.

Mein Kampf, completed three years later, was a turgid hotchpotch of ideas imbibed from Houston Chamberlain and other sources. Even his ally Mussolini was to grumble in 1934 that 'instead of talking about con-crete problems, Hitler only recited *Mein Kampf* from memory—that dreary book which I have never been able to read'. Yet buried in its 782 verbose pages was the implied death warrant of millions. The book called upon Germans to acquire a new *Weltanschauung* or 'vision of the world', multiply their numbers, keep their blood pure from mixture with other races, and seek *Lebensraum* ('living space') by conquest. Such a policy could mean only World War II.

At first *Mein Kampf* sold only a few thousand copies annually. After Hitler came to power sales rose to millions. It became common to give the book as a wedding present and to children leaving school. It was left lying about conspicuously, rather as families used to place a Bible where it could not be missed by visitors. Hitler became the most prosperous author in Germany. By then, however, he had other means of support.

He spent only a year in prison but came out with the martyr's halo so valuable in building up a subversive movement. His Party attracted more and more recruits. It had something for everyone, or nearly everyone.

Hitler and his henchmen: first left, front row is Himmler and next but one to him Hitler. Göring is at the extreme right and behind Hitler's shoulder is Dr Goebbels

When Hitler denounced the Jews the small trader thought of some big Jewish firm that was driving him out of business. The workman thought of the cunning Jewish capitalist who was exploiting his labour, forgetting that the Christian employer might be doing precisely the same. The disappointed professional man blamed his failure on the stranglehold the Jews were supposed to possess over newspaper ownership, the law, medicine, the theatre, the film studios, and the universities: it is quite true that the Jews had, by sheer ability and a natural tendency to hang together, won a remarkable predominance in Germany, but to blame them for everything was like attributing the Russian Revolution entirely to Jewish Marxists. Hitler did not hesitate to say any of these things. He knew that hatred was a powerful unifying force. He knew the advantage of telling people what they wanted to hear. By coupling 'Marxist' with 'Jew' he roused the enthusiasm of wealthy industrialists like the steel king, Thyssen, who began to contribute lavishly to Party funds: to such men Hitler offered an insurance against Communism and the hope that Jewish rivals would be driven out of business. By condemning the Versailles Treaty and suggesting that the splendid German Army had never really been defeated, **187**

Headquarters of the 'Storm Troops' in Nuremberg. The placard reads 'In standing out against the Jew, I am fighting for the work of the Lord'

only stabbed in the back by Jews and traitorous democrats, he won over the old officer class who a few years earlier would have looked down their noses at him.

No one recalled now that the Nazis had started as the 'German Workers' Party'. Though never fully at ease with the upper classes, Hitler had picked up some at least of the social graces, helped by his press adviser, Ernst Hanfstaengl, a sophisticated German-American from Harvard who was at home in those circles, German or foreign, with which Hitler was utterly unfamiliar. Until he saw the danger signals and slipped over the frontier, Hanfstaengl thought he could groom Hitler into a reasonable European statesman. He introduced him into the drawing-rooms of the influential and curbed his wilder statements. It was Hanfstaengl, remembering the American college cheer-leaders, who introduced those thunderous howls of *'Sieg Heil! Sieg Heil!'* An accomplished amateur pianist, who had to soothe Hitler with hours of Wagner, he also saw the value of a good marching song and knocked off a dozen for Party demonstrations.

Nazi strength was growing, and with it the exceptional position of the leader. To his followers he was no longer 'Herr Hitler', but *'Der Führer'*, just as Mussolini was *'Il Duce'*. Nazis ceased to say 'good morning', and **188** began to stamp and salute and bark *'Heil Hitler!'* By 1931 the Party was

Hitler's mountain retreat near Berchtesgaden in the Bavarian Alps

able to open new headquarters in Munich, an imposing mansion renamed the Brown House. This became a beehive of departmental organization, packed with those elaborate filing systems which delight the bureaucratic German mind, and multiplying 'jobs for the boys'. Even after the Nazis took over the government in Berlin, the Munich Brown House kept a lot of its importance. It was the capital of a state within a state, the vast Nazi movement, and handy for Berchtesgaden, where Hitler was to establish his mountain chalet, guarded by 20,000 troops.

It is time now to look at some of his principal lieutenants, that bizarre gang over which he had cast his spell and which was preparing to lift him to supreme power.

Chief of staff and commander of all the S.A. was Ernst Röhm, a stocky thick-necked ex-regular officer, his looks not improved by a bullet which had taken away part of his nose in 1914. Röhm's private morals were peculiar even by the slack Nazi standards but Hitler could not afford to dispense with his services until he had served his turn. Then on the notorious 'Night of the Long Knives' (30 June 1934) he drove in person to Röhm's hotel, roused him from sleep, and had him shot. Several hundred S.A. leaders and others were executed that night, or committed suicide, or were 'shot while resisting arrest'.

Of the original inner circle the two most famous later were Göring and Goebbels. Göring, a popular war hero, handsome and dashing when young, was undeniably brave and remained so till his death. He had a swaggering good-humour that, however crude, brought him closer to normal humanity than most of his comrades. He loved showing off, whether by keeping lion cubs as household pets or by devising even more resplendent uniforms for himself. When he became grossly fat such vanity was somewhat ill-advised; but at least, unlike the other Nazis, he occasionally contributed to the world's gaiety, as when he strung rows of clinking medals across his tight-stretched tunic, or levered himself into splendid white breeches and (as once happened) was incautious enough to nurse a lion cub on his lap too long.

Goebbels, his rival, was a complete contrast. Swarthy, undersized, limping from a childhood illness, he was the brain of the Party. Where Göring was jovial, Goebbels was waspish. In many ways he was a frustrated man. His limp had debarred him from military service and the memory rankled: he sometimes let people believe that it was due to a war wound. He was often unlucky in his numerous love-affairs, though he ended as a family man with six children. After a long university career, which had brought a doctorate of philosophy, he had tried vainly to win fame as a novelist and playwright. He had great skill with words, none the less. He was an orator second only to Hitler; indeed, if more reason and less rant were required, Hitler's superior. His writing found an outlet in

*Caricature of HermannGör-
ing by Kukriniksy (a team
of three Soviet artists)*

political journalism. Eventually, as Minister of Propaganda, he had the task of moulding the minds of all Germany to one pattern and of trying (less successfully) to impose the Nazi version of the truth upon the world.

Among the lesser personalities were three who (if they did not all achieve equal importance) became household names outside Germany for one reason or another.

Rudolf Hess, another ex-airman, swarthy, with black curly hair and bushy eyebrows, was fervently loyal, unambitious, and limited in intelligence. He served as Hitler's private secretary and eventually his deputy, though few expected him ever to inherit the leadership.

Far more formidable, though deceptively inoffensive in appearance with his scholarly pince-nez and good manners, was Heinrich Himmler, commander of the S.S., and in those days playing second fiddle to Röhm. Himmler excelled in patient and efficient organization. He built up files on everything and everybody, collecting the most embarrassing and long-buried secrets of friends as well as foes. These came in useful when he was made chief of the Gestapo, or Secret Police.

Lastly, by common consent the most odious, there was Julius Streicher, a former school-teacher with a perverted delight in cruelty and filth. The paper he ran, *Der Stürmer*, would have been notorious for its coarseness **191**

if not for its unceasing attacks upon the Jews. Streicher had been an early rival of Hitler, running his own anti-Semitic movement in Nuremburg, but he had soon jumped on the Nazi band-waggon and been rewarded with the post of *Gauleiter,* or regional leader, in that city.

In the democratic Germany set up with such high hopes after the Kaiser's fall, no single party equalled the Nazis in unity and will-power. The various factions wrangled on, even the Socialists fighting the Communists, blind to the growing shadow which was to plunge them all into darkness. In 1928 the Nazis won a mere dozen seats in the Reichstag, or Parliament. Two years later they won 107. Their support mounted with the unemployment figures: the Wall Street crash came between the two elections. In 1932 Hitler challenged Hindenburg, who had been President since 1925 and was now at eighty-three an almost legendary national figure. Hindenburg won, but over 13 million votes were cast for Hitler. As in Britain, a crisis-shaken people was looking for leadership.

Hindenburg was now senile. He scarcely understood what was going on, but with the obstinate prejudices of the Prussian *junker* or aristocratic caste he resisted the suggestion that this Austrian lance-corporal should become his Chancellor. But Hitler led the biggest party in the Reichstag. On 30 January 1933 the stiff-necked old marshal gave way. Hitler became Chancellor, leader of a 'National Government', German-style.

What would happen when he tried to govern? Would the other parties combine at this eleventh hour to defeat him? The matter was never fairly tested. The Nazis set to work at once to destroy their opponents, section by section. Communist meetings were banned, Communist newspapers closed down. Other parties had individual meetings forbidden or broken up by Brownshirts and their papers suspended without warning. All this was done with a show of legality, for Göring, now Minister of the Interior for Prussia, controlled the police throughout two-thirds of Germany. He used his powers to replace hundreds of officials with men from the S.A. and S.S., to enrol 40,000 Nazis as auxiliary police, and to threaten punishment against any reluctant to use their pistols against the 'enemies of the State'. An election was due on 5 March. There must be no doubt about the result.

The evening of 27 February brought a dramatic development: the Berlin sky glowed suddenly as the Reichstag building burst into flames. Hitler was dining with Goebbels. They got the news by telephone and drove through the city at sixty miles an hour. Göring, whose official residence adjoined the building, was in a state of furious excitement. 'This is the start of the Communist revolution!' he was shouting. 'We mustn't wait a minute. We must show no mercy. Every Communist official must be shot! Every Communist deputy must be strung up this very night!' There was in fact no sign of a Communist revolution or even a Communist, for those experienced politicians had been prudently going underground during the past week.

Even today some mystery still shrouds the Reichstag fire. At Hitler's birthday party in 1942 Göring boasted that he was responsible. Very possibly Goebbels first thought of it as a splendid way of discrediting the Communists. Two fires seem to have been lit almost simultaneously, one by a mentally subnormal Dutchman, Van der Lubbe, who held a Communist membership card but only the most inadequate equipment for burning down a Parliament House, and one by a detachment of Storm Troopers, entering by an underground passage which carried the central heating through to Göring's ministerial palace near by. It is supposed that the Nazis knew of Van der Lubbe's amateurish scheme and gave it every assistance, including (unknown to him) the S.A. squad with petrol cans and inflammable chemicals. Certain it seems that without such assistance the Dutchman would have burnt little more than his own fingers.

As for the four other Communists put in the dock with him at the famous 'Reichstag Trial', there was no evidence on which the judges could possibly convict them, though Göring (who conducted the prosecution in person) nearly died of apoplexy when he heard them acquitted. One, Ernst Torgler, leader of the Communists in the Reichstag, was kept in 'protective custody' until his death. The other three were Bulgarians. Disowned by their own country (then anti-Communist) they were granted Soviet citizenship by an unusually imaginative decision of Stalin's, and to **193**

'I am a Jew but I will not complain about the Nazis'

Göring's renewed chagrin whisked away to Moscow. One of them, Georgi Dimitroff, had conducted his own defence with a wit and courage that won him, Communist though he was, the admiration of newspaper readers throughout the world. Day after day he made rings round his duller adversary. It seemed impossible that he would be allowed to leave Germany alive, but the impossible happened. Years later, when Bulgaria went Communist, Dimitroff reappeared as her Prime Minister. Of the men who stood in the dock with him only the poor Dutch half-wit was found guilty and executed.

Months before this, the vital election had been held, almost before the ashes were cold. The Nazis had made good use of the affair. Their newspapers had screamed 'Communist Plot' and they had made wholesale searches and arrests, doing their utmost to terrorise all opposition.

In spite of this the German voters stood remarkably firm. The Nazis polled only 44 per cent of the votes. The Socialists, Communists and Catholics all crowded into the booths to support their parties. Hitler's sole hope of a clear majority lay with the Nationalists, a Right-wing party which had won just enough seats to tip the balance. He wanted, however, much more than the narrow majority of sixteen which their votes would give him. The Reichstag had been destroyed as a building: now it must be destroyed as a democratic institution. It must be persuaded to commit suicide. It must vote for a special Enabling Bill, surrendering its powers for four years to Hitler's Government. The snag was that such an exceptional measure needed a two-thirds majority, unobtainable if there was a genuinely free vote.

Hitler got his majority. When the Reichstag assembled on 23 March in its temporary meeting-place, the Kroll Opera House, the 81 Communist deputies were missing: either they were under arrest, like Torgler, **195**

The Reichstag burning

or they had been driven underground and were not such fools as to come out. About a dozen Socialists had been locked up by the police: the remaining 84 courageously 'stood up to be counted' in their opposition to the Bill. The Catholic Centre Party had trustfully accepted a Nazi assurance that whatever the new Government did would be subject to Hindenburg's approval. They were promised this in writing, but did not receive it. None the less, they voted with the Nazis and the National-ists. By 441 to 84 the Reichstag destroyed itself. Democratic republican Germany followed the Kaiser's empire into the dustbin. The Nazi dicta-torship of the 'Third Reich' had begun.

Hindenburg doddered on for another year, lost in muddled memories of old campaigns, unaware of what was happening to the nation that had trusted him: the boycott of all Jewish shops proclaimed on 1 April; the suppression of trade unions on 2 May; the week by week mounting terror of beatings and murders, the opening of Buchenwald and other concen-tration camps. Once, watching the endless marching of exultant Storm Troopers beneath his window, he is said to have mumbled: 'I did not know we had taken so many Russian prisoners.' On 2 August 1934 he died and no new President was elected. Hitler was now all-powerful.

Hitler addressing the Reichsta,

12 Dictators on the March

'We are entering a corridor of deepening and darkening danger,' Churchill warned the House of Commons in 1935, but even after two years of Nazi rule in Germany many in the West preferred to remain blind to what was happening.

People were bitterly divided on the issue of Nazism. Socialists and Communists, trade unionists and intellectuals, Liberals, Jews, Quakers and similar humanitarians naturally condemned Hitler's suppression of freedom. Others, whose political views were to the Right (like the British Conservatives) or who had no views at all, dismissed their protests as propaganda. Germany had been in a mess, they argued, and had needed a strong man to put things straight. Trade unions were a nuisance anyhow, so good luck to any one who could put them in their place. Many said much the same about the Jews, but under their breath: it did not do to sound anti-Semitic, of course, but wherever there were Jews there were Gentiles to be jealous of them. Again, they pointed out, Hitler was a barrier against Bolshevism. Finally, they declared with a great show of broadmindedness, what the Germans did in their own country was surely their own business.

But the concentration camps? The refugees who streamed out of Germany, their businesses confiscated, their careers ended, their worldly goods reduced to a suitcase, thankful if they could escape as a complete family? Were our own grandparents blind to all this, a later generation may ask, or too unfeeling to care?

As to what was happening in Germany no one then could know a tenth of what we have learnt since. Many Germans themselves have declared (some truthfully) that they had no inkling of what went on in the concentration camps or even that they existed. Foreign tourists came back with tales of unforgettable sports rallies and torchlight parades. Hitler had 'cleaned up Germany'. He was building superb *autobahnen* for the motorist. He was curing unemployment. These rosy holiday memories out-

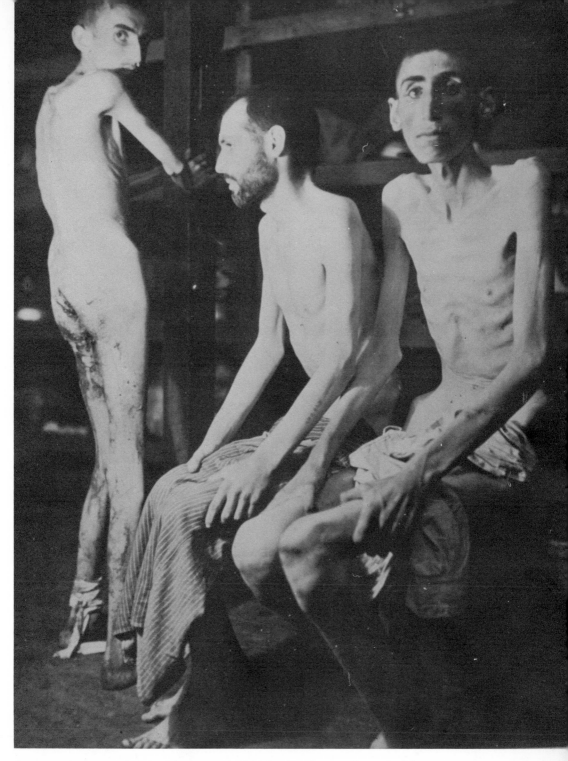

Concentration camp victims. Tattoo marks for identification can be seen on the arm of the man in the centre

199

balanced the refugee stories. Many people never met a refugee and would not have liked him if they had: if not a Jew, he would probably be a Red (perhaps both), and 'not our sort'. Anyhow, they concluded comfortably, there was 'so much propaganda', wasn't there? It was ironical that the Nazis, who more than anyone else had developed the art of unscrupulous lying, were protected by this widespread impression that 'propaganda' was really the weapon used by their victims.

True, Hitler had largely cured unemployment. What his foreign admirers were slow to realize was the price paid. How many vacancies had been created by the dismissal, flight, death or imprisonment of Jewish workers and other 'undesirables'? No Jew could be a teacher, public official, doctor, lawyer, journalist or farmer. He could not work in films, the theatre or radio. He was barred from the Stock Exchange. Soon he was barred from business in general. All this was legal. So were the notices, 'Jews Not Admitted', which often excluded him from shops and hotels, making existence difficult even if he had savings to live on. Less legal, but unchecked by the police, were the insults and physical assaults to which he was always liable. Small wonder that he fled the country if he could, but for many Jews it was impossible. The slightest taint of Jewish blood cost a man his job. Millions of Germans were feverishly hunting for old birth certificates and trying to discover their great-grandmothers' names before marriage. Many suffered merely for having taken Jewish wives.

A second crop of vacancies was created by banning women from industry. Women, according to the Nazi slogan, should devote themselves to 'Kinder, Kirche, Küche' ('Children, Church, Kitchen') with the emphasis on the first. Woman's primary duty was to bear future soldiers. 'Church' was added with the tongue in the cheek. Though the Nazis did not want to offend the Church unnecessarily, they were fundamentally pagan in outlook. They cared little whether the children were born of Christian marriages. They wanted the maximum number of pure-blooded 'Aryan' boys bred from the mating of healthy youths and girls. Just as the atmosphere of the slaughter-house developed in the extermination camps used for their enemies, so sometimes the morality of the stud-farm was encouraged in the holiday camps run for their young supporters.

Hitler also reduced the unemployment figures by expanding the armed services and the manufacture of munitions, uniforms, ships, vehicles, and other warlike equipment; by public works, like the motorways, often involving forced labour; and by rigid State control of finance and trade.

The Nazi attack on the freedom of the press, the arts and sciences, did not greatly worry the indifferent majority abroad. Let the Germans make fools of themselves if they liked, heaping thousands of books on public bonfires, books of such varied authors as Einstein and Freud, Jack London

Hitler Maidens

and H. G. Wells. Let them empty their picture galleries of 'decadent' canvases by Cézanne and Gauguin, Van Gogh and Matisse, which offended Hitler's taste; ban the music of the long-dead Mendelssohn as Jewish and that of their most original living composer, Hindemith, as decadent; distort scientific teaching to match their half-baked racial theories; close their eyes and ears to half the truth and beauty in the world. That was their look-out. Only a minority of people anywhere cared deeply for such things and pleaded that the whole of civilization was diminished by this relapse into barbarism.

It was the rearmament which began to disturb the British. As early as April 1934 George V, with clearer foresight than most of the governing class, talked to the German Ambassador with the 'no-nonsense' bluntness he retained from his naval days and which, as a monarch, he could afford to use. Germany, he said, was a danger to the world. If she went on like this there was bound to be a war within ten years. Why was she arming? Nobody wished to attack her, but she was forcing other countries to arm in self-defence. The Ambassador explained that Germany needed a bigger army to protect her frontier. The French had their impregnable Maginot Line, but Germany had nothing comparable. The King dismissed this argument as rubbish. Forts had been useless in the last war and would be even more useless in the future. Here the King was merely echoing a British expert in mechanized warfare, General Fuller, who seven years previously had prophesied that this Maginot Line would be 'the tombstone of France'.

In January 1935 the British Ambassador in Berlin was warned that 'the King feels that we must not be blinded by the apparent sweet reasonableness of the Germans, but must be wary and not be taken unawares'. Two months later Hitler reintroduced conscription, forbidden at Versailles. The victorious nations who had imposed that treaty did nothing. They were indeed entering the 'corridor of deepening and darkening danger'. In March 1936 Hitler marched his troops into the Rhineland, that strip of German territory which, as a precaution, the Versailles Treaty had demilitarized. No ammunition was issued to the troops, for Hitler calculated that neither France nor Britain would use force to turn them out; if they did, the Germans would stand no chance and would have to withdraw, so again there was no point in carrying ammunition. He had guessed right, however. France and Britain protested but did not move a soldier.

Hitler had found the right technique. If he tried for everything with a single grab even these Western democrats would be goaded to fight. If he nibbled slowly, no single act of aggression would seem to them worth a war. It was as easy as eating a German sausage. He merely had to cut the slices thin enough.

German sentries stand guard on a Rhine fortress, March 1936

In 1935 it was Mussolini's turn to provoke the crisis headlines with the Abyssinian War.

Ever since the late nineteenth century, when Italy looked round without much success for African colonies to match the French and British, she had gazed hungrily at Abyssinia, or Ethiopia as the inhabitants prefer the country to be called. An Italian expedition had been routed at Adowa in 1896. Ethiopia had remained one of the few independent African states, remote and backward, but in due course a recognized member of the League of Nations. The country is wild and mountainous. In 1935 it had no coastline, being separated from the Red Sea and the Indian Ocean by Eritrea (belonging to Italy) and the three Somalilands, French, British and Italian. The sole modern link with the outside world was a French-built railway, winding up from Jibuti to the Ethiopian capital, Addis Ababa.

There, five years before, in the presence of the Duke of Gloucester and representatives from many other nations, a sallow, silky-bearded prince, small in stature but of great personal dignity, had been crowned amid **203**

Italian troops on their way to embark for East Africa

scenes of exotic splendour Hailie Selassie I, 'King of Kings, Conquering Lion of Judah, Elect of God, Emperor of Ethiopia'. These magniloquent titles emphasize how remote his country was, mentally as well as in miles, from the twentieth century world. Household slavery still existed. The population was mixed in race, religion and level of culture. Some, like the Emperor, were Christian, others Moslem, others pagan. Great regions were semi-independent, ruled by princes rather like medieval barons. Haile Selassie was keen to start schools, hospitals and printing-presses, but he could not change a feudal country in five minutes.

An incident on the Eritrean frontier enabled Mussolini to pick a quarrel with him. The Emperor suggested arbitration: Mussolini refused. The Emperor then turned to the League of Nations: Mussolini argued that Ethiopia had lost her right to membership, since she had not yet abolished slavery. All through 1935 Britain and France tried desperately to patch up the quarrel so that they would not be forced to take sides against Italy. They might need Mussolini's friendship if it came to trouble with Hitler. So far the two dictators had not made the alliance which came to be known as the Rome-Berlin Axis. Though Hitler had imitated **204** Italian Fascism, Mussolini disliked him and considered that Nazism was

Haile Selassie, Emperor of Ethiopia, addressing the League of Nations

a debased version, 'the revolt of the old German forest tribes against the civilization of Rome'. Hitler was a 'horrible degenerate creature', a 'dangerous madman', and his movement was 'capable only of murder, slaughter, looting and blackmail'.

These words came somewhat oddly from the Duce, who on 2 October launched his long-planned invasion of Ethiopia. It was a two-pronged affair, with columns entering from Eritrea and Somaliland. The League at once proclaimed Italy the aggressor and imposed 'sanctions', in this case a half-hearted economic blockade which angered Mussolini without stopping him. Italian troopships could still sail freely through the Suez Canal. France, on the other hand, held up arms intended for Ethiopia, lest the Italians should bomb the French-owned railway by which they must be delivered. British and French foreign ministers, Sir Samuel Hoare and Pierre Laval, strove feverishly to strike a bargain that would give Mussolini some of his demands but not all. This Hoare-Laval Pact caused an outcry when its shameful terms became known. Hoare had to resign.

For eight months the Ethiopians resisted with savage courage, the little Emperor showing personal heroism at the head of the Imperial Guard. Mussolini also tried to direct his armies in person, but by remote **205** control, telegraphing detailed instructions from Rome, which did not help the commander on the spot. The invaders had the advantage in numbers and equipment, but had to contend with a most difficult country of desert, mountain and jungle, almost roadless and for one period lashed with tropical rain. If any Italians came out of the war with credit it was the engineers who drove a way for the armies. Otherwise it was a contemptible conquest, in which the Italian Air Force was used to spray mustard gas on their half-naked and helpless opponents. So Mussolini's armies blasted their triumphant way to Addis Ababa and the Emperor escaped to the French port of Jibuti with his family and close supporters, where they embarked in a British warship and eventually made their way to England. The King of Italy assumed the extra title of 'Emperor of Abyssinia'. Italy began her so-called 'civilizing mission', improving communications, exploiting the country's raw materials, and bringing out shiploads of somewhat scared and reluctant colonists. Mussolini had fulfilled his dream of winning an empire, but he was never able to do much with it.

Meanwhile a greater empire lost its ruler: George V died in January 1936, just after celebrating the twenty-fifth year of his reign. Those Silver Jubilee celebrations had surprised and moved the gruff old sailor—for that was what he remained, in spirit and manner, all his life. He had always concentrated on doing the right thing, never the popular thing. Yet in that final summer there rose a tremendous wave of affection for him, shown not only by the cheering crowds through which he drove, with the always stately yet also kindly Queen Mary at his side, but also in greetings, both official and private, from every part of the globe. It was some consolation amid the worries clouding the last year of his life.

Apart from general problems like Hitler, unemployment, and Gandhi's independence movement in India (treated in a later chapter), the King was specially troubled about his successor. David was forty-one, the only one of his children still unmarried. Officially he was not 'David' but 'Edward, Prince of Wales'; one day he would be King Edward VIII, for the British Crown is fettered by tradition and a sovereign is often known by a name different from the one used by his family.

The two had never got on particularly well. The Prince was less docile than his younger brothers. He resented his father's continual correction, 'nagging' as it seemed to him. Similarly as a young officer on the Western Front he was impatient with the generals who would not let him risk his life in the trenches. His father, he pointed out angrily, had other sons. One, the future George VI, did in fact take part in the naval battle at Jutland. But the Prince was sternly reminded that his own life was too precious for him to do as he liked.

206 Nor could he when peace came. Throughout the 1920s he was con-

tinually touring the world on good-will missions, keeping the Empire together and making Britain popular in areas like South America where British firms were anxious to sell more goods. These chores he did with a smiling cheerfulness which charmed everybody. He enjoyed his popularity, but he had to relax sometimes and even his modes of relaxation were criticized. He was a keen horseman but an unlucky one: after various falls he was told that the heir to the throne ought not to risk his neck in the hunting-field. Nor, it was murmured, his reputation by too great a fondness for night clubs and the company of the smart set. King George's relaxations were stamp-collecting and shooting pheasants in the muddy Norfolk woods, Queen Mary's were antiques and needlework. Their son preferred something livelier. They wished he would settle down, marry suitably and start a family, like the Duke of York, already the father of two princesses, Elizabeth and Margaret.

The King was even more disturbed when he learnt that the Prince had formed a close friendship with a married woman from America, Wallis Simpson. Mrs Simpson had divorced one husband there and had married an Englishman. Like many of his subjects, the King disapproved strongly of divorce. A divorced person who married again was not in his view properly married at all, if the previous spouse was still alive. True, Henry VIII had married Anne Boleyn, though his first wife was still **207** living, and otherwise there could have been no Queen Elizabeth, but that was all a long time ago. There was one crumb of comfort: legally, Mrs Simpson *had* married again, so at least there could be no risk of the Prince's wanting to make her his wife. No member of the Royal Family could marry without the sovereign's approval. No one, however, had power to forbid a sovereign's own marriage, so if the Prince came to the throne still a bachelor, it would be as well if his American friend were not available.

What the old King went to his grave without knowing was the real depth of affection between the two and the fact that Mrs Simpson's second marriage was virtually at an end, needing only the procedures of the divorce court to dissolve it officially.

When, to the usual fanfare of trumpets, the heralds proclaimed Edward VIII, Mrs Simpson was one of a select little group of his guests watching from the windows of St James's Palace. At the last moment the new King joined them. Always unconventional, he had decided to witness his own proclamation.

'Always unconventional. . . .' That is a key phrase to be remembered. Edward was impatient of red tape and pointless ceremonial. He disliked Buckingham Palace and all it stood for. At Windsor, even now he was King, he still preferred to slip away from the magnificence of the Castle to the quiet of Fort Belvedere, a sham fortress in the Park near by, which in recent years he had turned into his home, enthusiastically tackling its overgrown garden with his own hands. At Sandringham, his first order was to have all the clocks put right: since Edward VII's reign they had all been kept fast and this seemed to him absurd. He would use an aeroplane to save time (he was the first sovereign to fly) but if not in a hurry he would walk through London with a bowler hat and tightly-rolled umbrella like any other man. On free evenings he would drop in to see Mrs Simpson. In her company alone he found the sympathy he craved in the loneliness of kingship.

Throughout most of that year scarcely one person in a hundred thousand even knew of Mrs Simpson's existence much less of her destined role in history. People began to look forward to the coronation, fixed for May 1937. To them Edward was still the charming, popular figure he had been as Prince of Wales. Only in the inner circles were there subdued rumblings of criticism. Courtiers and officials disliked his changes. The new King thought too little of his dignity, they complained. He was inclined to meddle.

Meddling with Sandringham clocks and shortening tedious ceremonials was one thing. It was more serious when, as some politicians began to whisper, the King showed a tendency to meddle in more serious affairs. **208** One tiny incident was blown up out of all proportion as evidence of this.

King Edward VIII at a training centre for unemployed miners in South Wales

He made a tour of the South Welsh mining valleys and was sincerely moved by the sufferings of the unemployed. 'Something must be done!' he exclaimed. On the King's lips such words took on a new significance. They could be taken to imply that the Government was not doing enough (offensive to the Conservatives and their allies) and that somehow the King could influence the situation himself (offensive to any M.P. because it seemed like a threat to the authority of Parliament); in Left-wing circles spread a new kind of gossip, that the King was favourably disposed to the Fascist dicators and their drastic remedies for economic problems. So for various reasons, enthusiasm cooled and doubts sprang up, not in the country at large but in what we now call 'the establishment', the influential groups at Whitehall and in the Palace, in Fleet Street, the West End clubs and similar clearing-houses for inside information. Even the bishops lamented Edward's bad example of not going to church as regularly as his father.

It crossed nobody's mind that the King could be got rid of. They must make the best of him. But he would need watching. By tactful hints and obstinate obstruction his notions could be rendered harmless. **209**

Later the story was to be spread around (possibly to soothe certain consciences?) that he had never wanted to be King. This, though true enough of George VI, was not true of Edward VIII. He might not like the tedious reading and signing of the innumerable papers that arrived daily in the dispatch-boxes, but other aspects of kingship he enjoyed, particularly the chance to deal with people and stimulate changes. Whether or not he would have been a good king, he would certainly have been an interesting one; in his own view, a 'modern' one.

His friendship with Mrs Simpson continued. Her marriage was coming to an end. Mr Simpson had provided her with grounds for divorce. The case would be heard discreetly in a small country town. In six months she would be free to re-marry. Free, that is, in the eyes of the law, but not in the eyes of most religious people, for she would have two previous husbands still living.

King Edward, however, was planning to marry her. He could not see why he should not have the same freedom as any other Englishman, who could marry a divorced woman if he wished, though in a register office instead of a church. Why not the King? Edward failed to remember the basic difference between a sovereign and his subjects. As King, for example, he was officially head of the established Church of England. Again, any wife he chose would automatically become Queen of England and his consort throughout the Empire. She must be acceptable to all, universally respected. The fatal objection to Mrs Simpson was not that she was an American, nor that she was a 'commoner' without royal blood. It was that she had dissolved two earlier marriages. If she married the King, millions of his subjects would be unable to regard her as his real wife and their lawful Queen. Edward hopelessly miscalculated the feelings of ordinary people. He believed that his lifelong popularity would carry him through: that he would be fighting only his family and the leaders of Church and State, not the easy-going masses who had so often cheered from the pavement.

Those masses continued through the summer blissfully ignorant of Mrs Simpson's existence and of the King's intentions. The royal friendship was headlined, with all kinds of gossipy titbits and speculations, in the American and other foreign papers. 'Palace Car at Wally's Disposal', 'King Chooses Clothes to Match with Wallis' . . . so it went on, week after week, until the granting of the divorce in October was reported under the confident large-type prophecy, 'EDWARD WILL WED WALLY'. Not a whisper appeared in the British Press. Fleet Street knew. For that matter, so did thousands of people who had recently been abroad or received newspaper clippings from friends overseas. But if thousands knew something, millions knew nothing. The newspaper proprietors and editors
210 had made a bargain among themselves: no one would print a word.

Wholesale newsagents co-operated by censoring foreign magazines imported into the United Kingdom, and many a customer was perplexed to find paragraphs cut out. So, when the cat suddenly burst out of the bag, it was as great a shock as if it had been a lion.

The story broke with a sermon preached by a Yorkshire bishop who knew nothing of Mrs Simpson but was concerned by the King's apparent lack of religious feeling. The King, he said, needed 'God's grace . . . as we all need it. We hope that he is aware of his need. Some of us wish that he gave more positive signs of his awareness.' People who knew the inner story took these general remarks to refer to the King's association with Mrs Simpson. The *Yorkshire Post* and several other provincial newspapers were no longer willing to wear the gag agreed upon by Fleet Street. They commented on the bishop's rebuke and linked it with the gossip overseas. After that, the London papers could keep silent no longer. The astounded public found itself in the midst of a national crisis.

The next week was one of frantic comings and goings, Cabinet meetings and telegrams to the Prime Ministers of the various Dominions, urgent colloquies between the King and Baldwin, Baldwin and the editor of *The Times*, the King and Churchill, who supported him, the King and Mrs Simpson, until she fled to France. Edward was determined to marry the woman he loved. When Baldwin assured him that the Empire would never accept her as Queen, he suggested a 'morganatic' marriage, by which a woman may marry a royal personage without sharing his rank and titles. Impossible, said Baldwin, morganatic marriages were unknown in England. It must be one thing or the other.

Edward still believed that he would get his way. In 1929 Bernard Shaw had written a much-discussed play, *The Apple Cart*, in which a popular monarch had outwitted his ministers by threatening to abdicate. Edward declared that if he could not, as King, marry Mrs Simpson, then he could not carry on as King. He probably imagined that this challenge would do the trick. The nation would never let him go, he was too popular. But soon it was clear that, however sadly and reluctantly, the nation *would* let him go, rather than accept the marriage. A few leading politicians and newspaper owners, like Churchill and Lord Beaverbrook of the *Daily Express*, tried to form a King's party in his support, but they were outnumbered and outgeneralled by the massed support behind the Prime Minister. They, like the King himself, had for once miscalculated the public mood.

Once the anguish of uncertainty was over the necessary legal steps were taken with the smooth urgency of a surgical operation. In one bewildering week the ordinary citizen had to digest the first revelation of the King's private life and hear his broadcast farewell. Then he was gone, borne across the Channel in a destroyer through the December night, no longer **211**

Edward VIII but His Royal Highness the Duke of Windsor. The conferring of that new title had been the first act of the brother who now succeeded him as George VI. But when, after the due lapse of months, Mrs Simpson became the Duchess of Windsor, she was specifically denied the prefix 'H.R.H.' which would have put her on an equal footing with her new sisters-in-law. Resenting this, the couple made their home permanently abroad.

The drama was over. Sober folk shook their heads and sighed that the monarchy would never recover from this blow to its prestige. Nothing would ever be the same. There was much bitterness, some declaring that the ex-King had been the victim of a diabolical plot hatched by Baldwin, the Archbishop of Canterbury, and the editor of *The Times*, others that Edward was weak and unworthy, unable to put the sacred duties of kingship before his personal desires. Even thirty years later a woman could write to a Sunday newspaper, 'I think the day that King Edward VIII abdicated was the saddest in my life', while another still felt 'outrage and personal insult'. Most people soon recovered their balance. By Christmas irreverent children were singing new words to an old carol:

'Hark, the herald angels sing!
Mrs Simpson's pinched our King!'

212   The New Year brought thoughts of the coronation. The date could

Mrs Roosevelt, King George VI, Roosevelt's mother, Queen Elizabeth and President Roosevelt: a group taken in America in 1939

stand, little more was needed than a second throne in the Abbey for the Queen and different portraits on the souvenir mugs. George VI was a splendid man if painfully shy, and just like his conscientious father. Queen Elizabeth was gracious and charming, British and of noble blood. They brought with them a ready-made Royal Family in their two delightful daughters. Everything was going to be for the best. The nightmare was over.

Unfortunately, another kind of nightmare was about to begin. The onward march of the dictators had not slackened because of these domestic troubles in Britain.

The Spanish king had lost his crown, very differently, a few years earlier. Alfonso XIII had been driven in 1931 from a throne inherited at his birth in 1886. An election had swept the Republican parties to power and he had retired abroad to save his people from civil war. This came, none the less, five years later.

Young people today, hearing their elders refer to the Spanish Civil War, may well be puzzled by the intensity of the memories it still arouses. Since then there have been wars, civil wars, revolutions everywhere. Television newsreels have brought the stutter of machine-guns into every home. We have grown inured to the sight of tanks rumbling down the boulevards, men yelling, waving banners, running for shelter, drifts of **213** dark smoke from ruined buildings, lines of trudging refugees. What was so special, we may ask, about the Spanish Civil War?

The answer is that it was never 'just another civil war', the private affair of Spaniards. Men from all over the world went to fight and die in the sierras and at the barricades. Nine hundred Americans and 500 British left their bones in Spain. Why did they go, we ask again? Because it seemed to them a kind of crusade. They saw that the world-wide struggle between democracy and Fascism was coming. They had watched with helpless horror the Nazi triumph in Germany, the Italian invasion of Ethiopia. They had been disgusted by the timidity of their own democratic governments, the ineffectiveness of the League. When Fascism spread to Spain they thought they saw a chance, at last, for an individual to do something.

The 1936 elections for the Cortes, or Parliament, brought into power an alliance of democratic parties known as the Popular Front. This idea of a Popular (i.e. People's) Front had been adopted also in France, as the policy with which to combat Fascism, and it was warmly pressed in Britain where the official Labour Party, however, refused to co-operate with the Liberals and Communists. In Spain the Popular Front meant Liberals, Socialists, Communists, and Anarchists, those last an idealistic but violent group still numerous in Spain although almost unknown elsewhere. Against the Popular Front stood an assortment of Right-wing parties including the Fascist Falange, or 'Phalanx', and the Monarchists. There was an important religious factor too. Spain was a land of extremes. On the one hand was the immensely powerful Roman Catholic Church, on the other a mass of free-thinkers and atheists. Between these two sworn enemies lay scarcely any middle ground, only a few thousand Protestants and others. Since 1931 many churches and convents had been burnt by anti-clerical mobs and the Government seemed unable to prevent such outrages. Not unnaturally, therefore, most devout Catholics favoured the Right wing, though millions of others supported the Left. These wanted so much to tackle the backwardness of their country that they were ready, if need be, to work with the godless Communists. This religious factor in Spanish politics helps to explain the fanatical ferocity of the struggle when it came.

It came in July 1936. A revolt was planned by the Army, also mainly Right-wing in its views. The moving spirit was General Francisco Franco, Governor of the Canary Islands. Franco flew to Spanish Morocco, where many of the troops were serving, and the Nationalist rising began. Simultaneously the garrisons in Madrid and Malaga, Seville, Saragossa and other key cities, threw off their allegiance to the Government.

That day saw confusion everywhere. Socialists and Communists filled the streets, demanding arms to defend the Republic. Local officials often

General Franco in the midst of an admiring crowd

hesitated, afraid for their necks if they did the wrong thing. The workers took things into their own hands, seized what weapons they could, and hurled themselves at rebel-held barracks and police stations with a wild disregard for their own lives. With all its faults, the young Republic symbolized the hopes and ideals of the masses. Though the Nationalist generals had the advantage of surprise and most of the armed forces on their side, they did not win the swift victory expected. In Madrid and many other towns the rebels were overwhelmed. Their forces elsewhere in Spain would soon have been crushed as the Government rallied its supporters. But in Morocco Franco had complete control, with not only plenty of Spanish soldiers at his disposal but a Foreign Legion and the Moorish levies. His problem was how, without ships or aeroplanes, to get them across the Straits of Gibraltar.

Urgently he appealed to Hitler and Mussolini. Neither wanted a democratic Spain. Both weighed in with prompt assistance, troop-carrying planes for his immediate need, and then an increasing flow of arms and men when even his army from Morocco proved insufficient to win the day.

The Government in Madrid tried to buy arms from Britain, France and elsewhere. By normal international practice a government may buy arms from any other country with which it has friendly relations, whereas rebels cannot be legally supplied. Britain and France did not observe this rule. So nervous were they of getting involved in a sort of indirect **215**

Homeless refugees in Malaga, Spain

conflict with Germany and Italy that they proposed a Non-Intervention Pact. No one should help either side in Spain. It might seem unfair to the Republican Government, properly elected a few months earlier, but surely anything was better than turning the peninsula into a general battleground? Hitler, Mussolini and Stalin accepted the Pact, with no doubt many a quiet smile at the innocence of the British and French. None of them kept it.

For nearly three years the war waged. The Government held Madrid, though under constant rebel bombardment, Barcelona, most of eastern Spain running down to the Mediterranean, and a separate region of Basque territory on the Biscay coast. Franco held the rest. There is no point now in describing the different offensives and sieges, though at the time our newspapers, taking sides almost as keenly as the Spaniards, gave frequent maps of the ebb and flow. Franco's biggest effort was against Madrid. Four Nationalist columns advanced upon the city, but it would be taken, boasted one of his generals, by the 'Fifth Column' comprising thousands of secret sympathizers inside its defences. Thus was born a now-famous phrase. In fact, the 'Fifth Column' did not emerge into the streets until the war ended in the spring of 1939.

216

A Spanish soldier photographed at the moment of death. H
killed by a machine gun

It has been said that a million people perished. More sober estimates now suggest about 600,000, two-thirds violently in battle, air-raid or massacre, one-third by hunger, exposure and disease. Even allowing for unscrupulous propaganda on both sides, one can only be sickened by the appalling total of executions, lynchings, torturings and unmentionable atrocities that were undoubtedly committed. Civil war is usually crueller than other wars and the Spanish character has, along with its virtues, a streak of savagery. But the so-called 'non-intervening' nations have no reason to boast of the part they played.

Mussolini gave Franco the most help. At one time there were 50,000 Italian troops serving on the Nationalist side. From Italy too came 763 aeroplanes with their crews, vast numbers of guns, vehicles and other items. Ninety-one Italian warships and submarines helped to blockade the ports still held by the Government and cut it off from any foreign aid it could obtain.

Hitler sent fewer men but of better fighting quality. The German Condor Legion was always about 6,000 strong, plus thirty anti-tank companies. As no less than 14,000 Condor veterans attended a victory parade in Berlin, it is clear that its members were frequently changed. Germany used Spain as a training ground for the bigger war to come. Guernica was raided by Heinkels and Junkers during its crowded Monday afternoon market. For three hours successive waves came over at twenty-minute intervals, drenching the little town with machine-gun bullets, high explosives and incendiary bombs. They left it a smouldering shambles, with 1,654 townsfolk and peasants dead, 889 wounded. Göring admitted in 1946 that his Air Force had treated Guernica as a testing ground. Picasso, on the other hand, found there the inspiration for that terrifying mural which many regard as his masterpiece.

Stalin was equally cynical about Non-Intervention, but Russian aid to the Republicans was much smaller. Sheer distance made it harder to get through the blockade. Anyhow Stalin (as in China) put Russian interests before those of any foreign comrades. He wanted an alliance with Britain and France against Germany and he was not going to frighten them by seeming to bolster up Communism in Spain. He allowed a mere dribble of aid. Every tank and plane had to be paid for in gold. He sent few men, and those more for the experience than for any help they gave the Spaniards. Some were high-ranking officers under false names. A few years later they blossomed forth as Marshals of the Soviet Union.

Britain and France knew that no one else was observing the Pact, but they kept it faithfully, if that is the word. Neither side was given any help. In an extreme anxiety to avoid offending Hitler and Mussolini, every effort was made to stop private volunteers from going to Spain. Hundreds went none the less, making their way to Paris where the future Yugoslav

Part of the fortifications of Madrid, photographed after the war was over   **219**

Members of the XVth International Brigade

leader, Tito, had organized an illegal 'underground railway', whereby, issued with false papers and helped by relays of guides, they were passed across France and the Pyrenees frontier, like escaping prisoners of war a few years later. Most of these men came from the working class, most were Communist Party members if only for that short period of their lives, but there was a sprinkling of idealistic intellectuals. As well as the writers who went through the war with the Republican forces, like George Orwell and Ernest Hemingway, an overwhelming majority shared their sympathies. The poet W. H. Auden spoke for these when he said: 'The struggle in Spain has X-rayed the lies upon which our civilization is built'. A very few, like Evelyn Waugh, proclaimed their support for Franco. A few more, like T. S. Eliot and (surprisingly) H. G. Wells, tried to be neutral, but among the younger writers especially there was intense involvement on the Republican side. This may help to explain why the Spanish Civil War has left such a powerful lingering influence in the memory of a whole generation.

Thus, though the Republicans received no military units from abroad to match the Italian and German legions helping their enemies, they were able to organize their famous International Brigades, totalling about 40,000 men over the entire period. Nearly 3,000 Americans came and 1,000 Canadians. There were 2,000 British, 10,000 French, volunteers from about fifty countries in all. Many were exiles, eager to strike a blow **220** at Hitler and Mussolini. There were 5,000 Germans and Austrians, 3,350

Italians. Some 3,000 were of Jewish origin. The battalions were formed on a national basis and named after appropriate heroes, Garibaldi, Lincoln, Washington, and so on. The British seemed unable to select one, but after being visited at the front by the Labour Party leader, Attlee, they bestowed his name on No. 1 Company.

Idealism proved no substitute for the discipline and equipment of the regulars, Spanish and Moorish, Italian and German, on the other side. The Government too was disunited, with different factions striving against each other. The Communists especially maintained a private vendetta against all who challenged their attempts to take control. Many of the volunteers left Spain disillusioned. Early in 1939 the long agony ended in the collapse of the Republican cause. Franco's troops occupied Madrid, rivetting a dictatorship upon the country which was to remain immovable for a generation. Columns of Republican soldiers and refugees wound their way sadly across the French frontier, without much prospect (as it turned out) of ever seeing their native land again. The Civil War was over. The Second World War was now near at hand.

13 To Munich and Beyond

The dictators had not been idle elsewhere during the Spanish Civil War. Hitler was moving, as though on a line of well-spaced stepping-stones, towards his ultimate objective of world mastery. Mussolini, now more and more the junior partner, moved more hesitantly for all his brag. Small wars were all right, against weak enemies like Ethiopian tribesmen, but a major war was another matter. Psychologists tell us that strictly no one is 'normal'; but by the rough and ready standards of everyday life the difference between Mussolini and Hitler was that between a comparatively rational man and an unstable neurotic driven relentlessly forward by his delusions.

Germany was now arming at a hectic tempo. Churchill, though not in office, had exceptional facilities for collecting secret information about what was being done. He tried desperately to get the British Government to face the ugly facts. But Baldwin, always sluggish (except at rare moments like the Abdication) was now old and tired as well. Neville Chamberlain, who succeeded him as Prime Minister in 1937, was little younger and much less inspiring: his experience was in finance and home affairs, and he knew nothing of foreign policy.

Both leaders could excuse their slackness by pointing out that the voters wanted only peace and would not back a government that started to rearm. The Opposition, while it shouted loudest for a stand against Fascism, criticized any proposal to build up Britain's forces. This was not perhaps quite as illogical as the Conservative leaders made out: Socialists, Communists and others wanted first to be sure against whom these forces would be used. Suppose they were turned against Russia, as well they might be? Many people in high places felt closer in sympathy to the Germans than the Russians. Even those who did not wish Britain herself to fight Russia would be delighted to see Germany turn eastwards and do the job. This uncertainty as to how the National Government would use its arms put the Left in a dilemma. Mixed up as it was with pacifism and

Winston Churchill in the late 1930s

a distrust of Churchill as a life-long anti-Socialist and anti-Communist, it deterred them from supporting his appeals.

Hitler's next objective was the *Anschluss*, the union (expressly forbidden by the Versailles Treaty) of Germany and the small Austrian Republic. Austria had a Nazi Party which took orders from Munich but had no prospect of gaining power unaided. In 1934 these Austrian Nazis murdered their strongest opponent, the Christian Socialist Chancellor, Dollfuss. By 1938 Hitler felt strong enough to wind up the matter. Kurt von Schuschnigg, who had succeeded Dollfuss, was summoned to Berchtesgaden. In Hitler's study upstairs, the picture windows framing panoramas of the Alps, the Austrian Chancellor was browbeaten with one of the Führer's typical tirades.

'I need only to give an order,' he ranted, 'and all the ridiculous scarecrows on the frontier will vanish. Do you really believe that you could hold me up for half an hour? Who knows—perhaps I shall suddenly appear in Vienna overnight, like a spring storm. Then you will really experience something!'

When Schuschnigg could get a word in, he said: 'Of course, I realize that you can march into Austria, but we are not alone in the world, Chancellor. That probably means war.'

That was very easy to say, Hitler retorted, as they sat there in their armchairs. 'But don't think for a moment that anyone in the world is going to thwart my decisions! Italy? I have a perfect understanding with **223**

At a military parade in Berlin, Hitler declares Germany's right to re-arm

Mussolini. England? England will not lift a finger for Austria. And France? Well, two years ago I risked a good deal, marching into the Rhineland with a few battalions. If France had moved then, we should have had to withdraw. It's too late now for France. Think it over, Herr Schuschnigg, think it over well. I can only wait until this afternoon.'

With deliberate rudeness Hitler addressed the Austrian Chancellor by his name throughout, instead of his official title. The whole course of the dialogue (or more often monologue) was typical of countless other interviews with people he felt able to bully. Poor Schuschnigg, normally a chain smoker, was not even allowed to soothe his nerves with a cigarette while his host was in the room.

He had to agree to Hitler's demands, which still left his country nominally independent. But within a month the demands increased. Finally Göring telephoned: Schuschnigg must resign within two hours and the leader of the Austrian Nazis must be appointed Chancellor in his place, or the German Army would invade. Schuschnigg knew he was helpless.

224 He went to the President and resigned, but the President refused to play

Hitler in Vienna

the Nazi game by appointing their nominee. Let the world see that Hitler
was using naked force.

So the invasion began, but it was not the triumphant sweep into Vienna
which had been planned. On this first occasion (soon to be so tragically
repeated in other capitals) the much-vaunted new war machine rather
ridiculously broke down. Tanks and motorized artillery developed engine
troubles wholesale and the terrifying flood of steel froze into an undignified traffic jam. Many vehicles were loaded on to railway trucks so that
enough could reach Vienna in time for the scheduled victory parades. It
mattered little, for Austria could attempt no armed resistance and the
fiasco was quickly glossed over by propaganda. Hitler had gained his
objective, and added a useful 7 million people of Germanic stock to his
domain.

Schuschnigg was arrested and subjected to appalling humiliations and
ill-treatment, losing fifty-eight pounds in the first year of his imprisonment. He and his wife spent the war in concentration camps. Their names
were on Himmler's special list to be murdered at the last moment if they **225**

seemed about to be rescued by the victorious Allies, but this order was never carried out, and on 4 May 1945 the ex-Chancellor was able to write in his diary: 'At two o'clock this afternoon, alarm! The Americans! We are free!'

Czechoslovakia was next on the shopping list.

Her case was very different from Austria's. She was not a Germanic country. The Czechs and Slovaks formed a proud, independent Slav people. They had a highly-trained army of $1\frac{1}{2}$ million, a defensible frontier of mountains and forests, and a modern arms industry the envy of Europe. They had the courage to resist and the means to do so, until help came. France was their traditional ally and they looked eastwards also to their brother Slavs in Russia.

Churchill was now pressing Neville Chamberlain to make a 'Grand Alliance' with France and Russia, so that if Hitler committed another aggression they would fall upon him from both sides. Though still opposed to Communism, Churchill saw the world situation with a broader vision than the Prime Minister. Chamberlain thought the alliance 'a very attractive idea' but a look at the map persuaded him that it was impossible. He gave France no encouragement. He was chilly to the Soviet Union, where some very curious things had been happening.

These were the notorious 'purges' and treason trials begun by Stalin in 1936. Having outmanœuvred his rivals and become virtually a dictator, he was now strong enough to settle old scores. Marshal Tukhachevsky, long ago one of Trotsky's commanders but still apparently in high favour (he had just represented the Soviet Union at George VI's coronation), was suddenly arrested, tried with six other leading generals, and shot. The famous Old Bolsheviks went the same way, Kamenev, Zinoviev, Bukharin, Rykov. In successive waves about 5,000 Red Army officers and officials were put to death for activities against the Soviet State and treasonable contacts with the Nazis. In some cases there was real evidence against them, in others none. Innocent or guilty, it did not matter: they were men Stalin wanted out of the way. In the West the whole business was clouded over with mystery and horror. It did not encourage people to make friends with Russia. How much use was the Red Army, they asked, if it was as rotten with treachery as its Government declared? Churchill, though as disturbed as anyone, believed that Stalin had foiled a genuine plot to overthrow him and set up a pro-German government. Churchill still favoured an alliance with Russia. He was never afraid to 'sup with the devil' if necessary; he could always take a 'long spoon'.

It was unfortunate that Czechoslovakia's frontier with Germany, rugged by nature and strengthened with forts, proved a fatal weakness in another way. When the boundaries of the new state had been drawn in

Steps in Hitler's aggression

1919 they had been stretched to take in this mountainous western area although it had meant including 4 million German-speaking inhabitants, the descendants of colonists who had entered Bohemia centuries earlier. Neither they nor the region they inhabited, the Sudetenland, had ever belonged to Germany, but their language and racial origin were enough to make Hitler claim them as his own. The Sudeten Germans were encouraged to form their own Nazi movement, to complain more and more that they were oppressed by the Czechs, and to turn to the Führer as their natural protector. The Czechs, democrats under a humane and enlightened President, Benes, were ready to deal with reasonable complaints but stood up to Hitler's threats with courage.

This was the time when people began to speak of 'a war of nerves'. It was a technique based on psychology and now applied to political strategy by the Nazis. It consisted of alternately raising the tension by threatening speeches or ominous actions, like troop movements and mobilizations, and lowering it again by cancelled orders or reassuring statements. The technique could be elaborated by the deliberate 'leaking' of supposedly secret information which might be true or false. In time the victim became so nervously exhausted by the pendulum swing from fear to hope and back to fear again that he was thankful to settle for part of what his tormentor demanded. Half a loaf, says the proverb, is better than no bread. A dictator could usually get at least half a loaf if he spent a few weeks alternately screaming that there would be war if he did not **227**

Dictators 'side by side'

get the whole and protesting that he was not really hungry at all.

By early September 1938 the war of nerves over Czechoslovakia was well under way. At a typically hysterical Nuremberg Rally Göring roused the Nazi audience with his denunciation of the Czechs. 'This miserable pygmy race is oppressing a cultured people, and behind it is Moscow and the eternal mask of the Jew devil.' That same day the French Foreign Minister asked the British Ambassador in Paris a plain question. 'Tomorrow Hitler may attack Czechoslovakia,' he said. 'If he does France will mobilize at once. She will turn to you, saying, "We march: do you march with us?" What will Britain's answer be?' It took two days to get that answer from Chamberlain and his Cabinet. When it came it was vague and wordy. Britain would think about it when the time came. Hitler meanwhile was at Nuremberg himself, capping Göring's speech with threats and insults of his own.

We know now that some of the most frightened men in Europe were the German generals. If Britain was unprepared for war, so (despite all her hurried rearmament) was Germany. Her professional soldiers needed

Precautions against war: digging trenches in Hyde Park, September 1938

more time. If ordered to march against Czechoslovakia they had not enough divisions to hold the frontier against France. And there was Russia, whose determination was not in doubt. Her Foreign Minister, Litvinov, gave the League of Nations at Geneva a clear public statement that together with France she would go to Czechoslovakia's aid.

Chamberlain ignored this statement as if it had never been made. He would risk nothing for what he called, in a broadcast to the nation, 'a quarrel in a far-away country between people of whom we know nothing'. In his sincere quest for peace he offered to visit Hitler and discuss the problem. He had taken over complete, one-man control of British foreign policy, to the despair of his more experienced advisers. Three times in two weeks he flew to Germany, though he had never before set foot in an aeroplane and was in his seventieth year. He sat in that same study at Berchtesgaden where Schuschnigg had heard his doom pronounced, and there were occasions when he had almost the same difficulty in making his own voice heard.

Hitler, however, could change his manner at need. If the Sudetenland **229** were handed over to Germany, he said, 'This is the last territorial claim I have to make in Europe.' Chamberlain believed him.

Back in Britain many, including members of the Cabinet, did not. To hand over the mountainous borderland would be like tearing down one wall of a house. The rest of Czechoslovakia would be wide open. This was the moment to make a stand against Hitler. By 28 September it looked as though there would be war. Shelter trenches were dug in the city parks, and schools began evacuation to the country. Orders went out to mobilize the Fleet.

For the third time Chamberlain flew to Germany. A four-power conference was to settle the dispute. Mussolini and the French Prime Minister made up the quartet, but whereas the two Fascist dictators had met beforehand and agreed on their line, Chamberlain seemed almost to be avoiding the French. Russia was not invited. Nor was Czechoslovakia, though she was allowed, as a concession, to have two representatives waiting in another room, to be told their country's fate when it was decided.

Such was the famous Munich Agreement, signed at 1 a.m. on 30 September 1938, providing for the German Army to enter the Sudetenland on 1 October. An eyewitness described Daladier, the French Prime Minister, as 'a completely beaten and broken man'. Chamberlain was exhausted and yawning continuously. Hitler and Mussolini could not hide their glee. The unfortunate Czechs were simply handed a map of the land they had to give up and told by one of Chamberlain's staff that it was useless to argue. If they did, they would be on their own.

After a few hours' sleep Chamberlain went round to Hitler's private apartment for a personal talk. He produced a brief statement which he suggested they should both sign, three sentences expressing in general terms 'the desire of our two peoples never to go to war with one another again'. Hitler glanced at it. It tied him to nothing. He signed. As the secret records have since revealed, he had agreed with Mussolini only the previous day that sooner or later they would have to fight Britain 'side by side'.

Knowing all we know now, we may find it hard to realize that Chamberlain returned to London as a national hero. Relief was hysterical. A majority of the public, the newspapers, and the M.P.s welcomed the Munich Agreement.

When Chamberlain stepped from his plane he waved the statement Hitler had signed and read its harmless phrases to the crowd. He gave another recital from his window at 10 Downing Street.

'This is the second time in our history,' he declared, 'that there has come back from Germany to Downing Street peace with honour. I believe it is peace for our time.'

230

Chamberlain on his return from Muni

In fact, it was peace for eleven months.

Long before that period was up, even Chamberlain saw that he had been tricked. Dangerously late, the Government brought in conscription and a rearmament programme.

Czechoslovakia's doom was quickly accomplished. Within a week, under German pressure and threats against his life, Benes resigned the Presidency and fled to England. He went on to a university lectureship at Chicago, until events brought him back to London to lead his exiled countrymen in their struggle. On 15 March 1939 Hitler tore up the Munich Agreement by sending his troops into Czechoslovakia. There was no resistance: the Czechs had already lost their fortified frontier. Though Britain and France had guaranteed their new boundaries, not a finger was lifted to save them. Behind the German armoured columns came the Gestapo, the S.S. men, the Jew-baiters. As those columns clanked down the streets of Prague there were hopeless men who jumped from top-floor windows rather than suffer what was in store for them. Numbers escaped abroad and lived to fight another day, some as pilots from British airfields. Germany did not take over the easterly half of the country: she allowed her neighbour Hungary to occupy a long strip and Poland to take one small area, while the Slovak region became a separate puppet state. But all were equally at Hitler's mercy.

Meanwhile the Duce, jealous of Hitler's triumphs and anxious lest Nazi influence should creep too far down into Eastern Europe, seized the mountainous kingdom of Albania, no great prize in itself, but a possible spring-board for pouncing on Greece or Yugoslavia. He launched a surprise attack on Easter Sunday. The Albanians numbered little more than a million and were ill-equipped for modern war. It was all over in three days.

Italy herself was ill-equipped for any big European conflict. Mussolini was anxious to postpone one for at least three years. But Hitler was already making dangerous moves again. He was looking further east to that *Lebensraum*, or 'living space', of which he had written in *Mein Kampf*. He hoped to find it in the fertile cornlands of the Ukraine and southern Russia. It was not his plan to attack Poland, a country run by a Right-wing clique of Army officers, as anti-Russian (and some as anti-Jewish) as he could wish. Their Foreign Minister, Colonel Beck, was also anti-French, which was much less usual for a Pole. Hitler at first expected no trouble from this quarter.

There were, however, some details to be tidied up. The Versailles Treaty had given the new Polish Republic an outlet to the Baltic, a strip of land called 'the Polish Corridor' which had the effect of dividing East Prussia from the rest of Germany. To visit East Prussia without crossing

this foreign territory Hitler was compelled to go by ship, an unaccustomed experience which made him seasick and strengthened his determination that this state of affairs must be ended. He wanted to run a railway and motorway across the Corridor with extraterritorial rights, in effect a German Corridor bisecting the Polish. Secondly, there was Danzig (now Gdansk), the seaport at the end of the Corridor, which had been alternately Polish and Prussian throughout its history. Since 1919 it had been neither, a free city run by the League, with special trading facilities for the Poles. Its citizens however were mostly German. Hitler wanted Danzig. He was surprised to find the Polish Government unsympathetic, indeed positively stubborn.

His surprise was understandable. How could these Poles afford to quarrel with him? Their air force was out of date, their army brave but still in the horse-drawn stage. Their flat country could be quickly overrun. They faced Germans on three frontiers. To the east were the Russians, their ancient enemies, with whom they had made no effort to be friends. After defeating the Red Army in 1921 they had unwisely carved themselves a great slice of territory to which they had no genuine claim, so that eastern Poland was inhabited by 6 million Ukrainians and Russians, unlikely to be loyal if their Warsaw rulers got into difficulties. What did the Poles think they were doing?

Equally surprising was Chamberlain's sudden announcement on 31 March that Britain would help Poland if attacked. Six months earlier he had argued that it was impossible to help a 'far-away country' like Czechoslovakia. His change of front seemed almost impulsive. He was shaken by the angry realization that he had been tricked at Munich. It was only two weeks since the overwhelming of the Czechs.

Now it was Hitler's turn to be angry. When the news of the British declaration reached him, he raged round the room, his features distorted, his clenched fists banging the marble-topped table. He would deal with these Englishmen. 'I'll cook them a stew that'll choke them!' he howled. On 3 April he issued a top-secret directive to his Service chiefs, a plan 'to destroy the Polish armed forces' in 'a surprise attack'. He added: 'Preparations must be made so that the operation can be carried out at any time from 1 September 1939 onwards.' That was the exact date, five months later, on which World War II began.

What, it may be asked, was America doing all this time? Following their traditions and instincts her people were as reluctant as ever to be drawn into the quarrels of Europe. Roosevelt could never move more than a step ahead of his fellow-countrymen. And, great and wise though he was, and skilful in personal relationships, he was at his weakest when dealing with foreign dictators. He could not understand the breed. Between the White House at Washington and the Brown House at Munich there was a moral gulf his imagination could not leap.

Trying out gas masks in Britain

On 15 April he telegraphed to both Hitler and Mussolini a simple question. Would they promise not to attack the following countries? He listed Poland, Russia, Britain, France, and all the twenty-seven other countries which could conceivably be in danger. The telegrams were received with ribald sneers. Mussolini suggested that they were the result of Roosevelt's infantile paralysis, Göring that they were symptoms of mental disease. Hitler kept his laughter for a mass audience. He answered the American appeal in a brilliantly sarcastic speech, while deftly sidestepping the question.

The Russian Foreign Minister, Litvinov, always an enthusiast for collective security, now proposed that his country and France should back the British guarantee to Poland, and at the same time guarantee the safety of Rumania and the three little Baltic states, Estonia, Latvia and Lithuania. Chamberlain turned down the idea. These nations, the Poles especially, were nervous of letting Russian troops enter their territory even as friends. It was a genuine difficulty, though Churchill believed that in a crisis it could be overcome. It was nothing like Britain's difficulty in helping Poland if Russian co-operation were refused. Chamberlain however persisted: no pact with Russia but a guarantee to Poland that could not possibly be fulfilled.

Stalin now decided to switch his policies. He felt sure that Britain and France were not going to resist Germany. His concern, as always, was self-preservation. He must do a deal with Hitler. On 3 May he dismissed Litvinov, whose policy, based on the League and friendship with the democracies, had failed. Litvinov, as a Jew, was the last man to bargain

with the Nazis. In his place Stalin appointed his faithful lieutenant, Molotov.

'Molotov', a cover name adopted before the Revolution, means 'hammer'. It perfectly described the ponderous, expressionless, immovable man whose pasty face and monotonous 'No' were to become such depressing features of international conferences in the years ahead. Churchill called him a robot, and thought him 'the perfect agent of Soviet policy in a deadly world'.

The meaning of this move was not grasped in London. The Government, having dismissed Litvinov's proposals, made belated efforts to get some sort of military understanding with Moscow. Anthony Eden volunteered to go there. He had been before and got on well with the Russians. No other British envoy would have had as good a chance. But Chamberlain declined his offer and sent a Foreign Office official with strictly limited status and powers. It confirmed Stalin's conviction that Britain was not in earnest.

Throughout the summer leisurely, low-level discussions proceeded in the Kremlin. Simultaneously, but secretly, Molotov was negotiating with the Germans. On 23 August, like a thunderbolt from a clear sky, their Foreign Minister Ribbentrop arrived in Moscow. Late that evening a Non-Aggression Pact was signed in the Kremlin and Stalin raised his glass to propose the health of Hitler.

This pact, it has been said, was also a duel. Neither side had any illusions. Both were fencing for time. Stalin needed to reorganize the Red Army after its recent purges and to press on with the industrialization of his country, especially in the remote areas beyond German bombing range. Russia's survival in war had always depended on defence in depth. For this reason the clash with Germany, when it came, must begin as far west as possible. Along with the published pact was a secret agreement: Hitler would not take all Poland, but would stop at a predetermined line, and Russia would move into the eastern half, which she had lost in 1921. Likewise, Germany would not oppose her recovery of the Baltic states.

These arrangements were unknown to the world in general, but the pact itself suggested that the attack on Poland was near. Everywhere was bitter dismay. The Right wing, conveniently forgetting the Munich Agreement, complained that they had been double-crossed by Stalin: the Left, over idealistic and naive, too slow to understand the harsh realism of Russian policy, were like religious believers whose faith has been shattered overnight. But there was little time for gnashing of teeth. Again there were trenches to be dug, sandbags filled, hospitals cleared, gas masks checked, schools organized (holidays or no holidays) for instant evacuation.

In fact, though his army was poised to strike, Hitler still hesitated. The plans made in April were set in motion, then stopped. Mussolini was backing out of a situation he liked less and less. 'At our meetings,' he wrote, 'the war was envisaged for 1942, and by that time I would have been ready . . .' He was not coming in now unless compelled. One witness noted that Hitler was 'exhausted, haggard, croaking, preoccupied'. He still sought to avoid fighting the British, wondered why they would make no more agreements with him. 'Idiots!' he declaimed. 'Have I ever told a lie in my life?' By the evening of 31 August he was calmer and had persuaded himself that neither Britain nor France would fight. To convince his own people and others that he was acting in self-defence, a pre-arranged plan, 'Operation Canned Goods', was put into effect. At 8 p.m. a German radio station on the frontier was raided by S.S. men in Polish uniforms, who fired some shots, broadcast a threatening speech in Polish and made off. To add realism, concentration camp prisoners were drugged, smeared with blood, and strewn around as casualties. Later, the S.S. men were liquidated lest they gave away the trick. At dawn the German *blitzkrieg*, or 'lightning war', was launched upon Poland, and with it World War II began.

14 Britain Alone

People had often wondered, with fascinated horror, what would happen if war came. Since H. G. Wells's novel in 1933, *The Shape of Things to Come*, and the spectacular but terrifyingly plausible film based on it, they had braced themselves for immediate wholesale catastrophe. There might be no declaration of war. The heavens would open suddenly and death would rain down. The proud cities would topple, the panic-stricken inhabitants choke and drown in a sea of poison gas.

What happened in Britain in September 1939? The answer is, essentially, nothing.

In brilliant summer weather the special trains pulled out of the city stations, packed with thousands of children wearing name-labels and clutching suitcases, scared, puzzled, tearful, excited, exhausted, as the case might be. People dug shelters in their gardens, pasted strips of paper across window panes to reduce the risk of flying glass, and scoured the shops for black material, black paper, drawing-pins, and anything else that would serve to screen a light. The radio broadcast endless announcements, but no weather forecast lest this should help the enemy. Television was suspended until the end of the war, but as there were only 20,000 sets in the country this did not affect many of the public. For the first few weeks all places of amusement were closed. Large numbers must not congregate for fear of air attack.

And nothing happened. And when, after two days of impatient agitation in Parliament and much goading of the reluctant French Government, Chamberlain broadcast to the nation on Sunday morning, 3 September, explaining that Germany had ignored the British ultimatum and the two countries were now at war, still nothing happened, except a false alarm on the air raid siren in central London which sent everybody scuttling to shelter. No Nazi planes appeared. It was to be many months **238** before they did.

School children, wearing name-labels, were evacuated from London, and other cities

Meanwhile in Poland plenty was happening, and with bewildering speed.

The last August sun had gone down on a countryside as beautiful and quietly melancholy as the music it had inspired in Chopin a century before, a flat land of cornfields and birchwoods, sluggish rivers and dirt roads, white-walled cottages and Catholic churches. The first September dawn brought the screech of the dive-bomber and the rumble of gunfire along the horizon. The Luftwaffe began by blasting the Polish airfields: many Polish planes were destroyed before they could take off and the runways were made unusable. Outnumbered and outclassed, Poland's Air Force was practically obliterated in the first forty-eight hours.

Simultaneously the fast-moving German army poured across the frontier, irresistible as flood water from a crumbling dam. Nine armoured or 'panzer' divisions raced in front. Against these the Poles had a single armoured brigade. They had, however, masses of cavalry, still armed with sabre and lance, which they flung, heroically but hopelessly, against the tanks. They were as obsolete as Don Quixote himself.

Seven days saw the Polish armies destroyed as a coherent organization. A panzer division was at the gates of Warsaw, but the capital, though already severely bombed by the Luftwaffe, continued to fight back. The speed of the Germans' progress had surprised even themselves. They were getting on almost too fast. Soon they would have reached the line secretly **239** agreed with the Russians. Urgent messages went to Moscow, begging the Russians to move into their half of Poland. Stalin was reluctant to appear in the role of Second Murderer but soon he dared delay no longer. He ordered the Red Army forward on 17 September. His troops swept westwards almost without opposition and that same day they shook hands with the Nazis along the demarcation line. The Polish Government fled across the Rumanian frontier. Warsaw fought on, its radio station broadcasting defiance to the Germans and appeals to the allies for the help promised but never sent. On 27 September the city was bombed into silence. Only in the forests the Poles fought on as guerillas and saboteurs right to the end of the war. Those abroad formed new Polish units and served in later campaigns.

Hitler's policy was now to wipe out Poland's identity as a nation. 'The Poles shall be the slaves of the German Reich,' announced Hans Frank, the Governor General appointed to the conquered territory. Able-bodied Poles were sent to Germany as forced labour for farms and factories. Whole towns were emptied and refilled with German colonists. Himmler, the S.S. chief, directed this vast programme of deportation, often with barbaric inhumanity in winter temperatures of 40° below zero, so that many of these first 'displaced persons' died on the way. The Jews, very numerous in Poland, were herded into special areas, to await what was darkly referred to in Nazi documents as 'the final solution'. As Frank remarked, 'It is difficult to shoot or poison $3\frac{1}{2}$ million Jews, but we shall take steps to arrange their annihilation eventually.' A special camp was built at Oswiecim near Cracow: the world remembers it better under its Germanized name, Auschwitz. No one will ever know exactly how many men, women and children died in its gas chambers. One million, two, three, perhaps four? As Frank himself declared before he was hanged in 1946, 'A thousand years will pass and the guilt of Germany will not be erased.'

As for the Poles themselves, it would be enough (the Nazis decided) to exterminate the clergy, nobility and intellectuals. 'The men capable of leadership in Poland must be liquidated,' said Hitler. By the end of 1941 100,000 had been murdered and another 150,000 were in concentration camps. Because, even when a man is dead, his thought and spirit may survive on the printed page, all books on Polish language, literature, history and religion, must also be destroyed. The library of Warsaw University, which had escaped air raid and bombardment, was now deliberately burnt.

The Russians also carried out mass deportations. Their aim was not to exterminate or to colonize but to clear territory which (they were pretty sure) would be a battleground between themselves and the Germans within a year or two. Instead of their own western lands bearing the brunt

Warsaw was bombed into silence. The crosses mark graves among the ruins

Offices in Westminster protected by sandbags against aerial attack

of a Nazi attack, the occupied area would serve as a cushion. To the outside world they justified their advance into Poland as a measure of protection for the inhabitants against the Nazis. At the time few were impressed by the argument. Now, comparing the relative sufferings of the two halves of the country, we may see more force in it. But the harsh Russian action in 1939 certainly confirmed most Poles at the time in their traditional hatred.

In the West men called it the 'phoney' war. The Germans sat in their fortified Siegfried Line. The French stared across at them from their Maginot Line. The few British divisions took up their traditional position on the French flank and therefore had only the neutral Belgians to look at.

The Germans did not attack because they were heavily outnumbered and Hitler still hoped that Britain and France would back out, once Poland was finished. The French did not attack because they remembered the slaughter of the previous war and did not understand that conditions had changed: the odds now were on the bold attacker. If they had advanced with spirit, they could probably have overrun the vital industrial area of the Ruhr. Instead they contented themselves with little patrolling forays like boys playing Cowboys and Indians. The R.A.F. could have bombed the Ruhr but the French banned such a move lest it brought reprisal raids on their own factories.

At sea it was slightly more like the war people had expected. On the second day a U-boat sank the British liner, *Athenia*, with the loss of 112 lives including 28 American. Ten more British ships went down in the first week; then the losses diminished as Hitler applied a restraining hand and as Churchill took control at his old desk in the Admiralty after twenty-five years. Chamberlain had offered him the job, and the whole Navy had rejoiced at the official signal, 'Winston is back'. This time they could foresee no Jutland-style battles. Hitler had U-boats and a few dangerous 'pocket battleships' but nothing like the Kaiser's fleet.

In Britain there was boredom. School, work, amusement, everything seemed to be upset for nothing. The homesick evacuees complained because there were no fish and chip shops. Rationing came in, there were identity cards, the black-out turned the streets into gloomy canyons between masses of blank houses and unlit shop windows. 'The British can have peace if they want it,' said Hitler, 'but they must hurry.' There was some talk of negotiating, put about mainly by Communist supporters, who echoed the Moscow line that this was an 'imperialist' quarrel and did not concern the masses. It was an attractive argument. After all, Poland had gone now as completely as Czechoslovakia, Austria and Ethiopia. Britain had not fought for them. What use to cry over spilt milk? But this view gained little support.

Hitler saw that he would have to fight the West. He brought troops back from Poland and prepared an attack in November, but postponed it because of the weather. It was postponed fourteen times, then definitely put off until the spring. It was a particularly hard winter. The armies made themselves as snug as possible, the British singing a more than usually inane song popular that year, 'We'll hang out our washing on the Siegfried Line!' Their first casualty was a corporal on patrol in December. The only real fighting took place in the snows of the Finnish-Soviet borderland. Russia had put in a demand for bases in the former Tsarist territories along

An Air Raid Warden

243

the Baltic, and whereas the other little republics had yielded, Finland had resisted with surprising success. It took the Russians from December to March to overcome that resistance. This made them even more unpopular in America, where there were many people of Finnish origin.

The spring of 1940 came. 'Hitler has missed the bus,' declared Chamberlain smugly. Then suddenly the war in the West leapt into life.

First it was the turn of Norway and Denmark. Hoping to stay neutral, they had treated both sides with strict impartiality. They had prepared no defences lest Hitler should regard it as an unfriendly act and they had ignored warnings of Nazi moves being planned against them. On 8 April the Norwegian Government drafted a protest to Britain against the mines just laid off their coast. Had they but known it, the German invasion forces were already at sea. An hour before dawn on 9 April German war-ships entered Oslo Fiord. Similar naval forces and transports made for Bergen, Trondheim, Narvik, and other ports. The Foreign Ministers in Oslo and Copenhagen were roused from sleep to receive a German ultimatum demanding instant submission.

Denmark accepted after a token resistance by the royal bodyguard. King Christian X told them to lay down their arms, to save useless bloodshed. The Germans had landed in the city, their columns were pouring over the land frontier. Denmark was overrun in a matter of hours.

In Norway it was different. The Oslo shore batteries opened fire. A Norwegian minelayer, two minesweepers and a whaler with a single gun courageously engaged the enemy. A German heavy cruiser sank, tor-pedoed from the shore, and another cruiser was disabled. The Germans retreated. But meanwhile troop-carrying aircraft were touching down on the undefended airport and soon the city was theirs.

Hitler had given emphatic orders that both Kings should be prevented from escape. But whereas Christian stayed perforce in his palace at Copenhagen, setting his subjects a dignified example of pacifism through-out the war, his younger brother Haakon VII took a different line. When the Nazis entered Oslo the bird had flown, by no means unaccompanied. Haakon had escaped northwards in a special train with his family, the Government, and almost the entire Norwegian Parliament. The gold reserve of the State Bank followed by road in twenty lorries. A certain Major Quisling, one of the very few Norwegian politicians with Nazi sympathies, seized this chance to take over the government, thereby turning his own name into a new word for 'traitor'.

For a few weeks there were rifle battles among snow-dappled pine forests, fierce and often heroic naval actions on narrow lead-grey waters hemmed between mountain walls. The Norwegian Navy was quickly sup-ported by British, French and Polish warships. All suffered losses but the German Navy was really crippled, and this was to prove important a few months later. On land the advantages were all with the Germans. The King and his little army were harried from place to place. The Luftwaffe was literally 'gunning' for King Haakon in person and there were times when the spirited old monarch had to dive for shelter from its bullets. Allied troops landed at various points but could make no headway. When the struggle became hopeless, Haakon and his ministers embarked for Britain, where they established themselves as the lawful Norwegian Government, to continue the struggle as the exiled Poles were already doing. Before long they were joined by several governments in the same plight.

Hitler's latest triumph rocked the British public. Was their own Government still taking things too easily? On 7 and 8 May there was a momentous debate in Parliament. Nearly 100 Conservative M.P.s, disgusted with Chamberlain's leadership, either refrained from supporting him or even voted with the Opposition. One of his oldest friends quoted Cromwell's historic denunciation: 'You have sat too long here for any good you have been doing. Depart, I say, and let us have done with you. In the name of God, go!' The veteran Lloyd George rose like some Old Testament prophet with his mane of long grey hair, and the voice of the Welsh Wizard rang out once more in that Chamber so soon to be destroyed by German bombs: 'I say solemnly that the Prime Minister should give an example of sacrifice, because there is nothing which can contribute more to victory in this war than that he should sacrifice the seals of office.' The Government's majority was slashed sensationally. Chamberlain suffered a moral defeat.

Still, amazingly, he clung to office. He tried to strengthen his team by inviting in the Opposition leaders. They refused to serve under his leadership. Under Churchill, yes. Chamberlain did not want to retire for Churchill. He suggested Lord Halifax as Prime Minister. There was no enthusiasm. Halifax, as a peer, could have no place in the House of Commons.

For a day the whole thing hung in the balance. Then, on the morning of 10 May, the dreaded blow was struck: the Germans rolled forward along a line of 175 miles into Holland, Belgium and Luxembourg, three more countries that had clung too long to their hope of neutrality, refusing all warnings and offers of help while there was still time. When Chamberlain heard of this latest calamity he tried still to avoid resigning. It was made cruelly clear, however, that he must go. That evening Churchill was summoned to Buckingham Palace. The King looked at him with a friendly, almost teasing smile.

'I suppose you don't know why I've sent for you?'

'Sir, I simply couldn't imagine why.'

King George laughed. 'I want to ask you to form a government.'   **245**

The moment had come at last. After years as a prophet in the wilderness, watching helplessly while lesser men allowed matters to drift, Churchill was to have his chance. An unspoken question quivered in the air: was it too late?

Churchill was now sixty-five. By that age most men have retired. Few are expected to compete in energy and alertness with their sons and grandsons. Churchill, however, went to 10 Downing Street with the zest of a young man.

He had already formed the habit of going to bed for an hour or two every afternoon. With this siesta, he reckoned to pack a day and a half's hard work into one. He could carry on until 2 or 3 a.m. yet be awake again at 8, ready to read a sheaf of telegrams and to dictate replies and instructions from his bed. Often there would be a personal message from Roosevelt. Thanks to the difference in time between the two continents, Churchill was able to send a message well after midnight which the President could answer before he too went to bed. That answer was at Downing Street when the Prime Minister awoke. Roosevelt sent 800 such messages during the next five years. Even before the United States came into the war, he realized how closely the fates of the two countries were entwined. The easy friendship of the two leaders helped greatly to get things done, and done quickly.

It was not only with Roosevelt that Churchill liked to deal direct. He preferred human contact, hating official jargon and red tape. Yet he could distinguish between broad issues and details. He knew when to keep his own finger out of the pie, when to delegate a job to someone he could trust, whether soldier, civil servant or scientist. He formed a War Cabinet of five, with Attlee as his deputy. These five were spared the pettifogging routine of running departments and kept their minds clear for the problem of winning the war. Outside that inner circle Churchill chose the best man he could find for each post, whether or not he fitted into the conventional pattern of Parliament. A trade union leader, Ernest Bevin, became Minister of Labour. The unorthodox Conservative newspaper owner, Lord Beaverbrook, took the new Ministry of Aircraft Production, where his dynamic personality was ideal for a terribly urgent task. The Left-wing Socialist lawyer, Sir Stafford Cripps, went to Moscow as British Ambassador. Both Cripps and Beaverbrook later joined the War Cabinet.

There were almost daily meetings of this body for Churchill to attend. There were talks with the Chiefs of Staff. There was a working lunch every Tuesday at Buckingham Palace, when King and Prime Minister conferred as they ate, helping themselves, all footmen banished from the room, though sometimes the Queen lunched with them. More than once, after the air raids started, they had to carry their plates and glasses down to the

Churchill was sixty-five, an age at which most men have retired, when he became the nation's leader

Journeys were no time for relaxation

shelter in the basement. The King worked hard at the mass of documents continually laid before him and sometimes brought up questions that Churchill had not yet studied. That was not surprising.

Besides conferences and correspondence, minutes and memoranda, Churchill had to travel thousands of miles. Within weeks of taking office there were dramatic dashes to France, running the gauntlet of Nazi planes. As time went on that familiar face was seen, half cherub, half bulldog, in the North African desert, Persia, the Crimea, Newfoundland, Iceland, the White House and the Kremlin, wherever the needs of the war required. Usually a cigar was stuck jauntily between the firm lips and two fingers were held up in the V sign which became his characteristic greeting. It was V for Victory, 'victory at all costs,' as he told the Commons in his first speech as Prime Minister, 'victory in spite of all terror, victory, however long and hard the road may be.' Even occupied Europe knew all about 'V for victory'. The B.B.C. broadcasts identified themselves with the opening notes of Beethoven's Fifth Symphony, which matched the dot-dot-dot-dash of that letter in Morse.

All this work, together with inspection tours of Britain's defences and military training and a host of other things, left Churchill little time to spend in the House of Commons, but he always appeared when necessary to explain what was happening or to put new heart into the members. Both there and at the microphone, he could always match the moment **248** with his eloquence.

'I have nothing to offer but blood, toil, tears, and sweat,' he told Parliament on 13 May. By then the latest German *blitzkrieg* was in its fourth day. Tanks, dive-bombers, parachutists, airborne infantry were beating the life out of the defenders. The Dutch had opened their dykes, their traditional answer to invasion, but this could not stop a modern fighting machine such as the ingenious Germans had developed. The Dutch, however, were fighting back doggedly. So were the Belgians, and the British and French forces had surged forward to assist them.

The next day was a black one. Rotterdam was the first big western city to feel the fury of the Luftwaffe. The central area was obliterated, 800 civilians killed. By evening the Dutch had laid down their arms. Queen Wilhelmina and her government had escaped to England in a couple of British destroyers. That same day the Germans released a flood of tanks between Sedan and Namur, driving a vast and widening wedge between the main French armies and the Allied forces which had advanced into Belgium.

Churchill was roused from sleep at 7.30 the next morning to take a telephone call from the French Prime Minister. 'We are beaten,' said the shaken voice in Paris. 'We have lost the battle. They are pouring through.' That was the beginning of a tragedy which went on, by way of Dunkirk, to the fall of France.

The story can only be summarized here. The Germans did not swing round as in the old Schlieffen Plan in 1914: they drove straight for the sea. King Leopold of the Belgians surrendered against the wishes of his ministers. This won him lasting unpopularity and led to his abdication ten years later. Meanwhile it left the British and French forces in Belgium in a

Dunkirk: soldiers wade out to a waiting ship

Dunkirk: sailor assisting wounded soldier

very tight corner. They retreated to Dunkirk, spending several days on the unsheltered beaches under the continual threat of the German bombers. They were rescued by a makeshift evacuation fleet from England, in which naval craft mingled with Thames pleasure-launches, tugs, barges, fishing-smacks, yachts, and ships' lifeboats. The crews were equally varied, Admiralty officials playing truant from their desks to serve with amateur volunteers from every walk of life. In calm hot weather this extraordinary armada shuttled to and fro across the narrow seas, the soldiers wading out to meet it. The evacuation was not achieved without loss but it was a miraculous success. A third of a million men were ferried across to England, including two generals, Alexander and Montgomery, who were later to take a handsome revenge on the Germans. The British Army had lost its heavy arms and equipment but it survived to fight another day.

Holland and Belgium were overrun. The Germans could now turn south against France. The French tried to form a new line but they were punch-drunk with the weight of the Nazi onslaught, unprepared for this new war of movement, with its panzer thrusts, its parachutists, its leapfrogging of fortified positions. They had been hypnotized by their own Maginot Line, and as George V had foreseen it had proved entirely useless. The Germans had simply gone round it.

Now Mussolini ('like a jackal,' said Churchill) thought he could safely declare war. If he stayed out any longer he would not share in the spoils. So France faced a new enemy along her south-eastern frontier.

The French Government left Paris for Tours, then Tours for Bordeaux. Churchill flew backwards and forwards, trying to put nerve into them. For the moment he could offer little but words. Some British troops were back in France, some Canadians, some exiled Poles: not enough to affect the issue. He sent all the fighter planes he could, but refused to strip Britain of the last twenty-five squadrons essential for her own defence. He begged the French, if they could not continue the struggle in France, to do so from their African territories, just as he, if driven from Britain, would fight on from Canada. The French Fleet, too, must not fall into Hitler's hands. But Churchill got little satisfaction. At French headquarters all was confusion and despair.

Most of the politicians were in agreement with Marshal Pétain, hero of Verdun in the first World War but a feeble shadow of his old self, who now favoured an immediate surrender. One man, however, stood out head and shoulders (morally as well as physically) amid this dejected crew. Churchill was much impressed by a very tall, very quiet, newly promoted general, Charles de Gaulle, who advocated guerilla warfare if all else failed. An original military thinker, de Gaulle had preached for years the very theory of mobile warfare that had just been used to overthrow his country. He had been a lone voice then. He was a lone voice now, a junior, largely ignored, but not by Churchill, who murmured to him, 'Man of destiny!'

Pétain became Prime Minister and immediately, on 17 June, asked the Germans for an armistice. That morning de Gaulle went to his office in Bordeaux and made various appointments to see people after lunch. This was a ruse. He knew he was a marked man and Churchill had already authorized a plan to get him safely to Britain. He drove to the airfield with his friend General Spears who was returning to London. They shook hands, the engines roared, and in the last split second the Frenchman leapt into the plane. He was gone before anyone knew what was happening.

So, in June 1940, Britain stood alone. Not friendless, but for the time being essentially alone.

For the friends were far, the enemy all too near. Across the narrow seas she faced a whole continent dominated by her enemies. From the North Cape of Norway to the angle of the Bay of Biscay every harbour was in German hands. At her back the neutral and defenceless Irish Republic was a constant temptation to the Nazis, a constant anxiety to Churchill.

The Commonwealth was unshaken, but its troops could not arrive quickly. Many were needed elsewhere, for example to defend the Suez Canal (then a British zone) against an attack by Mussolini. For the moment the United Kingdom must depend mainly on her own man-power, with the few Commonwealth forces already in the island and the **251**

Britain's seaside resorts were made ready against invasion

Poles, Norwegians, Dutch, Belgians and Free French. These de Gaulle was energetically organizing in London, taking as his symbol the Cross of Lorraine, a reminder of Joan of Arc. Equipment was even shorter than manpower. So much had been lost on the Continent.

Here Britain's other friend, America, stepped in. Still neutral, she could not send a man. But Roosevelt asked his Service departments to prepare a list of everything they could spare. In a matter of days they were packing and shipping half a million rifles, 900 field guns, 80,000 machine-guns, and ammunition to go with them.

The whole world now awaited Hitler's invasion of Britain. There seemed a terribly strong chance that he would succeed where the Spanish Armada and Napoleon had failed.

Even before the collapse of France, Churchill had told Parliament: 'We shall defend our island, whatever the cost may be. We shall fight on the beaches, we shall fight on the landing-grounds, we shall fight in the fields and in the streets, we shall fight in the hills. We shall never surrender.'

In that spirit the people toiled through the summer. Beaches and cliffs were mined, wired, obstructed. Concrete pill-boxes and anti-tank barriers like dragon's teeth sprang up grey-white across the countryside. Farmers placed waggons and built haystacks in the middle of their fields to prevent aircraft landing. Signposts lost their arms, town names were removed from railway stations and painted out on commercial vehicles: if a parachutist came down, at least he would not know where he was. No church bells rang: they were to be kept to sound the alarm when the invasion started. Men too old for the regular forces or in 'reserved occupations' became Local Defence Volunteers and were soon renamed the Home Guard, an immense spare-time army with units in every village.

A Home Guard, 'an immense spare-time army with units in every village'.
BELOW: 'If a parachutist came down, at least he would not know where he was'

253

Until now Hitler's landlocked mind had shied away from serious thoughts of invading Britain. Surely she would see the hopelessness of her plight and ask for terms? When she proved too pig-headed to do so, he instructed his Service chiefs to plan Operation Sea Lion. Neither the generals nor the admirals went to work with much enthusiasm. Only Göring, as head of the Luftwaffe, was eager.

A plan was worked out. Huge numbers of transports would be concentrated along the French coast. The German Navy would protect a corridor across the Channel, roofed over by the fighters of the Luftwaffe. Landings would be made along the south-east shores of England. In the first week the troops should have reached a line running from Portsmouth to the Thames estuary. Göring meanwhile would have bombed London, spreading panic and jamming the roads with refugees (as in France) so that the defenders could not move their forces freely. The second objective would be a line running eastwards from Gloucester. When that was reached, resistance would be over, and Churchill (it was assumed) would

have fled to Canada.

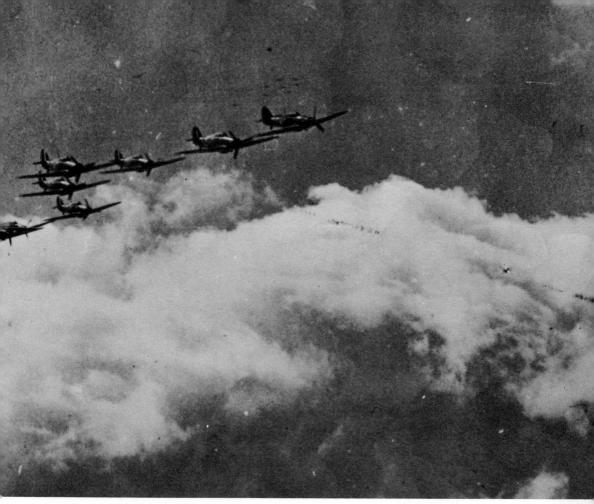

Battle of Britain planes: a squadron of Hurricanes followed by Spitfires

A black-list was prepared of 2,300 influential men and women to be seized at once by the Gestapo. These included not only politicians but authors, scientists and journalists. The list reads like a roll of honour, ranging from Bertrand Russell to Baden-Powell. H. G. Wells, J. B. Priestley, C. P. Snow, Aldous Huxley, E. M. Forster and Noël Coward were among the famous writers. Hitler meant to rule Britain by terror from the start. All males between seventeen and forty-five were to be deported to the Continent and hostages taken for the good behaviour of the remaining population. There would be the death penalty for failure to hand over one's radio set. All this is on record in cold print. There was even a scheme to kidnap the Duke of Windsor in Lisbon, with the optimistic idea of using the former King as a pawn against his brother.

Before any invasion, however, the Services chiefs agreed that the Luftwaffe must establish air supremacy. Nothing loath, Göring launched the attack on 8 August, thus beginning the Battle of Britain, which went on with only brief lulls until 31 October.

255

Civil Defence workers bringing out a victim from a London house shattered by bombs.
RIGHT: *The dome of St Paul's Cathedral lit by the flames of the burning city*

The Germans tried various tactics. They began with mass formations of bombers and fighter escorts high overhead. They evolved a 'box' system, completely surrounding their bombers at different levels. They sent waves of planes and single sneak raiders. They changed from day to night bombing. They varied their targets from shipping, ports and coastal airfields to inland airfields and aircraft factories. Then they switched to London, sending an average of 200 bombers every night for two months. Terrible damage was done, over 14,000 civilians killed. But the Germans did not achieve their object of destroying the Royal Air Force. Rather, the Luftwaffe was never the same again. It lost 1733 planes against 915 British, and as many were bombers the loss in men was even more to their disadvantage.

It was the Hurricane and Spitfire pilots, fighting their lonely battles miles up in the sky, heedless of danger and exhaustion, who inspired Churchill's famous tribute: 'Never in the field of human conflict was so much owed by so many to so few.' It is only fair now to bracket with them the scientists who had perfected radar to warn them of the approaching

enemy. Even so, the R.A.F. and their comrades in arms, the airmen from

the occupied countries, were stretched to the utmost. At times it was touch and go. Only the combination of heroism and scientific ingenuity made victory possible.

Baffled, Göring turned to a succession of raids on provincial cities, beginning with Coventry. The invasion of Britain was postponed until 1941. It was never seriously considered again.

What else must be recorded from those twelve months when Britain was alone?

Defeated France was only half occupied by the Germans, who held Paris and the Atlantic-facing coasts. Pétain's puppet government, at the little mountain spa of Vichy, was left in control of the Mediterranean half, provided they did nothing to offend their conquerors. There was, from the earliest days, an underground Resistance movement, known also as the 'Maquis', a word originally meaning the scrub covering the hills of Corsica and southern France. These people performed daring feats of sabotage. They also risked (and often lost) their lives helping British airmen and others to escape into Spain. By secret radio and the parachuting of agents from Britain they were kept in touch with the world outside. Many other Frenchmen accepted the new régime with apparent enthusiasm. They were known as 'collaborators'. Between them and the Maquis there was an undercover civil war which did not stop short of murder.

Churchill's great fear was that Hitler would capture the French Navy and upset the whole balance of power at sea. Warships anchored at Portsmouth and Plymouth were easy to take over and hand to de Gaulle. Those at Alexandria and in the French West Indies were neutralized by agreement. But the admiral at Oran in Africa refused to give any guarantee as to his future action. His fleet had to be bombarded into submission in perhaps the most reluctant action ever undertaken by the British Navy. Nothing could be done about the numerous ships at Toulon. There was always the risk that Hitler would take them over. He meant to when, two years later, he occupied this other half of France, but a party of French naval officers acted promptly and all seventy-three vessels were scuttled at their moorings.

In 1940 France's overseas territories acted in various ways. Morocco, Algeria and Tunis for the time being took orders from Vichy. Remoter possessions, in Africa and elsewhere, joined de Gaulle's Free French.

Africa became important with Italy's entry into the war. Mussolini sent an army along the north coast from Libya into Egypt, where Britain still had treaty rights to keep forces in defence of the Suez Canal. This attack was driven back by General Wavell's Commonwealth troops, mainly from Australia, New Zealand and India. Wavell could not press his victory. Some of his men were taken away for a brilliant campaign which enabled Haile Selassie to return as the liberator of Ethiopia. Another part **259** of Wavell's force had to be sent hurriedly to help the Greeks, on whom Mussolini had launched a surprise attack from Albania. Here the Italians were no more successful than they had been in Africa and the Greeks soon threw them back over the snow-clad mountains. Then, however, Hitler took a hand. German armies swept down into the Balkans and overran Greece. On the way, they had to overrun Yugoslavia as well, where a vigorous guerilla resistance was quickly started by Tito and others. The neighbouring countries of Rumania and Bulgaria became docile Nazi satellites. Having smashed the French Army, Hitler had troops to spare. He sent some to the Italians in Libya, and with their aid Wavell's depleted desert army was pushed back into Egypt.

These were just some of Churchill's worries as 1940 turned into 1941. There were many more. How, for instance, to get arms and supplies to Britain? And how to pay for them?

Once again the island was besieged. This time U-boats could operate from bases not only in Germany but along the whole conquered coastline. Britain could not use her former bases in southern Ireland. Convoys nearing Europe had to fear not only submarines but dive-bombers. The Battle of the Atlantic was a grim one. The strain on Britain's shipping resources was made greater by her having to use the longer sea route round the Cape. Though her Navy held the upper hand in the Mediterranean Mussolini and his German helpers made it too dangerous for merchantmen.

The United States, by far the greatest industrial country in the world, was the chief supplier of all that Britain could not produce in her own munition works, aircraft factories and shipyards, but dollars were needed to pay the ever-mounting bills. The British Government had dollars of its own, it had gold which was just as good, and many individual British citizens owned stocks and shares in the States. These investments were compulsorily taken over by the Government, 'conscripted' as it were like men, and their owners paid compensation in British money. Three hundred and thirty-five million dollars' worth of American investments were taken from private people in this way and sold by the Government to pay for essential supplies. Up to November 1940 Britain had paid cash for everything, to the staggering total of 4 billion dollars. But it could not go on. The purse was not bottomless.

In December Churchill sent one of his personal letters to Roosevelt. Roosevelt brooded over it alone for two days as he cruised through the Caribbean aboard an American warship. He knew that Britain was fighting America's battle as well as her own. It was stupid to let Britain go under because she could not pay any more for the means to fight. He found a brilliant solution in an old law which allowed the American Government at 260 its discretion to 'lease' equipment it was not using. Thus the system of

Lease-Lend (later Lend-Lease) was born, whereby everything from a warship downwards could be lent free of charge to Britain.

Thus the year of greatest peril, 1940, passed into 1941, with Britain alone but certainly not friendless. Then, on a fine Sunday morning in June, her people switched on the radio at breakfast time and heard a news bulletin which transformed the entire outlook: Hitler had launched another *blitzkrieg*, this time on the Soviet Union.

A Spitfire

15 The World in Arms

At first it seemed like Poland all over again but on a vaster scale. Hundreds of Russian aircraft were surprised on the ground and destroyed. Bridges were captured before they could be blown up. The panzers rolled eastwards, eating up even the great Russian distances.

The Soviet unpreparedness was unbelievable. For months Britain and America had been warning Stalin of the German build-up. In April 1941 the British Ambassador in Moscow had predicted 22 June as the date fixed by Hitler for his attack. But Stalin, so shrewd in some ways, was strangely deluded. Molotov was harder headed. There had been stresses and strains already in the new friendship with Germany; true to his name, he had 'hammered' the Führer with awkward questions as no other statesman had ever dared to do. Stalin, however, had taken more and more power into his own hands, and Molotov, always the loyal subordinate, accepted his master's optimistic views. Roused at dawn on 22 June to receive the German Ambassador's declaration of war, he was stunned. 'Do you believe,' he demanded, 'that we deserved that?' It was a curiously moral phrase for a Communist. Marxist philosophy does not usually take account of whether people 'deserve' or do not deserve what befalls them in history.

Churchill might well have thought that the Soviet Government 'deserved' this treatment. For two years Stalin's policy had been utterly cynical. He had given economic help to Hitler and snubbed every friendly gesture from the democratic nations. There was some poetic justice in what was now happening. Churchill, however, was too great a man to gloat and cry, 'I told you so'. He went to the microphone that same evening. 'Any man or state who fights on against Nazidom will have our aid . . . The Russian danger is therefore our danger, and the danger of the United States.'

In the opening weeks everything went well for Hitler. The attack was **262** part of his lifelong dream to win *Lebensraum* for the German people. He had

The Russian Front: the Red Army advancing

always coveted the exceptionally fertile 'black earth' region of south Russia, the coal and iron of the Donbas, the oil of the Caucasus. He had two reasons for acting at this time. First, the Russians had extended their power too much while he was occupied with the West. Secondly, he believed that the stubborn British were kept going only by the hope that some day they would have Russia as an ally. Smash Russia, thought Hitler, and the British will see the futility of further resistance. And Russia *would* be smashed by the end of the summer.

Many in the West believed the same. In 1941 Russia was thought of as a backward country in which illiterate ex-peasants wrecked any modern machinery supplied to them because they did not know an oilcan when they saw it. It was assumed that Socialism and Communism were foolish theories which did not work: it suited those who opposed such theories to believe this. Some even imagined that, because the Communists were a minority who had imposed their system on the country, the rest of the population would seize this chance to rise up and overthrow them. A British newspaper asked anxiously if Russia could fight on for six weeks.

This pessimism seemed reasonable enough at first. The new border-lands, Stalin's shock-absorber, were lost in two weeks. At one point the Germans had penetrated 300 miles. They were hitting the Russians along a front of 1000 miles, helped by the Finns in the far North (seizing their chance to avenge Stalin's attack in 1939) and by the Rumanians in the **263** south. Again and again the Germans blasted gaps in the defence line, swept through, and encircled towns and armies. Each day the pins on the map had to be moved eastwards.

Then, as the summer weeks turned into months, there were surprises for the Germans too. However many divisions they annihilated, however many droves of prisoners they rounded up, fresh Soviet armies materialized out of the heat haze. These unmechanical ex-peasants produced mammoth tanks, completely unforeseen by German military intelligence and immune to German anti-tank guns. When encircled, the Russian forces refused to admit they were in a hopeless position: they fought on. The population did not rise to welcome its 'liberators': for all the shortcomings of the Soviet system, its citizens fought to defend it as none of the invaded western nations had fought for their democracies.

Stalin had made many mistakes, committed many crimes, been a tyrant and a hypocrite, but as a war leader he held their loyalty. Shrewdly he appealed to the old patriotic emotions. There was little Marxist talk, little of Lenin and Trotsky's internationalism. This was a war for the fatherland. He invoked the memory of Napoleon's defeat in 1812. Even the persecuted Church was brought back into favour. If its prayers put heart into millions of Russians who still believed, if it pleased the British and Americans to think that religion was free in Russia, the cynical atheist in the Kremlin was quite prepared to allow the Church some temporary recognition.

As the Red Army fell back, he announced a 'scorched earth' policy. Everything, from railway trucks to grain stocks, must be ruthlessly destroyed rather than left to the enemy. His call was obeyed with a thoroughness only a Communist country could achieve. Grim-faced, the Russians went about their heart-breaking task, obliterating the achievements of their famous Five-Year Plans. Their first great hydro-electrical project, the Dnieper dam, had to be blown up.

Triumphantly the Germans pressed on. One by one the historic cities were by-passed, beleaguered, blasted into rubble. 'Golden Kiev' held off the panzer divisions for six weeks: it had to be subdued house by house. Odessa lasted still longer: suicide squads, driven literally underground, blew themselves up with the Germans they could hear above their heads. In Sevastopol, where the siege lasted eight months, Russian soldiers fastened bombs to their belts and hurled themselves at the German tanks. Leningrad and Moscow remained just beyond the invaders' grasp, but many Government departments were evacuated.

Hitler had told his generals that this campaign would not be fought according to the rules of war. Humane considerations did not apply to Russians. Now he ordered that no surrender by these two chief cities should be accepted even if offered. Leningrad was to be 'wiped off the

264

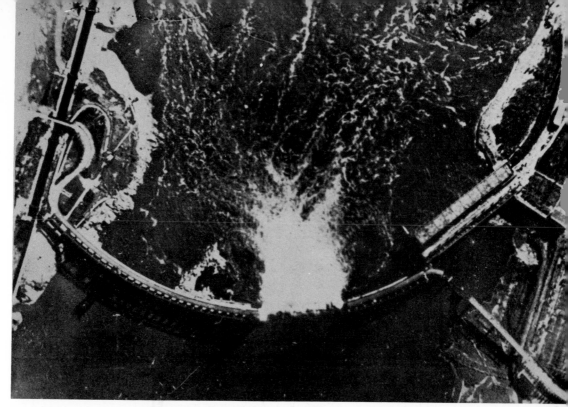

Destruction of the Dnieper Dam

face of the earth'. Germany could not worry herself with feeding survivors. 'This year,' Göring told Mussolini's son-in-law Ciano, the Italian Foreign Minister, 'between 20 and 30 million persons will die of hunger in Russia. Perhaps it is well that it should be so . . .' Of the Russian soldiers taken prisoner 2 or 3 million certainly died in captivity, many deliberately starved.

All captured Communist Party officials were lumped together with Jews for extermination. When Kiev fell there were 33,771 such executions in two days. At a moderate estimate three-quarters of a million were put to death in Russia in this way, Jewish women and children included, and this is only the total for more or less immediate massacre, quite apart from the millions disposed of later. The leader of one Extermination Group confessed to being responsible for 90,000 victims in a single twelve-month period in the Ukraine alone.

At first the prisoners were mown down in mass shootings. The psychological strain became too great for even the most hardened executioners. At Minsk Himmler ordered a demonstration shooting of a hundred men and women, to see what it was like. He saw. He nearly fainted with horror and became hysterical. He ordered that no more women and children should be shot, but gassed instead. Mobile units were provided, each van taking twenty-five victims.

Despite dazzling victories, the Germans were somehow falling behind their schedule. Hitler had counted on Russian collapse by the autumn, but the autumn brought only its usual heavy rains. The dirt roads became impassable. Even tractors were bogged down. The Luftwaffe had to drop coils of rope to the stranded columns. Then came the winter. The Nazis were not equipped for a winter campaign in Russia. It had not been part of Hitler's programme. Many froze to death. And out of the woods and marshes crept the guerillas, superhumanly tough, heedless of the weather, picking off stragglers as the wolves had done in 1812.

Hitler's generals were no happier than the frostbitten sentries. 'I realized,' said von Rundstedt, 'that everything written about Russia had been nonsense.'

On 7 December 1941 the outstanding Russian general, Zhukov, had just started a counter-offensive in front of Moscow. In Washington a Japanese mission was making a smooth-tongued pretence of seeking better relations with the United States. Thanks to a device called 'Magic', which enabled them to decode Japanese secret messages, the Americans knew that a surprise attack might be made on them at any time. They did not know when or where, however, and their latest naval intelligence reports were sadly inaccurate about the disposition of the Japanese fleet. It had entirely escaped them that six aircraft carriers, containing 360 planes and escorted by a formidable armada of warships, had stolen to within striking distance of Pearl Harbor, the Hawaiian base where ninety-four American naval vessels were anchored.

Just before eight o'clock that morning the first wave of dive-bombers came screaming over: two hours later the last wave was a line of specks vanishing towards the horizon. America's Pacific supremacy lay in ruins, beneath a pall of oily smoke. Four battleships were at the bottom of the harbour, fifteen other vessels sunk or badly damaged, over 3000 American servicemen dead. The success of the attack owed much to the work of the 200 secret agents directed by the Japanese consul in Honolulu; much also to the over-confidence of the U.S. military and naval commanders. To the American public the news came as a shattering psychological blow, from which recovery was slow and painful.

Churchill heard the radio bulletin that night at Chequers, the Prime Minister's official country home. Within minutes he was speaking to Roosevelt across the Atlantic. 'It's quite true,' said the President. 'We are all in the same boat now.' Japan had an alliance with Germany and Italy. Though Hitler would have preferred her to attack Russia, and (we now know) had not been told of the Pearl Harbor scheme, he would be forced to fight the United States himself. Churchill felt sure that the war was going to be won. He did not yet know the extent of the disaster. It would

Japanese attack on Pearl Harbor

have grieved him deeply, half American as he was. 'I went to bed,' he records in his memoirs, 'and slept the sleep of the saved and thankful.'

That was the long view. But much had first to be endured. Simultaneously the Japanese struck out in all directions. They already held the Chinese coast: the British island base of Hong Kong had to surrender to them on Christmas Day. Malaya was assailed: Britain's new battleship, *Prince of Wales,* and another, *Repulse,* were caught without air protection and sunk by bombs and aerial torpedoes. The great base of Singapore, designed for defence only against naval assault, fell to land attack by siege artillery and infiltrating infantry, under a blanket of dive-bombing. The Dutch were overwhelmed in Indonesia. The Americans maintained a long and heroic resistance in the Philippines, where about 36,000 troops (some Filipino) under the energetic General MacArthur kept a Japanese army of 200,000 at bay in the Bataan Peninsula for four months. When the situation became hopeless MacArthur was ordered to escape. He obeyed, with a vow to return, handsomely kept three years later, when he led the crushing amphibious invasion which reconquered the islands.

From these sweeping conquests the Japanese gathered in a great number of prisoners, especially British and Dutch, civilians, women and children, as well as fighting men. The sufferings of these captives were often terrible: Japanese troops were not themselves expected to surrender and they despised foreigners who did so. Also, in building their 'New Order in Asia', they set out to destroy the old idea of white superiority, taking pains to humiliate their captives in the eyes of the Burmese, Malays, and other people formerly subject to white rule. Besides the sometimes fiendish treatment given them for this reason, prisoners suffered merely from having to exist on a low Oriental diet under coolie conditions. Some 13,000 died as slave labourers building the notorious Burma-Siam railway.

By the spring of 1942 Japan's tide of victory had reached high-water mark. She was at the gates of India: she might soon attack Calcutta and Madras. Her fleets were within striking distance of Australia and even the Pacific coast of America was in danger. Then, in May and June, her progress was halted. The Battle of the Coral Sea, won by a combined American and Australian fleet off the Solomon Islands, removed the threat to Queensland. Off Midway Island, a month later, planes from American carriers inflicted the worst defeat on Japan in her naval history. Four of her precious aircraft carriers were sunk, with 200 planes and all their personnel, as well as several crowded transports. This ended the overwhelming superiority she had enjoyed in the Pacific since Pearl Harbor. America and her allies could begin the dogged step by step return to within range of the Japanese islands themselves.

268   Now everything was falling into place. The world was indeed in arms.

Chiang Kai-shek, leading China's resistance from the mountainous interior, became an ally of Churchill and Roosevelt. The next year he met them in Cairo. Stalin, his hands full with the Nazis, kept out of the Japanese quarrel, so that the Western statesmen had to journey on, without Chiang, to meet him in Persia. Otherwise, the nations had finished picking sides.

In 1942 and 1943 things were on the turn. The aggressors could still make frightening advances, but the advantage was passing from them.

Hitler still ranted incessantly, but everyone noticed how grey his hair had become. 'Hitler talks, talks, talks,' noted the Italian Foreign Minister. 'Mussolini suffers—he, who is accustomed to talking himself but has to keep more or less silent.' Göring was grosser and seedier than ever: he turned up in Rome in an immense sable coat, his fingers covered with rings. One of his new duties was to supervise the plundering of occupied Russia. Goebbels was needing all his ingenuity as a propagandist to convince the German people that everything was going well.

Even Goebbels could not explain away the air raids on their own cities, heavier and more terrifying each year. Göring's Luftwaffe had much reduced their attacks on Britain. These had been bad enough, with thousands of people killed and injured and widespread destruction of homes, factories, docks, and historic buildings like the House of Commons, but they were small compared with those now mounted by the R.A.F. and the U.S.A.F. In these the planes numbered thousands instead of hundreds, and dropped 'block-buster' bombs which obliterated vast areas. The historic 1940 raid on Coventry killed some 400 people: on one night in February 1945 an allied raid on Dresden killed 25,000. Such was the price paid by the Germans for their submission to Hitler's leadership.

The summer of 1942, however, saw his soldiers still advancing. In Africa General Rommel drove the British back into Egypt. In Russia there was a second surge forward. This time Hitler's target was limited. He had lost more than a million men and had to fill the gaps with Italians, Hungarians, Rumanians, even Spanish 'volunteers' sent by Franco. He wanted the oil of the Caucasus. Equally he wanted to deprive Stalin of it. Stalin's problem was to get military supplies. Everything from the outside world had to come by roundabout routes like the perilous Arctic convoys or overland from the Persian Gulf. Hitler therefore told his generals at all costs to capture Stalingrad, which had played such an important role in the Civil War as 'Tsaritsin'. If they captured Stalingrad, the Germans could stop all traffic on the River Volga and cut Moscow's lifeline.

An epic siege followed. At first, for the Russians, it seemed a forlorn hope. The broad river lay behind them. The city was thinly strung for miles along the west bank. The panzer columns drove against it, the Luft- **269**

Red Army men moving forward during street fighting in Stalingrad

waffe flew overhead, the enemy infantry came on in masses. The odds seemed all on the Germans. The Russians could only sell their lives dearly, contesting every yard of the littered ground.

Yet gradually the struggle became less hopeless. Reinforcements broke through. The Russian artillery cracked the German tanks like nuts. The sheer physical toughness of the Red Army man carried him on when the enemy began to flag. November saw a counter-offensive, launched in a blizzard. A new pattern began to emerge: powerful fresh Russian armies were converging on the Germans, and soon the besiegers might be themselves besieged. Hitler's generals begged him to withdraw while there was time. 'I won't go back from the Volga!' he screamed. Göring promised to **270** supply the army by air. It was impossible. Through December and

January the Germans were penned in an ever-shrinking space, frozen, starving, their wounds untended. Five thousand Russian guns were lobbing shells into the area. The temperature touched 24 degrees below zero. No help came or could come. Hitler merely radioed wholesale promotions and emphatic instructions not to consider the honourable terms of surrender which the Russians repeatedly offered. On the last day of January, however, the Germans disobeyed him. Ninety-one thousand dazed and frost-bitten scarecrows hobbled into captivity, including two dozen generals and the first German Field Marshal ever to be taken prisoner. They were all that was left of an army of more than 250,000 men.

Stalingrad was the turning-point on the Russian Front, foretaste of countless other victories to be announced from the Kremlin, with ceremonial salutes of guns, during the next two years. Meanwhile, in North Africa, there had been another transformation.

General Montgomery in North Africa

Montgomery, most dynamic and least conventional of the British generals, had taken over there. On 23 October 1942 he began the battle of El Alamein which threw Rommel out of Egypt. On 8 November the American General Dwight D. Eisenhower appeared at the other end of North Africa leading a powerful allied swoop upon the Vichy-held territories of Morocco and Algeria. Soon Eisenhower and Montgomery joined hands to push Rommel's Afrika Korps and their Italian comrades into the Tunisian peninsula. Rommel fought ably, but by 13 May 1943 it was all over: his 250,000 men were trudging through the sand to their prison camps and he himself had escaped to Europe. Better for him if he had surrendered! Within eighteen months he was suspected of joining a plot to kill Hitler. Faced with certain death, he took the poison offered him.

Africa was now cleared. Stalin was clamouring for the 'Second Front' in Europe. No Russian understood the appallingly complex problems of invading the continent. Before America and Britain could assail the

'Atlantic Wall' of the Nazi coastal defences they had to create armies, build ships and landing-craft, win the mastery of the skies, and solve all manner of scientific problems. They could not be ready until 1944. In the meantime they could at least press forward in the Mediterranean, strike at what Churchill called the soft under-belly of the Axis, and perhaps knock Italy out of the war.

Facing the Tunisian peninsula lay Sicily. In July the Americans, British and Canadians invaded the island and in a month of sometimes stiff fighting overran it completely. Even before that, their first successes knocked Mussolini off his pedestal. Italy was sick of a war which had cost her all her colonies and thousands of casualties. At a Saturday midnight meeting of the Fascist Grand Council the Duce found himself outvoted. A quite separate move had been planned by the elderly little King Victor Emmanuel: that Sunday afternoon Mussolini was arrested as he left the royal villa in Rome. At once the streets filled with wildly cheering crowds, tearing down his portraits and every emblem of Fascism. A new government, under Marshal Badoglio, set to work to extricate Italy from the war.

Here they, and the Allies, muffed their opportunity. Only the Germans in Italy acted with decision. They simply took over, disarmed any Italians who got in their way, and proceeded to treat Italy as a conquered country. The King and his new government fled southwards to Brindisi, in due course making peace with the allies and declaring war on Germany. They did not even take adequate care of their prisoner: an intrepid party of German parachutists landed at the remote mountain spot where the Duce was held and spirited him away in a light aeroplane to Munich. He reappeared in northern Italy a shadow of his old self, completely under Hitler's control.

As a result of all this the Allies had to spend another eighteen months painfully fighting their way up the long mountainous peninsula against determined German opposition, while the hapless Italian people, instead of taking themselves out of the war, found their country turned into a vast battlefield. Behind the lines, too, the S.S. applied the now familiar methods of terror: hostages, deportations and mass executions. In the north, especially, sprang up a ruthless and desperate Resistance movement, in which the Communists played an important part.

Resistance there was, indeed, wherever the swastika flag flew over occupied Europe. On the blacked-out boulevards of Paris, on the craggy heights of Yugoslavia and Greece, along Dutch canals and Norwegian fiords, many an unwary German came to an unpleasant end. Punishment was swift and savage. As the Resistance fighters were hard to catch, the hostages paid the penalty. A hundred hostages shot for each dead German **273** was the official rate of exchange. But when 'Hangman' Heydrich, Himmler's deputy, was assassinated in Czechoslovakia, the price was much higher: 1331 Czechs, including 201 women, were immediately executed, followed a few days later by the massacre of every man and boy in the village of Lidice. At Oradour in France, where hidden explosives were reported, the villagers were machine-gunned or burnt alive, only ten escaping out of 652.

Even these horrors seem small, however, against Hitler's systematic extermination of the Jews, which has given us a new word, 'genocide', meaning the murder of a whole racial group. The Nazis wished to get rid of about 11 million Jews, including a third of a million in Britain, not yet in their hands. The plan was to work them as slaves for a year or two, so that many would die from their hardships, and then apply 'the Final Solution', as it was confidentially referred to. The mobile gas units were replaced by Auschwitz and four other scientifically designed extermination centres, not to be confused with the thirty or so concentration camps. Crystallized prussic acid was used. Auschwitz had enough gas chambers to suffocate 6,000 people per day, and crematoria to destroy the bodies, once they had been relieved of gold dental fillings and anything else of value not stripped from them while alive. By mid-1945 half the plan had been achieved: 5 million Jews, more or less, had been wiped off the face of the earth.

Did they know what was in store for them? In many cases, no. Sometimes the Nazis went to infinite pains to keep them in ignorance. New arrivals saw lawns and flowerbeds, were welcomed with light music, were handed out picture postcards to send to their relatives, with the printed message: 'We are doing very well here. We have work and are well treated. We await your arrival.' Having addressed them, the victims were told to strip, fold their clothes neatly, and take a shower. They passed through a door marked 'Baths' and were locked inside the gas chamber. But it was not always done so discreetly. Others perished under conditions of nightmare brutality.

And those who knew what to expect, did they never resist? Sometimes. There is, for example, the story of the Warsaw Ghetto. Here in 1940 the Germans rounded up 400,000 Polish Jews in a tiny area of the city. These Jews worked under starvation conditions and were shot at sight if they crossed the boundary. By 1943 only 60,000 remained, in a reduced area measuring 1,000 yards by 300. The rest had died there or been deported for extermination elsewhere. The survivors guessed that their own time was near. They managed to smuggle in a quantity of rifles and pistols, even a dozen or so machine-guns. With bottles and petrol they improvised 'Molotov cocktails', like those invented by the Soviet guerillas. So, when the Germans ordered the final liquidation of the ghetto, they found that

Prisoners from the Warsaw Ghetto

for once they were not dealing with meek human cattle. Over 2,000 troops and police, with tanks and artillery, flame-throwers and dynamite, had to battle their way yard by yard. It took them a month to destroy the makeshift citadel. The last defenders died like rats in the cellars and sewers, but they died fighting. It was a better end than Auschwitz.

According to Nazi racial theories the slightest taint of Jewish blood was something to be got rid of at all costs. Even Hitler, however, would not decree the extermination of every person with mixed ancestry. He could not afford to lose their labour. It was therefore suggested that ablebodied young people of mixed blood might perhaps be sterilized by a brief exposure to radiation. They would thus be left fit for work but would never have children. Many brutal experiments were conducted on fully conscious subjects, but the Nazis never had time to apply the treatment widely.

Innumerable other 'scientific' experiments were carried out, not only on Jews and part-Jews but on Russian army officers and prisoners of many types, to discover just what a human being could endure before death. No page in history is more revolting. But we shall be foolish if we cover our eyes and ears and try to forget what was done. We need to know the worst of which Man is capable, as well as the best. These camps were not planned and run by fiends, but by thousands of ordinary men, including doctors, conditioned to do as they were told.

The full story of these atrocities was not generally known at the time. It came out later, when the victors found the damning evidence: the camps, the ashes and skeletons, the ghostlike survivors, the tons of captured documents ranging from medical records to private diaries. But more than enough was known to convince the Allied leaders that the Nazi tyranny must be destroyed without the waste of a day. The feelings of de Gaulle and the other exiles can be imagined. Roosevelt, Churchill and Stalin were just as eager. But each had to think of his own people's security. They were not knights errant assailing the Nazi dragon to deliver its hapless prisoners.

Churchill, especially, had to restrain his bellicose instincts. Europe's liberation must be calmly planned. In Norway, Belgium and Greece the British Army had paid a heavy price by dashing chivalrously to the rescue when it was not equal to the task. Let Stalin nag because the Second Front had not yet opened. Roosevelt and Churchill agreed that, when it did, there must be no chance of failure. They must go into western Europe with overwhelming force. Then, with luck, the war could be won in a few months.

So, while the Russians (following the Stalingrad victory) rolled the
Germans back across their country and the Anglo-American forces

An R.A.F. 'party'. Beaufighters shoot up a German convoy

pushed halfway up the Italian peninsula, preparations were made in Britain for a landing in northern France. The Supreme Commander was Eisenhower. Montgomery was to lead the combined land forces in the opening assault. As the spring of 1944 turned into early summer, all southern England became an immense armed camp, the British troops assembling in the easterly counties, the Americans under General Omar Bradley further west.

It was much more than a question of concentrating a large number of soldiers. Thousands of ships and landing craft, thousands of planes and gliders were involved. The Atlantic Wall was a defence line of fortified positions, mines and every kind of beach obstacle, known and unknown. The plan, Operation Overlord, was to drop three airborne divisions be- **277** hind these defences and to make a frontal attack with five more divisions from the sea. An infinite number of problems had to be considered, from the difficulty of landing tanks and self-propelled guns without docks and cranes to the choice of a sea-sickness remedy that would enable the infantry to get ashore in a condition fit to fight. Landing-craft were fitted with drawbridges so that tanks could drive straight out. Amphibious vehicles were invented, the famous American D.U.K.W.s. Once the armies had won a foothold two artificial 'Mulberry' harbours would be towed across the Channel in units and put together so that heavy equipment could be unloaded as easily as in a port. The vast amount of oil required for a mechanized army would not be unloaded at all, for it would be pumped through a pipe, 'Pluto', laid across the sea bottom from the Isle of Wight. The Germans knew nothing of these devices and reckoned that, so long as they could prevent their enemies from capturing a French harbour intact, no big build-up of Anglo-American strength would be possible.

A thousand and one details had to be studied. Tides and moonlight would be suitable on only a few days in each month, and if the weather was wrong at the last moment the invasion must not be attempted. As it was impossible to fix an exact date in advance the planners referred to it as 'D Day', relating everything to it as 'D minus 1 Day', 'D plus 3', and so on. Similarly, the time for landing the first troops was 'H Hour'. Everything must go in precise sequence. If moves were made out of order there would be muddle, possibly disaster.

Rommel, Montgomery's old desert adversary, commanded the defences. He must be tricked. Dummy ships and faked exercises were arranged to make him think that the blow would fall near Calais, not (as intended) on the Cherbourg peninsula. A last-minute heavy bombing of French bridges and communications would prevent his switching his forces when he learnt the truth. As things turned out his own advisers mistakenly assured him that no invasion was possible in early June, so he went off to see Hitler in Berchtesgaden.

Now the moment had come the weather was perilously uncertain. Eisenhower postponed D Day from 5 June to 6 June. After 7 June there would be no further chance for weeks. He had the paralysing sole responsibility of the decision on which all depended. He did not let himself be paralysed. He gave the word. That night the Germans noticed that the ether was crowded with coded radio messages obviously intended for the French Resistance. In Britain many a householder stirred uneasily in his bed, aware that the June night was throbbing overhead with endless air armadas. He came down to breakfast confident that 'something had started' and soon the B.B.C. news bulletins confirmed his guess.

278 The first parachutists and glider-borne troops touched down soon after

American troops make their way down the main stree
Carentan after the Normandy land

A Mulberry harbour, showing the main pierhead with two floating roadways on which cargoes are transferred from ships to motor lorries

midnight. Four thousand ships and innumerable smaller craft crossed the Channel during the brief midsummer darkness. The Allied navies guarded their flanks, ready to cover the landing with 640 heavy guns. Innumerable Allied fighters formed a protective shield above. At dawn the assault troops spilled into the shallows, cut their way through the beach obstacles, and raced inland to their first objectives.

The Germans were taken completely by surprise. They reacted with the toughness and discipline to be expected of them. From their prepared positions they raked the shore with an infernal fire. The Allied troops suffered heavy casualties. But they had waited so long for this moment, they knew they had the numbers, the equipment, the air and sea support, everything that could possibly have been planned beforehand to guarantee success. So, with a kind of berserk fury, they stormed the defences.

Soon the Allies had overrun a broad strip running several miles inland. Montgomery came ashore, set up his caravan headquarters in the grounds of a château, and by 12 June was entertaining the Prime Minister to lunch. Churchill vastly enjoyed being within range of the enemy. 'I had a jolly day', he told Roosevelt, 'on the beaches and inland.' Sailing home, he rounded it off by joining in the Navy's coastal bombardment. In his seventieth year (and indeed in his ninetieth) Churchill kept a streak of mischief.

The German generals were in dismay. Russia launched a formidable offensive within days of the Normandy landing: the Red Army surged into Poland, threatening East Prussia. They begged Hitler to let them draw back from the French coast, lure the Allies inland and defeat them on more favourable ground. As at Stalingrad, Hitler forbade withdrawal. He would defeat Britain with his 'secret weapon'. This proved to be the V1, a jet-propelled flying bomb, which now brought back to London and south-eastern England the horrors of the 'blitz'. Later came the V2, a rocket launched mainly from bases in Holland. Both caused heavy casualties and damage but neither halted the onward sweep of the Allies.

In desperation some German generals decided that Hitler must be removed and a non-Nazi government formed to make peace with the western Allies before the fatherland was overrun by the Russians. There had been many unsuccessful plots to kill the Führer. They were always patriotic plots, designed to save Germany, never to save Hitler's victims elsewhere. This time a bomb was planted under the table at his headquarters. By a combination of strange chances Hitler escaped almost unhurt. The conspirators were sentenced to a horrible and lingering death, every moment of which was filmed by his order and shown to him that evening. Goebbels had to cover his eyes to avoid fainting.

The Allies hoped to win in Europe by late 1944, and then to turn on

Japan, whose defeat might take a long time and cost many lives. It was

French forces move up on the Paris Chamber of Deputies where Nazi troops surrendered during the liberation of Paris

never easy to know what was best. Roosevelt and Churchill did not always agree, nor did Eisenhower and Montgomery, nor even, for that matter, Montgomery and Churchill. There were difficulties with de Gaulle, who was apt to stand on his dignity, although France could scarcely claim an equal voice with America and Britain. There is not space here to go into these arguments, but they existed, and had far-reaching political effects after the war.

Stalin was a special problem. The Western leaders might disagree but they trusted each other and remained loyal comrades. The Russians did not meet them in this spirit. Suspicion dogged their relationship throughout. Stalin's rigid Marxist philosophy taught him that the Americans and British were still capitalists. Churchill remembered that the Russians were still Communists and would use victory to spread Communism. Roosevelt was inclined to minimize this fear and to imagine that he could handle Stalin. We shall see soon how this affected the movement of the Allied armies across the Continent.

In those first summer months all seemed to go well, despite some criticism of Montgomery's apparent slowness in breaking out of the Cherbourg peninsula. Thereafter progress was swift, especially by the dashing **283**

Paris welcomes British, American, Canadian and French troops to the newly-freed city, August 1944

American tank general, Patton, who cut off the German forces in Brittany and penned them there with notable aid from 30,000 French Resistance fighters. In August there was another Allied landing in the South of France. Marseilles was taken. On the same day, following another light-ning sweep by Patton, the Free French entered Paris unopposed, and on the morrow delirious Parisian crowds cheered the tall figure of de Gaulle himself as he marched solemnly down the Champs Elysées. And all this time the Red Army kept up their hammering along the eastern front.

The Germans fought back doggedly. They stopped the Russians in front of Warsaw. Here there was a tragic and mysterious episode, when the Polish Underground rose against the German garrison, only to be bloodily suppressed when the Red Army advance was unexpectedly halted. Many say that Stalin deliberately allowed these Poles to be wiped out because they hindered his political plans for their country. Others say that the Poles acted too soon, without instructions, and that heavy German reinforcements made Russian help impossible. Whatever the truth, this event left rankling suspicions and recriminations long afterwards.

In the west there was a set-back when the Allies made a massive and imaginative airborne landing at Arnhem in Holland, hoping to get across the Rhine. These troops made a gallant stand for some days, surrounded by Germans, but the ground forces could not catch up with them in time. It was another six months before Arnhem was captured. When winter **284** came, the Nazis still held most of Holland; further south the Allies had

only just begun to dent the German frontier. They had not yet reached the Siegfried Line. The Germans had still enough spirit to make a powerful surprise attack through the Ardennes hills under cover of the December fog. This 'Battle of the Bulge', as it was nicknamed, was won, as Montgomery testified, 'primarily by the staunch fighting qualities of the American soldier', who took the full force of the enemy's onset and launched the massive January counter-offensive that sent the Germans reeling back again.

This was the last flick of the dying dragon's tail. The superiority of the anti-Nazi nations was now taking effect. Millions of avenging Russians swept into Bulgaria, Rumania, Hungary, Germany. They took Warsaw, Budapest, Vienna. The Resistance groups came into their own, especially in Yugoslavia, where as the Germans pulled out of the country it was liberated by Tito and his partisans. In Italy the Allies could see the Alps in front. In the west Eisenhower's armies crossed the Rhine and pierced the **285**

Churchill, Roosevelt and Stalin met at Yalta, in the Crimea, for the Three Power Conference in 1944

Siegfried Line. It seemed likely to be a race with the Russians for Berlin.

Afterwards, there was much criticism of American policy for not pressing on faster. Patton, who had made one of his characteristic lightning sweeps through southern Germany into Czechoslovakia, could certainly have been the liberator of Prague, but to please the Russians Roosevelt left this further triumph to them. So, one by one, the eastern European capitals slipped into the Soviet sphere.

By 12 April an American column was within sixty miles of Berlin, with nothing to bar its way but a few demoralized divisions. Much of the German resistance had now gone to pieces. Dozens of generals, hundreds of thousands of soldiers had surrendered, anxious only to fall into western rather than Russian hands. Eisenhower's main fear (ill-founded as it proved) was that Hitler would make a last stand in the mountains of the south. He was less concerned with capturing Berlin than with pushing

across Germany to link up with the Russians and prevent any such move.

Hitler and Eva Braun

So the Americans advanced no further towards the capital, where in fact they would have found Hitler still trying to direct his vanishing armies from an underground headquarters, fifty feet below the bomb-damaged Chancellery.

That same day, as Roosevelt was sitting for his portrait, he was suddenly taken ill. Within a few hours he was dead. When Goebbels heard the news in Berlin, he got out the best champagne. But the President's tragic death brought no benefit to Germany. Vice-President Truman took over and proved a most able successor. American policy, for good or ill, remained the same.

Even Hitler now saw that the game was up. He was a nervous wreck. He trembled and screamed, his eyes bulged, his rages were quite uncontrollable. On 20 April he celebrated his fifty-sixth birthday, no age for a statesman, but to his staff he appeared in some ways almost senile. He was issuing orders, most of them discreetly ignored, for the shooting of all distinguished prisoners and the wholesale destruction of German industrial plant and economic resources: like a defeated pirate he wanted to blow himself up with the whole ship. Himmler and Göring both slipped out of Berlin after that birthday party, Göring with all the looted art treasures he could salvage from his own home. Both men had private and separate intentions of taking over the leadership and making a peace deal with the **287**

Germany surrenders: General Eisenhower with the Soviet General Susloparov after the signing of the document of surrender

western Allies. Both failed. Both were to commit suicide by poison, Himmler after his capture by the British, Göring after his death sentence as a war criminal at Nuremberg.

Others were more loyal to the Führer. Goebbels, his wife and six children stayed. Eva Braun, whom Hitler had loved in his peculiar way for twelve years, had joined him in his subterranean refuge a week before: she was a quiet, pleasant enough but unglamorous young woman, devoted to him.

Russian tanks had reached the suburbs, Russian shells were crashing overhead. For some days longer the German troops held the enemy at bay. By the early hours of 29 April, however, the Russians were within a few blocks of the Chancellery. Hitler chose this moment to go through a marriage ceremony with Eva Braun, and to dictate his last testament, a long rambling document, hysterically blaming everything on the Jews. Later that day he learnt of Mussolini's death. After the collapse of resistance in northern Italy the Duce had tried to escape into Switzerland but he had been caught by Communist partisans, stuck up against a wall, and shot. His body was hanging head downwards in a Milan square for all to see.

V.E. Day: Churchill giving his victory sign, appears before a vast crowd in Parliament Square

Hitler was determined to avoid such an undignified fate. He would go out in fire, like some warrior of legend. He had his Alsatian dog, Blondi, poisoned. After lunch on the following day he and Eva disappeared into their private quarters. Hitler took a pistol, poked it between his lips and pulled the trigger. Eva swallowed poison and collapsed beside him. When there was a lull in the bombardment their bodies were carried up to the garden, laid in a shell crater, drenched in petrol, and set on fire. Goebbels and his wife waited one more day. Then, as they had agreed, they had their six children injected with poison by the same doctor who had disposed of the Alsatian. They said goodbye all round and walked up the steps into the garden where, on their own instructions, an orderly stood waiting with a revolver and shot them both in the back of the head. Their charred bodies were found by the Russians next day. By then the last of Hitler's followers had melted away, each to save his own skin as best he could.

Two days later Montgomery stepped out of his caravan on Lüneburg Heath and received the surrender of the German armies on the western front. On 7 May, at Reims, Eisenhower accepted the unconditional surrender of Germany as a whole.

Clement Attlee, Harry Truman and Josef Stalin at Potsdam; behind are their respective 'Foreign Ministers'—Ernest Bevin, James F. Byrnes and Molotov

Three nations' leaders had gone in three weeks. Now it was another's turn to go, not by death but by democratic vote. It was at last possible to hold a Parliamentary election in Britain, the first since 1935. When the count was made on 26 July it was revealed to the world's amazement and his own that Churchill had been overwhelmingly defeated, not personally (he remained an M.P. until 1964, dying in 1965) but as leader of the Conservatives. It was not that the British voters did not like Churchill, but simply that they were tired of the Conservatives. Through the grim years they had been buoyed up with hopes of a better Britain, a welfare state with wonderful new towns and social services, and though both parties had promised changes the voters felt that the Socialists were more sincere in their enthusiasm. So the Conservatives went down like ninepins and Clement Attlee became the first Labour Prime Minister with a clear majority. It was not Roosevelt and Churchill but Truman and Attlee who journeyed to meet Stalin at Potsdam, that old centre of Prussian militarism, and settle the future of Europe; and it was Truman and Attlee who had to finish the war against Japan.

How had that war been going since the tide of Japanese victory had been halted three years before?

There had been hard fighting at sea and in the air, on coral beaches and **290** in the jungle. In the Pacific the main burden fell on the Americans,

Europe in 1946

helped by the Australians. In Burma the British and the Indians fought first to prevent the invasion of India, then to reconquer the lost territories. And the Chinese battled on, helped by whatever supplies could be flown to them in their remote fastnesses.

The American strategy was one of 'island-hopping'. They would capture one base after another, drawing ever closer to Japan. Soon, however, the use of aircraft carriers enabled them to by-pass some of those islands, saving not only time but bloodshed, for the Japanese garrisons would never surrender. By late 1944 MacArthur was able to capture the important Philippine base of Leyte Island and when the Japanese Navy tried to interfere it was utterly crushed in a five-day battle. In February 1945 MacArthur liberated the Philippine capital, Manila. Simultaneously the British were driving back the Japanese in Burma.

Japan surrenders: on board the battleship Missouri *in Tokyo Bay, General MacArthur signs the document of surrender.* LEFT: *U.S. troops in jungle fighting*

MacArthur next pounced on Okinawa, only 320 miles from Japan. Its 100,000 defenders fought almost literally to the last man. It cost nearly three months and some 40,000 casualties. What would it cost to occupy Japan itself, against this fanatical people who believed in suicide and regarded their Emperor as divine? Churchill's own guess was 'a million American lives and half that number of British.'

Japan was now in such a plight that any ordinary country would have surrendered. Her cities were at the mercy of the U.S. Air Force: Tokyo and Yokohama had been largely destroyed by incendiary bombs. Her own navy annihilated, she could not stop the American Fleet from bombarding her coasts. The problem remained, how to administer the knock-out? Must every city be pulverized? Must every yard of every island be occupied by bayonet-point?

On 17 July, while Churchill was still Prime Minister, he was handed a cryptic message: 'Babies satisfactorily born'. He knew then that experiments in the desert in New Mexico had been successful: the atomic bomb was a reality. The idea of such a bomb, with its immense destructive power, had been occupying British and American scientists since 1940, at first separately and then jointly, the research work being combined in the United States. It had occurred to German physicists too, but mercifully they had switched their attention to rockets instead. **293**

It was Truman, with Attlee concurring, who decided to drop the bomb on the port of Hiroshima on 6 August. Before that, peace terms were offered to Japan and rejected. Then, day after day, millions of leaflets were dropped over Japanese cities, warning them of terrible raids to come. The bomb itself was still a secret, even from Stalin. When it was dropped it destroyed four square miles of the city by blast and fire. It killed 78,000 people and left many horribly injured.

Stalin's immediate reaction was to declare war on Japan and send troops over the Manchurian frontier. The next day the second bomb was dropped on Nagasaki: 24,000 people were killed, 30,000 injured, many dying later. This was too much even for the mentality of the Japanese Government. The nation which did not recognize surrender now surrendered unconditionally. The Emperor ordered his soldiers everywhere to lay down their arms, MacArthur took over the occupation of the country, and the surrender terms were ceremonially signed on the battleship *Missouri* in Tokyo Bay.

Only a few far-sighted people stopped to ponder what the atomic bomb might mean to the future of humanity. Most were still too dazed with joy because the second half of World War II had been won with such unexpected suddenness.

16 Sunset on the Empires

After World War I only the beaten empires broke up. World War II swept away the victorious empires also.

Imperialism was finished. One by one, across Asia and Africa, the flags of Britain, France, Holland and Belgium were hauled down. Only Portugal clung stubbornly to her small, backward empire.

Everywhere the former subject peoples demanded self-government. In south-east Asia two other factors made it impossible for the old order to continue.

The Japanese occupation had shattered the image of white supremacy. All the King's horses and all the King's men could not put it together again. The Asian peoples had seen white men surrender, labour as coolies, sometimes cry out under torture. The spell was broken.

The second factor was Chinese Communism. We saw how the Japanese invasion produced a reluctant alliance between Chiang Kai-Shek and Mao Tse-tung. When Japan collapsed, the dictator hoped confidently to deal with Mao. Instead, Mao dealt with him. Though Chiang had many advantages, including American lease-lend war material, Mao had a gospel that appealed to the masses. On his side was discipline contrasting with the low morale and increasing corruption of the Kuomintang. By 1950 the Communists had overrun the Chinese mainland. Chiang withdrew to the island of Formosa with large forces still intact. There he continued to regard himself as the head of the true Chinese Government and to cherish unlikely dreams of returning in triumph. The truth, however unwelcome to the West, was that China had become the world's second great Communist state, Russia's pupil for the moment but soon to be her jealous rival.

The effect on the former Western colonies was before long obvious. Where the old imperial power hesitated to move out, the struggle for independence was supported by the Chinese Communists with funds, arms and guerilla training. Where the West tried to leave behind it little **295**

The Far East 1939

democratic states, modelled on Europe and America, Mao wanted a
fringe of Communist satellites like those Stalin had created for Russia. So
throughout most of south-east Asia small but murderous campaigns
dragged on, whether it was the inhabitants hastening the departure of
their old white rulers or (more often) a Chinese-backed Communist movement harassing a Right-wing section supported by America. Mao's role
grew more important as he strengthened his control on China, but the
Colonies would have won their freedom in any case.

The Dutch never regained control of the East Indies at all. Long before
296 the war there had been an independence movement, led by a young

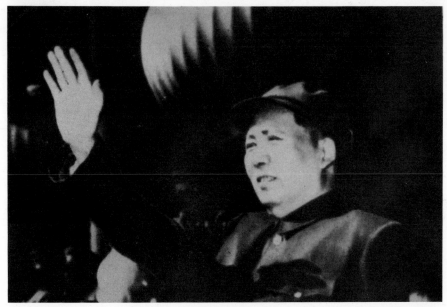

Mao Tse-tung

engineer, Achmed Soekarno. In 1945 he proclaimed the Indonesian
Republic. After five years of fighting and negotiation the Dutch gave way.
Indonesia was admitted to the United Nations, the improved world
organization formed after a conference opened by President Truman at
San Francisco on 25 April 1945 to replace the League. Soekarno became
one of the most powerful (and stormy) figures in Asian politics.

The French similarly had to get out of Indo-China after years of
gruelling jungle warfare. In 1954 the states of Laos, Cambodia and
Vietnam were created, but this brought no peace. Revolutions, civil wars,
plots and assassinations continued. South-east Asia had become a chess-
board on which China opposed America. Their 'pieces' ranged from
Japan herself, now a regenerated democracy approved by the West, to
puppet leaders of Left or Right-wing sympathies in the smaller countries.

Mostly it was an undercover struggle, pawn against pawn, in one corner
of the board. Korea, however, provoked a major conflict. This former
Japanese dependency had been temporarily divided into two republics
along the 38th parallel. In 1950 the North Koreans, encouraged by Mao,
attacked South Korea, under its unscrupulous and unattractive dictator,
Syngman Rhee. The United Nations came to his rescue, because, remembering how the weakness of the old League had led to disaster, they
did not wish any country to fall victim to aggression. The war swelled in
volume. Mao poured in Chinese 'volunteers'. American, British and other
U.N. contingents were thrown into the opposite scale. Through three hot
summers and three icy winters the wretched inhabitants saw their penin- **297**

United States Marines under shell-fire in Korea

sula scorched and pulverized by the bombardment of equally unhappy warriors brought from the other side of the world. When MacArthur favoured bombing China, thereby risking war with Russia, President Truman dismissed him from his command. A peace was patched up in 1953. The problems remained.

What of the other liberated countries? The Philippines achieved the independence that America had already planned. The British left Burma. In Malaya there were difficulties about the handing over. This rich rubber-growing, tin-mining peninsula was made up of various native states and Singapore, a separate problem. The population was mixed, part Malay, part immigrant Chinese, giving Mao a chance to poke a Communist finger into the pie. There was jungle warfare with 'terrorists', helped by China. Not till 1963 was it possible to form the independent state of Malaysia, which (unlike Burma) chose to remain in the Commonwealth, the free association newly substituted for the vanishing Empire.

Vanishing it was, even in regions where neither Japanese troops nor Chinese agitators had penetrated. It is time to look back some years to **298** India, the greatest imperial territory of all.

The Mahatma Gandhi

India's struggle was personified in an insignificant-looking little barrister, Mohandas Karamchand Gandhi, known later as the Mahatma, or 'Holy One': a wizened, bony, almost monkey-like man, with eyes twinkling behind cheap spectacles, a vegetarian, a pacifist, a Hindu who loved Christian hymns, a product of London University and the Inner Temple, who had practised in the courts of Bombay and Johannesburg but chose to go barefoot in a loin-cloth and spend years in prison.

In any other country he would have been dismissed as a crank. But in India spiritual values counted above the material. His non-violent methods, the fast, the sit-down strike, the peaceful boycott, were ideal for the Indian people. They were ideal also against a government like the British, basically humane and sensitive to public opinion. Against Nazis or Japanese soldiers they would have had less success. A typical act was Gandhi's peaceful march to the sea, where he started to evaporate water and make salt until arrested for infringing the government monopoly.

His followers gradually took over the National Congress, founded in 1885 with British encouragement to interest Indians in the affairs of their country. Britain always meant India to have self-government within the Empire. Britain had given her law-courts, railways, schools, universities, and hospitals, but she had also taken much for herself. Many Britons had **299**

a sincere love of India. Others went there solely for what they could get, despised the Indians, and often humiliated them. There were two sides to the picture, but few people saw both. By 1916 the Congress Party was agitating for Home Rule and rejecting the limited share of government offered by the British as a halfway stage. In 1937, however, its leaders accepted ministerial posts in the provinces and showed considerable ability.

Gandhi took no office. He remained free, a spiritual guide to his devoted followers, a dangerous agitator to his exasperated opponents. His position was unique. Viceroys consulted him. A Round Table Conference in London would have been useless without the little man in the loin-cloth.

His lieutenant, Jawaharlal Nehru, was completely different. He had been educated at Harrow and Cambridge. A Hindu like most Congress members, he discarded his religion and adopted a scientific Socialist outlook, and did not imitate Gandhi's saintliness. Yet the two men worked well together, and while Gandhi lived Nehru never disputed the leadership. Nehru spent thirteen years of his life in prison for political activities, yet he never lost his admiration for many aspects of British life.

When war came Congress withdrew all its members from the various provincial governments. Then, when Japan attacked and Indian loyalty became vital, Sir Stafford Cripps was sent out to offer complete self-government after victory was won. It was too late. The offer was turned down by both Congress and its rival organization, the Muslim League led by the handsome and fiery Mahomed Ali Jinnah. Both Muslim and Hindu leaders expected Britain's defeat by Japan. Gandhi described the offer as a **300** 'post-dated cheque on a failing bank'.

They were wrong. Britain won, with much help from the loyal Indian Army and very little hindrance from the few Indians who attempted rebellion. In 1946 the newly-elected Labour government (including Cripps) immediately tackled the problem of independence.

A problem it was. Some 400 million human beings were involved. Power over them could not be dropped like a hot brick. It must be handed to some one suitable. But to whom? Not to Congress: Jinnah and his 70 million Muslims would die rather than accept the rule of a mainly Hindu party. Still less, for obvious reasons, to the Muslim League. Gandhi and Jinnah could reach no agreement. There were other difficulties, such as the Indian princes, but the Hindu-Muslim enmity, often breaking out into bloodshed, was the chief stumbling-block.

There was only one solution, rough and ready, regrettable, but at least workable: the huge country must be divided.

Such a solution produced new problems: where would the dividing lines be drawn, what would happen to the millions of Muslims left in the Hindu portion, and *vice versa*, and to the princely states, especially Kashmir, where the ruler was Hindu and the people mainly Muslim; how would the army be divided, the financial assets, and everything for which the existing Indian Government at Delhi was responsible? It would have been hard enough to arrange with the friendly co-operation of all. That, to put it mildly, was not forthcoming.

A remarkable man was sent out as the last viceroy, with the urgent task of disentangling all the knots. Earl Mountbatten was a descendant of Queen Victoria and uncle of the future Duke of Edinburgh. He had already distinguished himself as supreme Allied commander in south-east Asia. Now, with a combination of tact, charm and ruthless energy, he proved equally effective. He won the respect of both sides. Firmly and good-humouredly he imposed independence upon them. On the appointed day in 1947 India and Pakistan came into separate existence, and so popular had he become that Congress asked him to stay on as India's Governor General.

The division was not made without much violence and suffering, as pessimists had foretold. There were appalling massacres of Hindus and Muslims, perhaps half a million, who found themselves left on the wrong side of the line. Millions of refugees had to seek new homes. The leaders appealed for tolerance and an orderly transfer of populations, but too often they could not control the mobs. Gandhi announced that he would fast 'unto death' unless the bloodshed ceased. Within four days the disorder was so much reduced that he was able to end his fast. Such was the unique respect that Indians paid to spiritual power. Yet Gandhi had his enemies, particularly the more exclusive Hindus who disliked his ideas of universal brotherhood. In 1948, as he moved smiling through a **301**

Gandhi's funeral procession, Delhi

crowded garden at New Delhi to his evening prayer meeting, a young
Hindu stepped forward and shot him at point blank range. Gandhi was
seventy-eight and weak from his fast. In half an hour he was dead.

Nehru then exercised the full leadership of the new India until his
death in 1964, making some mistakes and disappointing many people, but
on the whole earning himself a high reputation as a world statesman.
Pakistan also lost her original leader, for Jinnah died a few months after
Gandhi's murder. The new Muslim state then suffered a succession of
political crises. In 1958 Ayub Khan became president, a Sandhurst-
trained Indian Army officer, without the patriot's usual record of anti-

British agitation.

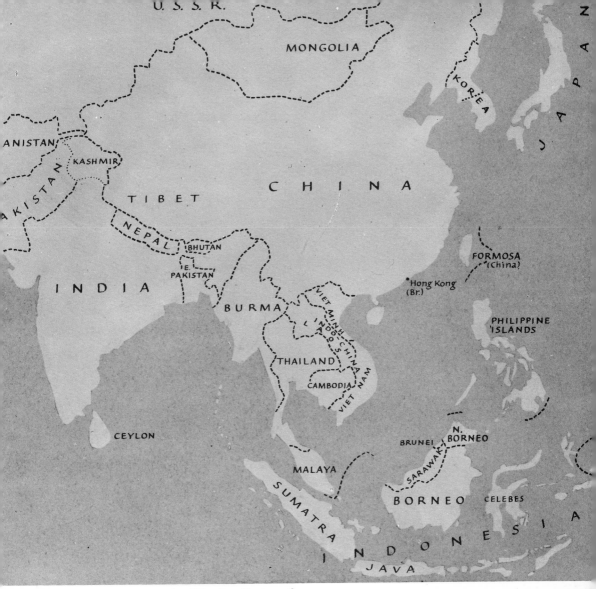

The Far East, 1965

So Britain stripped off her possessions, one by one. Often a basic pattern repeated itself. Promising young men were educated in Britain or on British lines, learned British principles of equality and free speech, and could not see why these were not always practised in her overseas territories. They formed nationalist movements, defied the Government, went to prison, came out popular heroes. When at last Britain granted independence, yesterday's jail-bird became today's prime minister. So it had been with Nehru. So it was in Kenya with Jomo Kenyatta, in Ghana with Nkrumah, in Cyprus with Archbishop Makarios.

Britain's apparent stupidity was much criticized. Why jail or exile these leaders when their triumph was sure to come? Why battle against Eoka **303**

TANGIER
International
SPANISH MOROCCO
Madeira
Port.
Canary Is. Sp.
IFNI
Sp.
MOROCCO
Fr.
RIO DE ORO
Sp.
TUNISIA
Fr.

British Occupation
in Suez Canal Zone

ALGERIA
Fr.

LIBYA
Italy

KINGDOM
OF
EGYPT

FRENCH WEST AFRICA

ANGLO
EGYPTIAN
SUDAN

FREN
SOM

GAMBIA Br.
PORT.
GUINEA

NIGERIA
Br.

Br.
Fr.

ITALIAN
EAST
AFRICA

SO

SIERRA
LEONE Br.

LIBERIA

GOLD
COAST Br.
TOGOLAND

CAMEROONS
SPANISH
GUINEA

Br.

FRENCH EQUATORIAL AFRICA

Fr.

UGANDA
Br.

KENYA
Br.

BELGIAN
CONGO

RUAND
Belg.

CABINDA
Port.

TANGANYIKA
Br.

ANGOLA
Port.

NORTHERN RHODESIA
Br.

NYASA
Como
F

SOUTH
WEST
AFRICA
S.A.

BECHUANA-
LAND
Br.

SOUTHERN
RHODESIA
Br.

MOSSAMBIQUE
Port.

MA

SWAZILAND Br.

UNION OF
SOUTH
AFRICA

BASUTOLAND Br.

In the Katanga province of the Congo in 1962, women are seen crowding up for food issued by UN

terrorists in the hills of Cyprus or the Mau-Mau secret society in the Kenya bush? The answer was not simple. A few more years might be vital in educating a country to run its own affairs. The Belgian Congo showed what happened when a European power was suddenly withdrawn from a disunited and backward population: the country relapsed into anarchy, with sickening atrocities that required the interference of the United Nations. There had been slaughter between Muslim and Hindu in India. There was to be more between Jew and Arab as the new state of Israel was carved out of Palestine. There was slaughter in Cyprus, Greek against Turk, and in British Guiana, Negro against Indian, and in several other colonies. Whatever the Empire's shortcomings, it had kept law and order. Independence too often brought violence and the suppression of those very democratic liberties for which the people had clamoured. With mixed feelings, from real sorrow to a bitter 'I told you so!', the British watched events take their course. The situation was that of parent and child, the parent never admitting that the child is quite grown up, the child rebelliously insisting that it is. The child usually gets its way in the end and learns, sometimes painfully, by its own mistakes. Unfortunately the mistakes of a young nation cause infinite misery.   **305**

Africa 1937

This washing line in Jerusalem is just in front of the wall which divides the city between Israel and Jordan

France's possessions went much the same way. She clung desperately to Algeria, which contained a large French population and was extremely important to her economic prosperity. It made no difference. There had been a tremendous upsurge of Muslim feeling throughout North Africa and the Middle East. The rebels found many sympathizers, notably President Nasser of Egypt, the self-appointed champion of Arabs everywhere. For years French manpower bled away in Algeria. Government after government fell as it failed to settle the problem. Eventually de Gaulle returned to politics from his retirement after the liberation of France. He gave up the useless struggle. Thousands of indignant French settlers, who had spent their whole lives in Algeria, had to abandon everything and move to the motherland they scarcely knew.

Palestine had always been a special problem: formerly Turkish, 'mandated' to Britain (not given) by the old League of Nations. For centuries it had been an Arab country, but since 1919 Jews had flocked there in the hope of creating a national home. After the Nazi atrocities the surviving Jews were even more anxious to settle there, and the British authorities found it hard to keep the peace between them and the Arabs. When the British had to leave in 1948 there was civil war. The Jews proclaimed the new state of Israel, which America and Russia at once recognized. Egypt, Syria, and other neighbouring countries rushed to help their brother Arabs, but a truce was arranged through the United Nations: the Jews held their ground, the rest of Palestine joined the little kingdom of Jordan, and Jerusalem became a divided city. The Arabs, however, refused to accept this as permanent and vowed that one day Israel should be destroyed.

This region has remained one of the world's regular trouble centres. In **306** 1956 President Nasser took over the Suez Canal, still legally the property

The Queen entertains the Commonwealth Prime Ministers, 1955

of the Anglo-French company which had built it. The outbreak of fresh fighting on the near-by border with Israel brought British and French forces into action against the Egyptians. It looked as if they would seize the Canal. But the United States disapproved of such high-handed methods and Russia (her support having shifted to the Arab nations) was outspoken in her threats. Britain and France had to climb down.

The Suez crisis produced a temporary coldness between Britain and America and a furious disagreement among the supporters of the Conservative Government. A breakdown in Eden's health forced him to give up the premiership he had recently taken over from Churchill, and Harold Macmillan moved into 10 Downing Street. The Conservatives had regained power in 1951 and were to hold it till 1964, when Harold Wilson brought Labour back to office with a tiny overall majority of four.

Whatever the party in power, however, no one could alter the historical process that was going on. These years witnessed the death agonies of the old empires, the birth cries of the new states. Fresh names were enrolled among the United Nations and on the list of independent countries in the British Commonwealth. Republics they might be, but most of Britain's old territories valued the special connection with London and each other. **308** They accepted George VI as figure-head of that Commonwealth, and

The Duke of Edinburgh and Jomo Kenyatta at celebrations of Kenya's independence

likewise (after his sudden death in his sleep in 1952) his daughter Queen Elizabeth II, but the British monarch no longer reigned over them as parts of an empire.

This sort of Commonwealth was something completely new. When, every few years, the leaders assembled in London for their informal conference, the Prime Ministers of Britain and Canada, Australia and New Zealand, were heavily outnumbered by the African, Asian and West Indian representatives, who could not strictly regard Britain as 'home' but who none the less had been deeply influenced by British ideas.

It proved impossible to fit South Africa into this new pattern. For many years the former Dutch or Afrikaner inhabitants had been increasing their domination there, outnumbering as they did the settlers of British stock. The entire white population was in turn outnumbered by the Bantu and the 'coloureds' of mixed race. The Afrikaners sought to maintain white supremacy by a policy of *apartheid* or segregation. *Apartheid* led to disorder and repression. South Africa's critics declared that she was becoming a **309** police state, with a racial philosophy as fantastic as Hitler's. Her leaders could scarcely sit happily at a conference table with the dark-skinned statesmen of Ghana, Nigeria, Uganda, Kenya, Jamaica, Trinidad, and the other new countries. South Africa, already a republic, left the Commonwealth.

Racial conflict was not, of course, confined to the old empires. In the United States, too, in the 1960s Negro equality became an urgent issue convulsing the nation. A Civil Rights Bill, making discrimination illegal, was introduced by President Kennedy in 1963, made law after a long and bitter fight in Congress, and signed by President Johnson in 1964. The provisions of the law were obstinately resisted in some states, but it was firmly upheld by the Supreme Court.

17 Cold War and Co-Existence

The winding up of the old colonial empires has been described first because it was the end of a story which had begun long before 1945. Now we come to two other consequences of World War II: the spread of Communist power and the atom bomb.

As in 1918 victory left the fighting men of the West with only one desire, to get home and pick up the pieces of their former lives. Neither Truman nor Attlee could have held those millions in uniform against their will. Stalin, however, had no such problem. The Soviet peoples were conditioned to discipline and direction. The Red Army would stay patiently where it was until released.

Even in the war's most desperate hours Stalin never forgot the basic issue, Communism versus Capitalism. His shrewd eye was always on Russia's ultimate advantage. He calculated every move with a view to the post-war situation, so that Russia would be strong and the West weak.

Churchill had foreseen this. As junior partner in the Anglo-American alliance he had only limited powers to prevent it. Now, swept from office by Labour's landslide victory, he was a private M.P. again, though the world listened more carefully to his warnings than ten years before. Early in 1946 he spoke at Fulton, Missouri, with President Truman nodding approval in the chair.

'A shadow has fallen,' he said, 'upon the scenes so lately lighted by the Allied victory. Nobody knows what Soviet Russia and its Communist international organization intends to do. . . An iron curtain has descended across the Continent. Behind that line lie all the capitals of the ancient states of Central and Eastern Europe. Warsaw, Berlin, Prague, Vienna, Budapest, Belgrade, Bucharest and Sofia, all these famous cities and the populations around them lie in what I must call the Soviet sphere . . .'

Thus Churchill coined one of his unforgettable phrases, 'the Iron Curtain', and for many years it was to be cruelly accurate. Censorship and restriction of movement were clamped down relentlessly upon the terri- **311**

tories occupied by the Red Army. Only Communist-controlled governments were tolerated. Czechoslovakia, with her strong democratic traditions, tried at first to assert her independence, but in vain: in 1948 the
democratic leader, Jan Masaryk, fell to his death from his office window
at the Foreign Ministry and Benes resigned his Presidency to the Communist Gottwald, himself dying soon afterwards.

Of the other countries Austria was eventually set free on the understanding that she remained strictly neutral and did not become an ally of
the West, while Yugoslavia (Tito courageously defying Stalin) insisted on
practising Communism in her own way. Yugoslavia had never given
Stalin any chance to occupy her territory. When in 1956 the Hungarians
sought a similar independence by a desperate uprising, they quickly learnt
the danger of such action in a country still containing Russian forces. After
a few days of delirious liberty in Budapest, when the outside world held its
breath and hoped against hope, the Red Army rolled in and crushed all
resistance, setting up a new government even more their puppet than the
one before. Poland and the other satellites took note. They might be
allowed certain little liberties and national variations, but if they quarrelled with the Kremlin on any major question it would be the worse for
them. This remained the position until the 1960s, when the disagreements
between Russia and China gave the smaller Communist states a chance to
play off one against the other and win some freedom of choice for
themselves.

Germany was always a special problem. The Russians had been allowed
to take Berlin but had been forced to let the Western allies share in its
occupation. Berlin, like Germany, had at first four zones, Russian,
American, British and French. Unfortunately, the city lay deep in the
Russian zone of Germany. The Western allies could reach it only by
crossing Soviet-occupied territory. For this purpose they were assigned
certain specified highways and 'air corridors'. The arrangement could
always be upset, and frequently was, whenever the Russians wished to
make trouble, either by holding up motor convoys or 'buzzing' aircraft.

The intention had been to reunite Germany as soon as a peace treaty
could be signed, but it became increasingly difficult to agree on such a
treaty. The West insisted on free elections so that the Germans, purged of
old Nazi influences, should have a chance to rebuild democracy. Stalin
knew that on a free vote there would be no future for the Communists he
had placed in power in Eastern Germany. So two separate states grew up,
neither recognizing the other: the Russian zone became the German
People's Republic, a typical Communist puppet state, and the three
Western zones combined as the Federal German Republic, with a capital
at Bonn.

312   It annoyed the Communists that West Berlin should act as a shop

The Berlin Wall: citizens of West Berlin waving to their loved-ones on the other side

window for democracy and capitalist prosperity. They tried to dislodge the Allied garrisons whose protection alone prevented the West Berliners from being absorbed into the Communist state surrounding them. Had it come to war these garrisons would have been in a hopeless plight, but Stalin dared not use such drastic methods. He therefore evolved the tactics of the 'cold war', a condition of hostility and obstruction which stopped short of military attack. In June 1948 all road convoys were halted between Berlin and Western Germany: only by shooting their way through and starting a war could the Allies have sent motor trucks to the city. They countered this move by transporting all supplies by air: only by shooting down the planes could the Russians prevent them. The famous Berlin air-lift lasted until February. In those eight months a million tons **313** of supplies were flown to the beleaguered city. Then Stalin saw he was beaten and called off the blockade.

Twelve years later, with the Western garrisons still firmly established and the prosperity of West Berlin continually showing up the low standards in the eastern sector, the Communists built a wall to end once for all the movement of Berliners from one zone to the other. Long before this, Churchill's metaphorical 'Iron Curtain' had become a real barrier running across Europe, with barbed wire and electrified fences, watchtowers, guard dogs, and the whole paraphernalia of the prison camp. But nothing shocked the world so much as the Berlin Wall which kept families divided for years on end, able only to wave to each other across a grim sort of No Man's Land. Many Berliners were mercilessly shot down in desperate attempts to cross the barrier, but there were also many heroic and ingenious efforts that succeeded.

Why did the 'cold war' never become 'hot'? In those first years after 1945 the Western armies would have been no match for the countless divisions that Stalin kept ready. The answer lies in the second new development mentioned at the beginning of this chapter. America held the atom bomb, with power to inflict unimaginable destruction upon Russia if she invaded the West.

Stalin did not rest until his own scientists discovered the secret. No one any longer sneered at the Russians as inefficient ex-peasants. That favourite illusion of the 1930s had been blasted out of existence by the formidable tanks, guns and aeroplanes which had appeared in the 1940s. The Russians had the brains and the resources for great scientific projects, as they later demonstrated by their remarkable achievements in space. They also had the help of German scientists (just as the West had) and an elaborate spy system. By 1949 Stalin had the bomb.

Thereafter it was a continuous race between West and East to seize or keep supremacy in this terrible new field. The atom bomb became the hydrogen bomb. Still more alarming possibilities were discussed. Aeroplanes were no longer essential; the bomb became a nuclear warhead, which a rocket would carry accurately to its target across thousands of miles. Such a rocket could be launched from concealed, invulnerable sites below the ground or from submarines perpetually gliding to and fro beneath the sea. When man-made satellites were sent into orbit round the earth for scientific observations it became possible to conceive of 'bombs' kept circling the globe for months or even years, ready to be directed down on to enemy targets when the ultimate emergency arose.

Such was the terrifying progress of nuclear physics and electronics. A new nightmare language was coined with words like 'overkill', meaning that Russia and America now possessed more than enough destructive **314** power to wipe each other out. 'First strike' casualties were forecast in tens of millions. Complex warning systems were devised. There could be no real defence against nuclear bombardment and the effects of radiation, threatening generations still unborn. The only defence, it was argued, was to make sure that, if Russia pressed the button for such an onslaught, an even heavier hail of projectiles would descend on her own territory. This was the hotly-argued theory of 'the deterrent'. Two enemies in a small room might fight with knives or pistols, but if they had only a hand grenade apiece would either pull out the pin and blow himself up along with his opponent?

Stalin died in 1953. He had no obvious successor. After some jockeying for position among the top men in the Kremlin, Nikita Khrushchev emerged as leader but by no means the absolute dictator that Stalin had been. The power and ferocity of the secret police were curbed. They became the servants of the Government again, not its masters. Though it was still hard to divine what was happening in the recesses of the Kremlin, it was evident that Khrushchev had to listen to his colleagues and retain their support. Unsuccessful opponents like Molotov did not die or disappear as in Stalin's day. They were allowed to retire or accept harmless lower posts.

Born in 1894 of peasant stock, bald and stout, liable to indulge in jovial clowning or ill-mannered tantrums as the mood took him, an affectionate family man and a doting grandfather, Khrushchev was a far more human figure than Stalin. He loved life. He wanted it to continue and to improve. He knew that the people were impatient for the earthly Paradise promised them forty years earlier. Khrushchev was the first Soviet leader to concern himself immediately with better living conditions, the first to admit that Russia could learn from capitalist efficiency in producing food and goods.

He remained a convinced Communist, never doubting that Marxism would one day spread all over the world. 'We shall bury you yet,' he once assured some Western journalists. Some of his other sayings were happier and revealed a sense of humour. He loved the peasant proverbs in which Russian abounds. 'Only crows fly straight,' he told the Yugoslavs, explaining that in politics the line must not be too rigid. Another time he said: 'One cannot repeat dogmatically what Lenin said all those years ago. We live in an age when neither Marx nor Engels nor Lenin is with us.' Obvious though this was, it marked an important advance in Russian thinking. Khrushchev did not wholly denounce the policies of his late master but he revealed things that astounded the Soviet masses. Stalin's body was removed from its place of honour beside Lenin, his statues were pulled down, and his name removed from the countless towns and streets to which it had been given.

Unlike Stalin, Khrushchev came out into the open, travelling tirelessly **315**

President Nasser and Nikita Khrushchev

through capitalist and Communist countries alike. He particularly courted President Nasser and the Arabs, giving them economic aid in developing their countries. He spoke always to suit his changing audience. Sometimes he called for friendship and trade with the West, at other times he relapsed into threats and abuse, using all the old-fashioned claptrap of early Communism. Only a few of the world's masses had any chance to compare one kind of speech with another, so he could afford to change his tune. While seeking peace with the West, he had still to hold the allegiance of those masses, themselves completely ignorant of the altered situation since the invention of the atom bomb. He must still breathe fire and fury when they expected him to. He must not seem to be losing his revolutionary ardour. He had not only to hold his position against Russian rivals with a Stalinist pre-nuclear outlook: he had to hold it against Mao Tse-tung, who shared their outlook, and was now trying to win for China the leadership of the Communist world.

For all his warmth and humour, Khrushchev was as ruthless a Communist as Stalin had been. He showed that in his crushing of the Hungarian revolt. He had no qualms about seizing every advantage for his side and interfering in any part of the world where he could add to the difficulties of the Western governments. This he demonstrated particularly in Cuba.

Cuba, largest of the West Indian islands, lies only 130 miles from Florida and has always been of special concern to the United States, concern which has increased since that distance can be bridged by planes or rockets in a matter of moments. Like many Spanish-American republics Cuba has seldom known democracy as understood in Washington and London. Most of her governments have changed by revolution. Many have been corrupt dictatorships. A new situation was created, however, by a dynamic Left-wing leader, Fidel Castro, who unseated Batista's dictatorship in 1958 and seized the government. He began by insisting that he was not a Communist but soon (meeting only with hostility from the West) turned to Moscow and made his régime indistinguishable from those of Eastern Europe. Before long, to America's alarm, Cuba became a Communist stronghold, bristling with Soviet weapons and packed with Russian 'military advisers'. Long accustomed to having a wide ocean between them and the nearest possible enemy, the Americans found themselves like a man with a pistol poking into his ribs.

This happened during the tragically short presidency of John Kennedy. After a second term under Truman, America had a Republican again for eight years in Dwight D. Eisenhower, whose wartime popularity would (it was said) have won him the office whatever party label he had chosen. When the Democrats came back in 1960 a whole new era seemed to open for America. Kennedy was brilliant, good-looking, and young, the first of the great world leaders to have been born in the twentieth century, a complete change from Truman and Eisenhower, Macmillan in Britain, de Gaulle in France, and all the other aging statesmen. With his beautiful and cultured wife Jacqueline, with his handpicked circle of intellectual associates, Kennedy looked as if he would transform the whole outlook of his country. He was a figure of hope, especially to the rising generation.

To the Cuban crisis he brought the strong nerve and energy of a man in his prime. The complicated situation boiled down to this: the United States demanded that the Russian bombers and rockets should be removed from Cuba and no more brought in; Russia retorted that the United States had no right to interfere with Cuba's 'defences'; America declared a blockade and announced that her Navy would stop any ships **317**

John Kennedy and his wife 'He was a figure of hope, especially to the rising generation'

carrying arms to Cuba; Russia said that any attempt to obstruct her ships on the high seas would be resisted with force. It was a situation which, before the invention of the atom bomb, would have meant war. For a day or two of unbearable tension the world listened to successive news bulletins reporting the inexorable advance of the Russian vessels into the forbidden area of the Atlantic. Would Kennedy back down? Or Khrushchev? Or would it indeed be the start of World War III? It was, at the eleventh hour, Khrushchev who gave way. Russia withdrew from Cuba. Clearly, like the West, she did not want an atomic war. Khrushchev was apparently sincere when he talked of 'co-existence': for all his bluster he recognized the great fact, the capitalist and the Communist nations must somehow learn to live side by side.

Kennedy might well have proved the ideal man to handle the Russians. They always respected strength in an opponent and Kennedy, with his quick flexible mind, was better equipped than the older American politicians to achieve an understanding with them. But in his third year of office he was cruelly shot down as he drove through the streets of Dallas, his murderer, the unbalanced Lee Oswald, being himself shot dead by an impulsive night-club owner soon after his arrest. Vice-President Lyndon Johnson took over, an extremely able if very different type of politician.

318 The Kennedy line of firmness with co-existence went on, and in 1964

Assassination of President Kennedy

Johnson scored a devastating victory over the extremely Right-wing Republican candidate, Barry Goldwater. Less than a month earlier Khrushchev had been quietly and peacefully 'retired' by his colleagues in the Kremlin inner circle, but there too it seemed that the policy of co-existence was to go on unchanged.

Co-existence grew easier for both sides to swallow as gradually, whether they liked it or not, the old sharp differences between Capitalism and Communism were blurred. When, in 1945, the British Labour Government had launched its vigorous programme of social change, several key institutions and industries had been put under public ownership: the Bank of England, the coal mines, electricity, gas, the railways and steel. Business in general was left to private enterprise, but henceforward any government had the whip hand. It could influence the economic life of the country not only by laws and taxes but by this control of money, fuel, power and transport. Britain was now a 'mixed economy', partly capitalist and partly Socialist. When Churchill and the Conservatives regained office in 1951, they could not unscramble the eggs. Only one or two Labour measures, like steel nationalization, were reversed.

Still less did the Conservatives try to wipe out Labour's other changes. Plans for a national health service and for 'social security' against unemployment, old age and widowhood, had been prepared by the wartime **319**

President Lyndon Johnson

coalition Government. So had a new scheme for the schools and a higher leaving age. The voters, rightly or wrongly, had placed more faith in Labour's determination to fulfil these dreams. But the more progressive Conservatives were sincere in their support of the 'welfare state' as it came to be called, and though rival politicians continued to argue they all knew in their hearts that they could not go back to the 1930s, let alone the 1910s. The welfare state had really begun long before with Lloyd George and his Liberals. It would go on developing, faster or slower, whoever was in power.

So too with the whole idea of 'planning', once almost a dirty word, suggesting ruthless programmes imposed by Communists. The war had accustomed the British to all sorts of changes hitherto distrusted. It had taught them that great and worth-while efforts must be planned. The rebuilding of bombed cities was an obvious example. Others were the construction of fast highways, bridges, and nuclear power stations, the transfer of overcrowded populations to new towns, and the encouragement of firms to move into areas like Northern Ireland or north-east England where serious unemployment lingered.

Elsewhere, as Macmillan declared when he followed Eden as Prime **320** Minister, many people 'had never had it so good'. Children fresh from

The nose-to-tail queue to the coa
any fine summer Sunday in Br

school drew the kind of wages on which their father had brought up a family. Workers began to own cars and take foreign holidays. People married earlier and had more children. Money was seldom the main problem, for the bride often continued with a job; the usual difficulty was finding a home, since all the building could not keep pace with the rising standards expected and the increased population. Apart from the birth-rate, the plentiful work in Britain attracted immigrants from the poorer Commonwealth countries and the flow of Britons to Canada and Australia was more than counter-balanced by the influx of Indians, Pakistanis, West Indians and others.

In countless ways British life was altering, not always for the better. As working hours shortened there seemed less to do with leisure, except to watch television. Many people, especially the young, complained of boredom. Others, especially the old, complained of the young. Disappointingly, material progress had not produced the radiant Promised Land of which the Socialist pioneers had dreamed. There was disillusionment and a strange new hostility between the young and the old, something more than has always been natural. But this did not happen only in Britain. It could be seen in America, where the idea of the welfare state was bitterly resisted especially by the Republicans and where 'socialized medicine' like the British National Health Service was denounced as the thin end of the Communist wedge. It could be seen in Communist countries where there was little affluence and old-fashioned discipline had been retained with a new Party twist. It could be seen in Sweden, where there had been no war and no sudden change in everyday life.

Western Europe made a remarkable recovery after the devastation. Indeed, the more a country had to rebuild from the ruins the better able it was to modernize its industries, communications and housing and compete with those whose old-fashioned equipment was still intact. This recovery was helped lavishly by America. Her Marshall Plan, developing into the Organization for European Economic Co-operation, helped sixteen war-ravished countries to start again, and would have included the Communist bloc if Stalin had allowed. As it was, those states had to go without American help and gear their programmes to Moscow's. Often, instead of receiving Soviet aid, they were themselves drained of raw materials and manufactured goods to help Russia's recovery.

During the war it had seemed unthinkable that Europe would ever split up again into completely separate states. After 1945 Churchill was one of many who tried to create the United States of Europe. The 'Iron Curtain' cut out the eastern half of the Continent, but various Western groupings came into existence. A 'Common Market' was formed by France, West Germany, Italy, Belgium, Holland and Luxembourg, with a plan to abolish trade barriers. Britain tried to join but was kept out

U.S. Peace Corps teacher instructing Ethiopian children in English

largely by de Gaulle, who as President of France became more and more an autocrat, determined to remain the dominant figure in any European association. For defence there was N.A.T.O. (North Atlantic Treaty Organization) in which Western Europe combined with America and Canada to maintain armed forces against Communist aggression. The equivalent S.E.A.T.O. (South-East Asia Treaty Organization) faced China through the so-called 'Bamboo Curtain'. Peaceful co-existence seemed possible if the two sides did not trespass across such demarcation lines or meddle too dangerously where no line existed, as in the 'uncommitted' countries like India.

In those countries there were as yet no difficulties arising from affluence or the welfare state. Hunger, poverty, illiteracy, disease, and other age-old problems still awaited solution, and the famished millions lost no sleep over the atom bomb. Here, as in devastated Europe, economic aid was urgently needed, and the Communists vied with the West in offering it. 'Whoever solves the land question will win the peasants,' Mao Tse-tung had said long ago. 'Whoever wins the peasants will win China.' Dangerously late the West began to realize that this applied to vast areas of Asia, Africa and Latin America. The best way to stop Communism might be to help abolish the conditions that made the masses turn to it, rather than to bolster up with arms and money their often unpopular and corrupt governments. Besides all this, aid was given by the United Nations, by **323**

charitable funds, and by voluntary service schemes under which young people went out to work among the inhabitants of the developing countries. To them, as to many of their elders, the war on want seemed infinitely more worth fighting than any other kind. If the opposing halves of the world could agree on co-existence what other difficulty could not be overcome?

So passed the first two-thirds of the twentieth century. What will the final third be like?

That will depend partly on those who are now boys and girls. They will make the history. Some may eventually write it. We much older ones, who have lived through the century so far, can hardly expect to hear the end of the story. If our experiences have taught us anything we have learnt the folly of prophesying. No one can sketch out even roughly how affairs will go between now and the year 2000. It is reasonable, though, to mention some factors sure to influence 'the shape of things to come'.

The stresses and strains of Communism and anti-Communism will long be with us, providing periodical alarms, but every year it should be a little easier to make co-existence work. At the time of the Spanish Armada many worthy Catholics and Protestants could not bear to consider a permanent 'co-existence' of their differing religions. They had to, in the end. Short of a muddle or mischance (which the present nuclear-armed powers seem most anxious to guard against) there is no more reason why the two twentieth century ways of life should not learn to put up with each other. Much depends on China: how fast she matches her huge population with industrial and military growth and how fast her leaders learn, as the Russians did in time, that even the biggest nation cannot afford to start throwing nuclear bombs.

The old Prussian statesman Bismarck once soothed a younger colleague with the words: 'Let us leave a few problems for our children to solve. Otherwise they might be so bored.' Whatever else can be said for the final decades of this century there should be no shortage of problems.

Nationalism and race will provide plenty. What will happen to Israel, hemmed in by hostile Arab neighbours? Will South Africa persevere in her lonely but determined policy of *apartheid*? Will the United States accomplish the final emancipation of the Negro without serious political upheaval? Will Britain herself face racial conflict following the influx of immigrants?

We may be sure of dramatic scientific advances, in space travel, surgery and a hundred other fields. Old problems will be solved by brilliant inventions: new problems will be created. Doctors and drains have already lengthened the average life span. Now, if multiplying mankind is not to perish from hunger, more food must be produced and fewer babies. Both involve a world-wide effort, primarily to educate the ignorant and fatalistic masses of the East. The world's land area must be better used, soil erosion prevented, water conserved, farming methods improved. At the same time we must not use scientific aids (such as pesticides) so as to upset the balance of nature and create a worse situation than before. Mankind must learn to use its new power safely, and this will require agreement between the nations. Shall we for instance see a mighty co-operative effort to 'farm' the oceans and produce enough food to banish the fear of world famine? Or shall we witness only the extermination of the whale through uncontrolled fishing by the rival countries?

Fresh chapters of economic history will be written as projects like these are undertaken or (at our peril) shirked through lack of energy and imagination. So too, in the social and political fields, stimulating challenges confront us.

Our cherished democracy, for instance, with all its assumptions of freedom and equality: can we be quite sure that it is humanity's best form of government and the one to which the non-democratic nations will turn eventually? Or will the twentieth century A.D. see the end of the brave experiment that began in the sixth B.C.? Many ex-colonies, launched into independence with ready-made systems modelled on those of Britain and the United States, have quickly abandoned them and turned to **325**

one-party or even one-man rule. Some fresh history will be written there, perhaps in blood. Meanwhile the long-established democracies have a growing problem of their own: how to make the millions of voters shoulder their responsibility and think of their elected governments as 'we' instead of 'they'. Issues have become so complicated, rival propaganda at once so convincing and so confusing, that many ordinary citizens are tempted to throw in their hands and let their destiny be decided by the alleged expert. If this tendency is not reversed, democracy will assuredly die.

Social history will be made by the manner in which every individual lives his life; above all by the extent to which he insists on remaining truly an individual, exercising his own will, taste and conscience. Some prophets threaten us with a drably uniform world in which every home has become like every other, every town, every country the same; all this as a result of State controls, standardization of industry, business amalgamations, and subtle brainwashing by the advertisers. The vision could be true. Our Main Streets and High Streets already display a lack of local variety which would have bored the stranger wandering along them in 1900. The traveller of those days would find modern France less distinctively French, Italy less Italian, as a monotonous mass produced culture begins to infect even the loneliest Greek islands. Social history would become very easy to write if this process continued until every nation bought the same goods, wore the same clothes and thought the same thoughts, or ceased to think at all. But not everything can be exported as easily as Coca Cola. If enough young people insist on having minds of their own the various communities can keep those fascinating differences which make life and foreign travel worth while.

If Bismarck were alive today he would have little cause to worry lest the next generation be bored through lack of problems. In any case, he might well shrug his shoulders and say: 'It will be your own affair now if you are bored. Your fathers and grandfathers have done their best—or, you may complain, their worst. You carry on from here, whether you like it or not, I am afraid. This is *your* century now. *You* have to finish it.'

*he vast and increasing population
' the East, illustrated by the crowd
atching Jawaharlal Nehru's fun-
al procession in Delhi, May 1964*

Still a problem in 1965: a 'refugee camp'

Postscript

Every older reader who has lived through part of this period will have some fault to find with the account given here. He will complain that much has been left out and much (in his opinion) over-simplified, that justice has not been done to this statesman and the importance of that event has been ignored. He will want to warn the younger reader: 'There is more than one interpretation. There was a lot more to it than this, you know.'

He will be right. The author would entirely agree.

Absolute historical truth can never be discovered. The more recent the events, the harder it is to agree on exactly what happened or why. Many facts about the twentieth century are still buried in public and private documents that will be kept secret for years to come. However, a mass of material is published. It *is* possible to trace the general course of contemporary history and it has been done with scholarly care in innumerable books. There is little uncertainty now about the actual events, though they often prove very different from what was reported by press and radio at the time. About the causes and consequences there may often be room for honest disagreement. In a short account like this it is obviously impossible to present all the pros and cons. The author can only make up his own mind on the evidence and tell the story accordingly.

At the end of a volume like this it is customary to print a bibliography, listing all the books which the author has found helpful. In this case it is impracticable: it would require too many pages. A list of 'Recommended Books for Further Reading' would be almost equally difficult to compile, for there are hundreds of biographies and memoirs and individual studies of this foreign country or that historical episode. It is much simpler for the reader to go to his local bookseller and librarian, state his special interest, and see what they can offer. If every reader of this book is sufficiently stimulated to study a more detailed account of even one aspect, one of its main objects will have been handsomely achieved. For it was not intended to say the last word on any subject, only the first.

GEOFFREY TREASE

Colwall, 1965

Some Key Dates

1901   Edward VII succeeds Queen Victoria. Theodore Roosevelt (Republican) becomes President of U.S.A.

1904–5   Russo-Japanese War. Russian Revolution fails.

1906   Liberals' landslide election victory opens era of social change in Britain.

1910   George V becomes King.

1912   Chinese Revolution. Woodrow Wilson (Democrat) becomes President of U.S.A.

1914–18 World War I.

1917   America enters the war. Bolshevik Revolution.

1919   Treaty of Versailles. League of Nations founded.

1922   Mussolini establishes Fascism in Italy.

1923   Lenin dies: leadership passes soon afterwards to Stalin.

1924   First Labour Government in Britain.

1925   Death of Sun Yat-sen: Chiang Kai-shek takes over in China.

1926   General Strike in Britain.

1929   Wall Street crash begins world economic crisis.

1931   Fall of Britain's second Labour Government. Japanese begin aggression against China in Manchuria.

1932   Franklin D. Roosevelt (Democrat) becomes President of U.S.A. and launches New Deal.

1933   Hitler establishes Nazi dictatorship in Germany.

1935   Mussolini invades Ethiopia.

1936   Edward VIII becomes King but abdicates in favour of George VI. Franco starts Spanish Civil War.

1938   Hitler's aggression against Austria and Czechoslovakia.

1939   Invasion of Poland starts World War II.

1940   Dunkirk. Fall of France. Battle of Britain.

1941   Hitler invades Russia.
           Pearl Harbor. Japan's attack brings America into the war.

1944   Allies invade European mainland.

1945	Complete victory. First atom bombs. Death of Roosevelt, Mussolini and Hitler. Churchill defeated in British Election by Labour. United Nations founded.
1946	Churchill's 'Iron Curtain' speech.
1947	Independence of India and Pakistan.
1948	Gandhi murdered. Berlin Air Lift.
1950	Korean War begins.
1951	British Conservatives regain power for next 13 years.
1952	Elizabeth II becomes Queen. Eisenhower (Republican) becomes President of U.S.A.
1953	Stalin dies. Khrushchev soon emerges as new leader.
1956	Suez Crisis. Anti-Soviet revolt in Hungary.
1960	John Kennedy (Democrat) becomes President of U.S.A.
1963	Kennedy assassinated. Vice-President Lyndon Johnson takes over.
1964	Khrushchev deposed by colleagues. In Britain Labour wins narrow election victory. Johnson wins Presidential Election with landslide victory over Republican Goldwater.
1965	Churchill dies.

Acknowledgements

Acknowledgments are due to the following for permission to reproduce pictures on the pages indicated: Associated Press Ltd, v, 118, 131, 165, 167, 168, 175, 184, 203, 209, 215, 216, 219, 228, 265, 287, 306; Mrs Judy Blofeld, 23; Mr Vincent Brome, 220; Camera Press Ltd, 94, 98, 192, 285, 293, 300, 313, 319, 326; Central Press Photos, 128; Mr Winston Churchill, 323; Courtauld Institute of Art, 112; Fox Photos Ltd, 189, 194, 199, 247, 302, 318; Gernsheim Collection, 5, 76, 97, 113, 224; Greater London Council, 6, 7, 12/13; John Hillelson Agency, 217; Imperial War Museum, 32/3, 36/7, 41, 44, 47, 48/9, 51, 52, 55, 56, 57, 59, 60, 61, 63, 66, 67, 73, 74, 100, 191, 197, 241, 249, 250, 254/5, 258, 261, 263, 267, 270/1, 272, 277, 280/1, 283, 284, 286, 289, 292; International Photo News, 154; Keystone Press, 72, 124, 156, 205, 213, 225, 253, 256, 257, 279, 290, 294, 297, 298, 309, 320; London Express Pictures, 316, 321; *Punch*, 7, 10, 14, 101, 104; Radio Times Hulton Picture Library, viii, 2, 8, 9, 11, 16, 17, 21, 25, 27, 28, 29, 34, 35, 39, 45, 65, 69, 79, 81, 83, 86, 92, 95, 103, 108, 110, 113, 117, 119, 121, 127, 137, 139, 141, 142, 148, 150, 153, 158, 159, 161, 166, 170, 171, 173, 177, 179, 181, 187, 188, 195, 204, 207, 212, 223, 229, 231, 234, 235, 238, 239, 242, 243, 248, 252, 253, 299, 308; Rex Features Ltd, 91; Arthur Rothstein from Brown Brothers, 163; *The Sun*, 328; *Tatler and Bystander*, 71; *The Times*, 324; Mr Nigel Viney, 76; Underwood& Underwood News Photos Inc, 68; United Press International, 18, 123, 169, 182, 201, 275, 288, 305; Wide World Photos, 162.

Index

339

Kaplan, Dora, 129
Kemal, Mustafa, 58
Kennedy, Mrs Jacqueline, 317, **318**
Kennedy, President, J. F., 310, 317, **318**, 318, **319**
Kenyatta, Jomo, 303, **309**
Kerensky, A., 90, 93-5
Khan, President Ayub, of Pakistan, 302
Kolchak, Admiral, 125
Kitchener, Lord, 47
Korea, 27-8, 297-8, **298**
Kornilov, Russian C-in-C, 93
Krasin, 121
Kremlin, The, 116, **124**, 124, 236, 315, 319
Krupskaya (Lenin's wife), 77-8, 84
Khrushchev, Nikita, 4, 315-7, **316**, 318, 319
Kuomintang, 149, 295
Kut, 58, 67
Kwang Hsü, Emperor of China, 143, 147

Labour Party in Britain, 23, 115, 172-4, 178, 180, 290, 301, 308, 319, 320
Laos, 297
Lansbury, George, 173-4, 180
Latvia, 105, 124, 234
Laval, Pierre, 205
Lawrence, D. H., 111
Lawrence, T. E., 58, 65, **74**, 67, 75
League of Nations, idea of, 76; mandates of, 103-4; protests at Manchurian Incident, 156; ineffectiveness of, 204-6, 214; replaced by United Nations in 1945, 297
Lend-Lease, 260-1
Lenin, 4, **91**, **94**; his personality, 77; his background, 78-9; leaves Switzerland, 77-8; arrives at St Petersburg, 78; expelled from University, 80-1; wins gold medal at St Petersburg, 82; and Marx's *Capital*, 82; as lawyer, 83; imprisoned, 84; spends 3 years in Siberia, 84; travels to England and Switzerland, 84; publishes 'Iskra', 84; leads Bolshevik Party, 84; changes party name to 'Communist', 1919, 85; gets aid from Germany, 78, 85; his policy and difficulties, 91-2; driven into hiding, 93; works underground from Finland, 93; returns to Russia, 93-4; takes command on 8.11.17, 96; signs peace treaty with Germany, 96; grapples with problems, 112; his skill, 122, 129; withdraws Govt to Moscow, 124; troubles, 125-6; his New Economic Policy, 127; awareness of his destiny, 129; and music, 129; shot at in 1918, 129; suffers stroke in 1921, 129; his way of life, 129; further strokes and paralysis, 130; considers successors, 130-1; dictates his testament, 131; dies, 131; his funeral and lying in state, **131**; 132; cult of, built up by Stalin, 132; his testament kept secret, 132; quoted by Khrushchev, 315
Liberal Party in Britain, 22-3, 24, 25, 115, 172, 198, 320
Li Lien-ying (Head Eunuch to Empress of China) 143, 145, 147
Libya, 29, 260
Lidice, 274
Liège, 43, 53
Lithuania, 105, 124, 234
Litvinov, Russian Foreign Minister, 229, 234, 236

Local Defence Volunteers *see* Home Guard, 252

Lockhart, Bruce, 95, 129
Lodge, Senator, Henry Cabot, 105
London, Armistice Day 1918 in, 99, **100**
London, Jack, 12
Long March, the, 155
Ludendorff, General von, 53, 54, 70-1, 72, 73, 75
Lusitania, 61, 66
Luftwaffe, 239, 249, 250, 254, 255-9, 269-70

MacArthur, General, 268-91, 294, 298, **293**
MacDonald, Prime Minister, Ramsay, 172, 173, 176, 178-80
Macmillan, Prime Minister, Harold, 19, 42, 180, 308, 317, 320
Maginot Line, 202, 242, 250
Makarios, Archbishop, 303
Malaysia, 298
Malaya, 268
Manchuria, 27-8, 156
'Manchurian Incident', 155, 157, 294
Mao Tse-tung, 14, 151; escapes from Chiang Kai-shek and sets up Soviet, 153-4; eludes capture, 154; makes the Long March, 155; reaches N. China, 155; in 1945-50, 295, **297**, 297, 298, 316, 323
Maquis, 259
Marconi, 9
Margaret, Princess of England, 207
Marshall Aid, 322
Marx, Karl (Political Philosopher) 82-3, 110, 123
Mary, Queen Consort of England, **177**, 206, 207
Masaryk, Czech President Jan, 312
Masurian Lakes, Battle of, 54
Matisse (impressionist painter), 111
Max of Baden, Prince, 73, 75
McKinley, President, 4, 19-20
Mein Kampf (Hitler), 186, 232
Michael, Grand Duke, of Russia, 90
Midway Island, 268
Millionaires, American, 19
Molotov, (Russian Politician), 236, 262, **290**, 315
Monroe, President, 19
'Monroe Doctrine', 19
Montenegro, 30
Montgomery, General, 250, **272**, 277, 282, 283, 285, 289
Mosley, Sir Oswald, 140, 142, 172, 173
Motor Car, in Britain, 7, 8, **100**, 101-2, **321**; in USA, 25, 101-2
Mountbatten, Earl, 301
Mulberry Harbours, 278, **280-1**
Munich Agreement, 230, **231**, 236
Mussolini, Benito, 4, 112, 134; his background, 134-5; lacks intellect, 135; edits *Avanti*, 135; wounded in WWI, 135; edits *Il Popolo d'Italia*, 135; starts Fascist Party in Milan, 1919, 136; elected to Parliament, 136; his power causes strike, 136; invited to form Govt, 138; wins clear majority in 1924, 139; his uses of violence, 139, **139**; Western Powers approve of, 140; ends feud between Pope and State, 140-2; as colonizer, 142; notes Manchurian Incident 1931, 157; grumbles at *Mein Kampf*, 186; starts Abyssinian War, 203-6; dislikes Hitler, 204-5; supports General Franco, 215; moves parallel to Hitler, 222, **228**; and Munich Agreement 1938, 230; invades Albania, 232; attitude of, to USA in 1939, 234; attempts to

343